THE THIRD REICH

THE
THIRD REICH

BY HENRI LICHTENBERGER

Translated from the French and edited by

KOPPEL S. PINSON

With a foreword by

NICHOLAS MURRAY BUTLER

THE GREYSTONE PRESS

NEW YORK

1937

Printed in the United States of America
by the Haddon Craftsmen, Inc., Camden, N. J.

Contents

Contents

Contents

Editor's Preface

THE French edition of Professor Lichtenberger's work appeared in the spring of 1936 under the title, *L'Allemagne nouvelle*. It was published by Ernest Flammarion in Paris as one of the series of works in the collection, Bibliothèque de Philosophie Scientifique. The present English version, however, is more than a translation of the French text. Professor Lichtenberger has supplied several additional sections which did not appear in the original Paris edition. The Editor has also revised the text and added numerous notes in order to bring the work up to date as well as to illuminate various problems which are of particular interest to the English-speaking reader. The footnotes added by the Editor are in all cases indicated as such.

Completely new in this edition too is the collection of documents contained in the Appendix as well as the Bibliography. Both are the work of the Editor, for which he assumes sole responsibility. The documents were chosen to illustrate some of the more important aspects of the political, social, religious and cultural phases of Nazi Germany. Attention was given particularly to documents of the kind which did not receive wide dissemination in the press and which were, therefore, not easily accessible to the English-speaking reader. In practically all cases the documents are presented in full. Only in the case of the poignant address of Ernst Wiechert on the "Poet and his Times" were a few sentences omitted here and there, because the allusions were peculiarly local in character and of no significance to a foreign reader. Unless otherwise indicated, the English version of these documents was prepared by the Editor.

It is the hope of the Editor that this version of Professor

Editor's Preface

Lichtenberger's text combined with the supplementary material by the Editor will provide both the student and the serious layman with a guide to the understanding of one of the crucial problems in our present-day world. World peace and world prosperity have come to depend in a very large measure on developments in Hitler Germany and nothing is more essential than a dispassionate and clear comprehension of Nazi aims, principles and policies. We trust that this work will contribute to such clarification and understanding.

New York City,   KOPPEL S. PINSON
May 15, 1937.

Foreword

UNDER conditions such as now exist, it is quite impossible for any German scholar to write an objective and dispassionate review of that which has happened in Germany since the Armistice. It would seem to be almost equally impossible for any French scholar to accomplish this task, but Professor Lichtenberger has done precisely that. Born himself in the disputed territory of Alsace, he has been a lifelong student of German philosophy, German literature and German institutions. At the present time he is Professor at the Sorbonne and Director there of the Institute of Germanic Studies. He has been for many years a valued member of the European Committee of the Carnegie Endowment for International Peace. His works on the philosophy of Nietzsche, on Richard Wagner, on Heine and on German thought and literature have been accepted as outstanding contributions to the knowledge and appreciation of modern Germany.

In the present volume Professor Lichtenberger passes in review with sedulous care and objectivity the events of the past twenty years. It is safe to say that nowhere else will the English-speaking peoples find a more accurate, a more comprehensive or a more just examination and interpretation of the Germany of today. Professor Lichtenberger is a scholar far too thorough and far too wise to indulge in a criticism which is merely violent and emotional. He shows himself wholly able to weigh the arguments in favor of policies and practices in which he does not believe and which he can not accept. Like the trained historian which he is, he sets these judiciously but firmly in their proper light.

NICHOLAS MURRAY BUTLER

Columbia University
in the City of New York.
June 1, 1937.

BOOK I

The Rise of
National Socialism

1. The Rise of National Socialism

1. Pre-War Germany

IN 1907 when I wrote *The Evolution of Modern Germany*, the second Reich was still at the height of its power and prosperity. An imposing group of German historians, economists, sociologists, philosophers, technicians and writers of every sort were then engaged in drawing up the balance sheet of the preceding century, and they marvelled at the work which had been accomplished.

Germany, indeed, had every reason to be proud of the prodigious progress which she had made during the nineteenth century. On the political side, there was the unification of the Reich, prepared and effected by Bismarck, and the victories of 1866 and 1870. From the point of view of civilization the Germans were conscious of having greatly increased man's mastery over nature. They had solved the problem of sustaining 65 million people on the same German territory which in 1800, at a time when living conditions were more difficult than in our age, had been inhabited by only 25 millions. They gloried in their transformation of a poor agrarian country into a formidable manufactory which was provided with highly perfected industrial and commercial equipment and which maintained itself by the industry of its workers and the revenues from its acquired wealth. They took pride in their order and discipline, their diligence and tireless energy and in their scientific thoroughness. All these virtues enabled them, amidst the universal unbridling of competition, to assume a foremost place among modern indus-

3

trial nations. Optimism was the order of the day. On the eve of the World War, Arnold Steinman-Bucher wrote his book *Das reiche Deutschland*. William II, in his addresses, railed against the *"Schwarzseher,"* the pessimists and prophets of evil, who insisted on seeing difficulties and predicting catastrophe.

In spite of this official enthusiasm, however, there were some distinctly unhealthy symptoms. There were, in the first place, the critics of the left. Many liberals, democrats and socialists, in Germany as well as abroad, looked upon Wilhelmine Germany as militaristic and feudal, imperialistic and harshly realistic, absorbed in power and riches and disdainful of all democratic and humanitarian ideology. As such they considered it an anachronism in modern Europe, unlikely to survive any serious and violent transformations in the impending future.

Such reservations and attacks, moreover, came not only from opposition parties or individuals treated readily as "subversive"; discontent also spread among much wider sections of public opinion. Despite loyalty to the monarchy and respect for authority, sentiments which are so deeply rooted in the German spirit, there was a visible increase, toward the end of the reign of William II, in the number of skeptics who asked whether the emperor would be able to maintain his traditional role as arbiter among the parties; whether he would be able to remain the sovereign of the entire nation; and whether he would be able to steer clear of making himself the prisoner of a privileged coterie or the toy of the capricious impulses of his own individual temperament. There was no doubt that an appreciable section of public opinion showed signs of weariness and formulated more and more emphatic protests against a regime of personal government, against the instability of the "new course" and against the abuses which flowed from it. Memoirs of the period which have recently appeared indicate that even in the highest spheres of society,

4

within the inner circle of leading personalities, the feeling had been constantly increasing that something was "rotten in the state of Denmark."

German thought, long before the end, had weighed the fragility of the European order and the dangers which were threatening the material and spiritual equilibrium of modern society. It had perceived and denounced the rise of economic materialism, the exclusive cult of science and technology, the disappearance of older ideal "values" in politics as well as in morality, the perils engendered by the frantic development of industrialism, the terrible pressure of expansionist imperialism, and the growing violence of collisions between exasperated nationalisms. The German spirit was not deluded as to the "problematic" aspects of the magnificent but precarious edifice of the Wilhelmine Reich.

The revolt against the reigning order and the expectation of a vast cataclysm which would swallow up a world doomed to ruin had its prophet in Friedrich Nietzsche, who was perhaps the most creative thinker of our age. Nietzsche, the merciless psychologist of "decadence," and the philosopher of the "transvaluation of values," who scorned Marxism and anarchistic communism, parliamentary democracy and Anglo-Saxon eudaemonism, the religion of technology and of efficiency and capitalism and its cult of riches,—Nietzsche, this intrepid negator who earned for himself the title of the first nihilist of Europe, the iconoclast who philosophized with blows of the hammer, the seer who pronounced anathema against the state,—Nietzsche divined the decay of the Reich when it was at the apogee of its pan-Germanic exaltation and he predicted that Europe would enter into the classic age of war and into an era of formidable social cataclysms. Nietzsche, I say, embodied within him all the doubts, all the revolts which were stirring within the German soul beneath its surface optimism. Profoundly "unreal" in the age of William II, he was at first ignored and then attacked, often with bitter violence. Against him were the satisfied and the mighty; on the one hand those who felt content in the capitalist society with its gross materialism, and, on the other hand those who preached the ideal of discipline, subordination and obedience. Official Germany looked upon him as a disordered mind or as almost a madman, as a dangerous iconoclast or as a funereal rhetorician. Even in 1914 a distinguished critic assured me that the vogue of Nietzsche was really but a fad which was already in the state of decline and that scarcely any one took the poet of Zarathustra seriously. The war and the events following the war have shown in startling fashion the clairvoyance of that visionary genius in whom the *mauvaise conscience* of his time was incarnate.

2. *The Significance of the Revolution of 1918*

It is not within my province to discuss here the beginnings of the World War and its progress, nor the reactions which it aroused in the German soul. But in order to understand how National Socialism was born it is necessary to grasp the significance of the revolution of November, 1918, which represented the culmination of the great cataclysm.

The characteristic feature of this revolution was that it was not the result of active pressure on the part of the revolutionary masses. It appeared rather as a collapse which the country experienced in a most passive manner. The four years of war had completely ruined the imposing edifice of the Reich of William II. The emperor, the Chancellor, the Reichstag and the parties had gradually lost the confidence of the country. Authority came to be concentrated entirely in the hands of the General Staff. This really meant in the hands of Ludendorf, who was in supreme command not only of the military operations but also of the general political affairs of the Reich. On the day on which the General Staff confessed its weakness and asked for the immediate conclusion of an

6

armistice, the Empire, the ministers, Parliament, everything collapsed at once without any resistance. It was not a powerful movement of the masses, however, which overturned the imperial edifice. It gave way of its own accord under the pressure of a group of agitators who never had the opinion of the country behind them. The Germans somehow found themselves suddenly before an abyss. When they saw thrones and governments falling around them, when Workers' and Soldiers' Councils sprang up on all sides, when the cities resounded with the crackling of machine guns and the explosion of grenades, the onlookers of the overturn believed that they distinguished in the sky the bloody gleam of the "great night" so long heralded by the prophets of the revolution. And in a cold fit of anguish they wondered if the bolshevist wave which had submerged Russia would now flow down from the Vistula to the Rhine; if Germany in its turn was not going to experience all the horrors of civil war and the calamities of general anarchy. For a time the terror of the red specter haunted the minds of the people.

The instigators of the revolutionary movement were a small minority. They were divided into two disparate groups. There were, first, the Independent Socialists who, under the leadership of Kautsky, Bernstein and Haase had seceded in 1915 from the Majority Socialists and in 1917 had formed a special group. Secondly, there were the extremists who, under the stimulus of Liebknecht and Rosa Luxemburg, had created in 1917 the Spartacus group and who together with the Russian bolsheviks were preparing for the world revolution. After the defeat of the strike, undertaken at the beginning of 1918 for the purpose of putting an end to the war by checking the manufacture of munitions, these militants of the left resumed their propaganda among the workers. They organized the workers, procured arms for them and established "shock troops" in the factories to fight the police. These were the individuals who in November, 1918, established connec-

7

tion between the diverse elements which had rebelled against the authorities. These elements included sailors revolting against their officers, soldiers on leave who were resolved at all cost to prevent the continuation of the war, and proletarians determined to bring about a rising of the poor masses of Europe against the possessing classes. Such were the elements whose chiefs, in particular Liebknecht, Barth, Ledebour, Kurt Eisner, etc., assumed the leadership of the movement in Berlin and Munich.

The revolution of 1918 was completely checked. The causes for this are not difficult to discern. In the first place there was a lack of outstanding leaders, men of will and action and fearless, able organizers, who might have been for Germany what Lenin and Trotzky were for Russia. Moreover certain perceptible differences developed between the Independents, who were very radical republicans but never communists and still less anarchists, and the Spartacists, who were in favor of an intimate alliance with Russian bolshevism in order to establish complete socialism by means of the proletarian dictatorship and systematic terror. Lastly, and above all, these extremists were never able to attract to their side the great party of the Majority Socialists whose prudent opportunism instinctively reacted against all hazardous adventures and who, from the first moment, sought contact with the bourgeois parties and the elements of order in Germany, i.e., the army and the bureaucracy.

Under such circumstances the German revolution was from the very beginning destined to certain defeat. In the first moments of popular excitement the Majority Socialists temporized and agreed to share power with the Independents. This accord, however, was soon broken and immediately thereafter the main body of the Socialists made common front with the moderate and conservative elements against the desperate assault which a handful of fanatical communists or impractical idealists made upon the bourgeois society. The

8

Majority Socialists were victorious in this struggle but not without meeting cases of very lively resistance. The violent repression of bolshevist agitation, however, does not represent a very glorious page in the history of that epoch. It was often brutal and marred by such ugly episodes as the murder of Liebknecht and Rosa Luxemburg. It worked, however, toward the complete destruction of all extremism. Very quickly the organized German workers came to understand the fundamental difference which separated Germany from Russia and they foresaw the irreparable catastrophe which the sudden realization of communism, such as had been established in Russia, would bring on Germany, a country of scientifically organized big industry.

On the whole the revolution of 1918 was little but a troubled interlude caused by the passing crisis of nervous disequilibrium, engendered by the physical privations of the war and the psychic shock following the defeat and collapse of the Reich. It did not win the sympathy of the mass of workers. In the bourgeois world it aroused passionate antagonism. A realization of the violence of this bourgeois resentment may be gathered from reading the vehement protest against the November revolution of a man like Stresemann, who later became one of the champions of the Weimar republic and of the policy of conciliation. He would have pardoned these rioters with all his heart, wrote Stresemann, if when confronted with the conditions of the armistice and of peace, they, like the French revolutionaries of 1792, had preached to all their followers a struggle to the finish for their endangered country. But they never thought of doing anything of the kind; they lacked completely the sense of national dignity. They basely insulted the army, continued Stresemann, which, "with brow covered with laurels," had succumbed to exhaustion. They trampled upon the flag, tore the cockades from the fighting men returning from the front and covered with opprobrium a corps of officers the like of which no other nation possessed. The cowardice with which the men of the revolution accepted the national disaster, the baseness of spirit with which they heaped abuse upon an army which had fulfilled all its duties and which until the end had acquitted itself nobly in an unequal struggle, inspired unlimited contempt in Stresemann. For him the 9th of November inaugurated "the period of national shame and moral degradation of our people." The very violence of these invectives was typical. It enables one to understand the intensity of the reaction of the average German against the November revolution and to anticipate one of the profound psychic sources from which National Socialism was later to draw its fundamental strength.

3. *The Weakness of the Weimar Republic*

The Weimar republic which was founded by the National Assembly elected on January 19, 1919 and which received as its charter the Weimar constitution signed on August 16 by President Ebert, was in no way a product of the "revolution" of 1918. It might rather be viewed as the first act of a counter-revolution directed against the small group of revolutionists who had brought about the collapse of the old regime. The support of the republic was derived in the first place from the Majority Socialists who had united with the petty bourgeoisie to wipe out the extremists. In addition there was the left proper, which was divided into two rival groups, the Democrats and the People's Party. Finally there was the Catholic Centre Party which, as under the old regime, did not hesitate to assume a preponderant influence in the government, and which furnished to the republic the greater number of its leaders.

We cannot go into the history of the Weimar republic here. It is sufficient to indicate how it was undermined and then destroyed by the second wave of the counter-revolutionary assault, the nationalist wave. We may begin by summarizing the general causes of weakness which were inherent in the republic from its inception and which ultimately led to its destruction.

The first and most serious weakness was the unsound character of the Social Democratic Party, the party which had from the beginning constituted the major element of the coalition and which, although not forming an absolute majority of the National Assembly, commanded 163 deputies elected by eleven and one-half million votes. The Social Democratic Party had a program, an ideal, and a solid organization. But in action it manifested an almost complete impotence. It is easy to plead extenuating circumstances for it. It was embarrassed by the revolutionary attitude of the extremists and by the necessity for clearly distinguishing itself from the Marxist communism which had triumphed in Russia but which Germany did not want at any price. It had been paralyzed by the necessity of compromising with the bourgeois parties which remained strong enough to check all radical reforms that might frighten the middle classes. It might, therefore, be unjust to be too severe with the Social Democrats. It remains true, nevertheless, that they were taken unawares by the events and that when power was offered them they recoiled before responsibility and practiced a policy of prudent opportunism, confining themselves to defending the interests of the working class and the "conquests of the revolution." The leaders whom the Social Democrats elevated to power lacked "stature." They were men of good intentions, good tacticians, at times intelligent intellectuals, but in general, more often shrewd trade union secretaries rather than veritable leaders. The Social Democrats may deserve recognition for having been resolutely opposed to every hazardous experiment with bolshevism and this was probably good for Germany. But this is only a negative merit.

11

They did not know how to play the leading role which had devolved upon them.

The bourgeois parties did not meet the test of power with any more good fortune than the Socialists. After a vain effort to constitute a large republican party of the left, they split up into Democrats and German People's Party and they were weakened by internal dissensions and personal quarrels. Personalities of the first order were rare among them. Max Weber died too soon; Rathenau was assassinated before he was able to show his measure. Stresemann alone remained.

Stresemann had the very great merit of sensing the need for Germany to pursue a policy of conciliation in foreign affairs and of "sacred union" in domestic affairs. A National Liberal and an imperialist in his origins, he felt as a good realist, however, that nothing could be accomplished in Germany without the participation of the Socialists on one side, and the right on the other. He was equipped with uncommon courage for this well-nigh impossible task. Treated with contempt by the Socialists, he wore himself out in vain efforts to win over the Nationalists. The latter abandoned him on all decisive occasions and the extremists would even have assassinated him if the occasion had presented itself. He died trying to prevent his own party from slipping toward the right. His policy of *rapprochement*, earned for him the passionate hatred of his adversaries of the right and at the same time he was always looked upon with a certain mistrust abroad, especially in France. He was accused of "finesse" and duplicity and it is indeed true that Stresemann was as "national" and as "German" as the fanatics who fought him to the grave. But he differed from them. Of those who knew him intimately, more than one feels that this defeated man who worked himself to death merited more than the injuries, anathemas and disdain which were heaped upon him in his own country and abroad. But he was a defeated man and nothing of his work has survived. With his end, the bourgeoisie, of which he was the most notable exponent, was completely bankrupt.

The Weimar republic above all succumbed under the crushing tasks which circumstances imposed upon it. It had to liquidate the war and the consequences which proceeded from the war; i.e., the armistice, the Versailles Peace, reparations, the Ruhr invasion, the fall of the mark, the ruination of the middle classes and the unprecedented economic crisis that shook the world. The Weimar republic was not responsible for these calamities. It was the men of the old regime and their mistakes that had brought about the ruination of Germany. It was the army chiefs and Ludendorf in particular who had imperiously called for an armistice. But neither one nor the other was called upon to find the means of warding off the disaster. This is understandable. Ludendorf could not be sent to negotiate the armistice with Foch nor could William II be charged with signing the peace treaty. It was the "civil officers" who, during the war had been stripped of all power yet, in the hour of distress, remained bravely to take the reins of government into their hands. But it was inevitable that the men who accepted this unenviable mission should be ruined in public opinion when they found themselves forced to advocate the acceptance and execution by their fellow citizens of the very severe conditions which were imposed upon Germany. The innocent ones continued to pay for the faults of the guilty.

The impossibility of the task of the new men was rendered complete by the fact that while they bore the responsibility for the sacrifices imposed by the victors, they never thereby gained the confidence of the Allies themselves. Democrats have often alleged that the Entente should have dealt kindly with the Weimar republic and its policy of fulfilment. By the severity of the conditions imposed and by the persistent mistrust which they showed to their German partners, the Allies

13

are in part responsible for the collapse of the very republic whose advent they favored.

This thesis obviously has substantial basis in fact. It runs counter, however, to a persistent doubt found especially in France. Some wondered, and they still wonder, whether there really was much of a change between the pre-war Germany and the new republican Germany; in other words whether the German "revolution" had really been a "crisis of conscience" and the index of a change in the very mentality of the German. They wondered whether Germany had driven out her old leaders because she sincerely repudiated her imperialist past or simply because they had been wrong in not being successful. A suspicion persisted that the revolution of 1918 was nothing but an instinctive defensive attitude assumed by the Germans. Feeling themselves lost they hastily cringed low in order to avoid collapse; but they remained invincibly faithful to their realistic temperament and to their policy of force. Their democracy from that time on was considered to be a function of their weakness. It was felt that in the measure in which they would regain their forces they would return to their true nature, to their imperialist mentality and to their ambitions of world expansion. This deep-seated doubt increased in proportion to and in measure with the increase of the second wave of the counter-revolution, that of nationalism, which ended by submerging the entire country in the triumph of Hitler.

4. From the German Nationalists to Hitler

In attempting to define the tendencies of the German Nationalists it must be noted, in the first place, that they pursued a purely negative policy which consisted of pitiless criticism of their opponents of the left. The criticisms levelled by the German Nationalists at the pacifist democrats was of the following nature. The democrats, they said, believed during the war in the possibility of a peace of compromise; they had faith in American mediation and, by this hope, delayed the inauguration of submarine warfare which, if unloosed immediately and thoroughly, could have starved out England. Moreover the democrats had, on July 17, 1917 voted the famous Reichstag declaration for peace, at the moment when the Allies were on the verge of defeat. Finally, by their defeatist propaganda, they had destroyed the morale of the troops and delivered to the army a "dagger thrust in the back." At the moment of defeat, they allowed the ignominious November revolution to come to pass and cast overboard their Emperor and their constitution. In the foolish hope of obtaining a peace of justice they had placed confidence in Wilson, signed the armistice and accepted the Peace of Versailles. After the defeat, always deluded by the false hope of alleviating the hardships of Germany, they recommended the policy of fulfilment, humiliated the country in vain and introduced into the nation a spirit of discouragement and abdication. During the invasion of the Ruhr they restricted themselves merely to passive resistance, only to resign themselves eventually to pure and simple capitulation. In accepting the Dawes Plan, they had granted to the Allies the right of control over German economic life, and in signing the Young Plan and the Hague accords they had subjected future generations to tribute for sixty years and placed the very existence of Germany in peril.

The tactics of the German Nationalists thus consisted in always drawing a comparison between the glorious past and the distressing present, consequently developing among the Germans a nostalgia for the imperial epoch. They sought to wean the people away from the leaders who had directed the liquidation of the war and to persuade them that they had nothing to lose; patience and resignation would serve them nothing, faith in justice was illusory and hope in a League of Nations a chimera. They thus led them to suppose that hate alone could bring about the regeneration of Germany and that an energetic "no" must be the reply to the unreasonable demands of the victors. It was necessary to brave the risks of a new bold stroke or else, they held, to retire w' 'n one's own borders and recoup strength while awaiting the hour of deliverance. They were realistic pessimists, believing in the final prevailing of might, in the eternal struggle of men and peoples for power and envisaging no other prospect for the future of Germany than the revival of the movement of 1813 and a regrouping of world forces which would permit the demolition of the order established by the Peace of Versailles.

From the point of view of domestic policy the Nationalists were unalterably hostile to the Weimar constitution. They detested this "rational" republic which applied the false principle of equality to collective groups as well as to individuals, which replaced the states, these "little fatherlands" dear to the heart of the German, by the *Länder*, void of all real sovereignty; which, in place of the Prussia of the Hohenzollerns—a dominant power in Europe—had substituted a diminished Prussia, upon which had been superimposed a republican form, a democratic electoral system and a parliamentary government. They detested a regime which destroyed the principle of authority, substituted a president and a party man for a German emperor, and which, while ruining the monarchy, was also destroying religion by preparing the separation of church and state and by dechristianizing public life. They never wearied of denouncing the defects of parliamentarianism with its favoritism and corruption, with its demoralization of the German bureaucracy, its ruination of state enterprises and its toleration of scandals like those of the Berlin municipal administration. They insisted that it was necessary to put an end to the "socialist fraud," to drive out the band of profiteers who exploited power and led the country to ruin. As a remedy for all these evils they

16

advocated the restoration of the monarchy, or at least of a strong central power, and the establishment of a corporate state with representation of workers of every category.

In foreign affairs, the policy of the German Nationalists was no less "revolutionary." It was grounded in the resentment aroused by defeat and revolution and in the instinctive pessimism of malcontents who did not accept the consequences of defeat. They sought to substitute for the policy of fulfilment a policy of decided resistance to a treaty which they believed could not be executed. This alone, they thought, could, after a violent and passing crisis, lead to positive results. From the start German Nationalist policy was oriented clearly against France, whom they accused of destroying Europe by her incoercible imperialism, by her severity in imposing impossible reparations and by her implacable desire to hold Germany in bondage under the pretext of assuring European security. The German Nationalists vehemently denied the charge that they were desirous of a war of revenge. They were, indeed, sufficiently realistic to sense the formidable dangers which a warlike adventure would bring to their country in their then unarmed state. When one noted, however, the opposition which they displayed to disarmament, the stubbornness with which they secretly prepared for the restoration of Germany's power, the care with which they spread the war spirit among their fellow citizens, it was difficult to maintain any illusions as to the future for which they were waiting and preparing. They counted on the hour to strike sooner or later with a new call to force and they worked with all their energy to prepare the great masses of the people for this decisive crisis.

All, to be sure, were not animated by the same intransigeance. There were extremists who dreamed of an alliance with the bolshevists and a crusade of the half-starved against Western capitalism, as well as fanatical racialists who wished to substitute the cult of Wotan for bolshevism. There were adventurers and desperadoes who engineered *coups de force*, setting up free corps, reviving the Holy Fehme or practicing political murder, as well as moderates who stretched out their hands to the People's Party and to big business, who agreed to collaborate with Stresemann, who sincerely disavowed every idea of a revolution inside or a war outside the country. But in a general way one may say that whereas fanatics scarcely ever manifested their action except by *coups de force*, without thinking of the morrow, the moderates, when they were associated at various times in the government, were invariably disavowed by the larger section of the party as well as by the voters, so that they finally disappeared completely from the political arena. The majority of the party developed an increasingly radical opposition to the Weimar regime. The substitution of Hugenberg for Count Westarp as party chief marked in a visible way the moment when the German Nationalists drew closer to the National Socialists and thus facilitated the internal changes which brought the Nazis to power.

5. Hitler and the Beginnings of National Socialism

Among the groups carried up by the great nationalist wave, that of the National Socialists was destined for the highest position. Its beginnings go back to the troubled period which immediately followed the revolution of 1918. Since the National Socialist Party is the individual and original creation of one personality, Adolf Hitler, we must first see how the political ideas of this great leader of men were formed.

We are amply informed concerning the spiritual development of Hitler by the detailed account of his youth provided in *Mein Kampf*.* From this we learn that his first experiences led Hitler in a direction which placed him in violent opposi-

---

* Rudolf Olden in his *Hitler* (New York 1936) holds the thesis that Hitler's *Mein Kampf* is a romanticised autobiography created to meet the political needs of the Nazi movement. Olden has attempted to reconstruct the account of Hitler's life by the utilization of other materials.—*Ed.*

18

tion to socialism and democracy but which also diverged very appreciably from the ways of the German Nationalists.

Hitler is an Austrian, but in his leanings he is exclusively and passionately German. His childhood enthusiasms go back to the exploits of the German army in the war of 1870-71 and to Wagnerian opera. He remained aloof from and even hostile to Austrian particularism. He had a decided repugnance for the Austro-Hungarian Dual Monarchy, viewing it as a state formed of heterogeneous elements, dominated by Slav influences, in a stage of complete decadence and doomed to inevitable catastrophe. He manifested no dynastic or monarchist enthusiasm, and had nothing but aversion for the Hapsburgs, whom he considered entirely too favorable to Czech and Slav influences and completely indifferent to the interests of German race, language, and culture. While yet a boy he saw no other salvation for Austria except in the destruction of the Austrian state.

Hitler belonged neither to the peasant nor to the working classes. He was the son of a petty customs official but he refused at any cost to enter upon the career of a functionary and aspired rather to become a painter or an architect. An orphan at 13 years of age, he came to Vienna where he was forced to renounce his artistic ambitions and go through the hard school of poverty; he shared the life and suffering of the people and earned his bread first as a simple day laborer, then as a draughtsman and water color painter.

As a manual laborer, he relates, he came into contact with socialists and he was immediately disgusted by the narrowness of their views. He studied Marxist doctrine and it inspired only a decided aversion in him. Above all he experienced the tyranny of trade unionism as expressed in the formula "Either be one of us or have your head broken." He decided that socialist brutality must be answered by an equal measure of brutality. "The terror in the workshop, in the factory, in the meeting local and in the mass demonstrations,"

he wrote, "will always be successful as long as it is not met by
an equally violent terror."*

At the same time that Hitler became an anti-socialist he
also became an antisemite. His encounter in the streets of
Vienna with a Jew in a kaftan and black earlocks led him to
perceive intuitively the racial difference which set the Jews
apart. He felt that the Jew was not a German but that he belonged to another species with which he had no bond of
solidarity. Little by little he familiarized himself with the
Jewish question: he studied antisemitic literature and came in
touch with Austrian antisemitism as found in Schönerer, the
leader of the Christian Socialists, or in Lueger, the famous
mayor of Vienna. Gradually he came to view the Jew as a
fermenting agent of moral and social decomposition, as a
vitiating factor and public corrupter, demoralizing public
opinion through the theatre, letters, the cinema and the press.
At the same time he came to believe that the Jew was also the
spiritual father of Marxism and that he uses this nefarious
doctrine in order to destroy public order. In this combination
of Judaism and Marxism, Hitler saw the fundamental danger
threatening the modern world.

His observations of public life, on the other hand, taught
Hitler contempt for democracy and parliamentarianism. In
Austria he witnessed a lamentable caricature of them. Had
he been in Germany he might perhaps have become a reactionary monarchist. But he lived in Austria where the Hapsburgs were worth even less than Parliament, and he ended by
spurning both majority rule and dynastic legitimism. He
wanted a leader, not elected by the majority but chosen freely
by the people and in whom all national aspirations were to be
incarnate.

In 1912 Hitler went from Vienna to Munich. Munich was
a city of purely German race, customs, language and culture,
and provided an environment which was open to the great cur-

* *Mein Kampf*, p. 46. All references are to the edition of 1932.

rents of opinion. Here Hitler's ideas on international politics became fixed. He soon came to feel intuitively that German foreign policy was based on a ruinous foundation, the Triple Alliance, and he sensed its decay. He foresaw the inevitable defection of Italy as well as the treason of the Slav elements in the Austro-Hungarian empire. The system of alliances whereby the Reich was seeking to make its situation in Europe secure was therefore deceptive and would not provide any real security for it.

Moreover it seemed to Hitler that the Reich was confronted with the formidable problem of an annual increase in population of 900,000 persons. Malthusianism in Hitler's eyes was a crime against race and there could be no thought, therefore, of restricting this population increase. But how were they to be fed? By home colonization? By exploiting every parcel of arable land? It would be a way, but it was insufficient. Moreover it had the disadvantage of favoring pacifism and Germany's falling back on itself, but nature wishes war. Was it to be achieved by a world policy at once commercial, industrial and colonial, such as was practiced by William II? This was a grandiose plan but impossible of realization, since it entailed a break with England, who was jealous of her economic supremacy. It would be much more worth while, then, to pursue an agrarian policy of a greater Germany. Frontiers are not sacred. They rest on the right of the strongest power. German territorial expansion could be fruitful, however, only in the direction of the east. There Germany should resume once again the crusade of the Knights of the Teutonic Order against Russia. This, said Hitler, represented the only possibility of conquering the necessary territory to assure the subsistence of an increasing population. It was necessary, therefore, for Germany to orient herself deliberately toward that solution. She should sacrifice her alliance with pacifist and conservative Austria and seek at all costs the friendship of England by renouncing excessive economic ambitions and the construction of a large navy. These had only aroused British mistrust.

The outbreak of the world cataclysm in 1914 filled Hitler with great enthusiasm. He was convinced that the war was not imposed upon the masses but that the great majority of the people wished it to come. As for himself he exulted in seeing that there were other things in the world than rivalry for trade routes. He enlisted not in the Austrian but in the Bavarian army for he desired at all cost to participate in the grand struggle which had broken out. The stake in this struggle, he held, was not little Serbia, nor even the fate of Austria, but the existence of the German nation. He immediately adapted himself to the calling of a soldier. He felt deeply the grandeur of the military virtues of courage, endurance, obedience and devotion to one's country. He was happy and proud to belong to an army which he considered the finest in the world, an army in which the maximum of organization was allied with a maximum of war spirit, courage and sacrifice. He had one regret, namely that in the high places they had too much regard for the civil officials. He had a horror of parliamentary institutions, of the babblers of the press, of socialists and Jews. He reproached the government with paying too much attention to them. He hoped that the patriotic awakening which was cementing the nation would result in the dissolution of the Reichstag and the placing under lock and key of the Marxist leaders and Jews who were preparing the revolution. While the better Germans were falling at the front, it was necessary "to crush the vermin" behind the lines.

He then constructed for himself a simplified story of the War in every point analogous to the legend of the "dagger thrust in the back" which was widespread among rightist circles. The German army, according to Hitler, remained unconquered. It had annihilated the Russians and forced them to sign the peace of Brest-Litovsk. Then, however, came the great treason of the Jewish Marxists, who wished at any price to prevent a German victory. Just at the moment when the army was gathering all its forces in order to make the decisive thrust on the Western front, there came, first, the munitions strikes, then the general strike and finally the November revolution fomented by a set of cowards and traitors. The German sword had triumphed in the east. In the west the criminal hands of the Marxist Jews had prevented the delivery of the decisive thrust and had thus brought about the collapse of the country.

In the great distress which, Hitler says, filled his heart in this hour of great catastrophe, he felt germinating within him the resolution which was going to determine his future. It is of no use, he thought, to construct houses on a dishonored earth. He renounced his ambition to become an architect. It was necessary to make amends for the Emperor's mistake of having extended his hand to the socialist leaders. "There was no coming to terms with the Jew, there was only the harsh either-or. As for me, I determined to become a man of politics." (*Mein Kampf*, p. 225.)

6. The Putsch of 1923 and the Regeneration of the Party

The first five years of Hitler's political apostleship, terminated by the Munich putsch of November 8 and 9, 1923, was a period of sustained efforts which met with a resounding and what appeared to be a decisive check.

One reads at length in *Mein Kampf* of the beginnings of Hitler's career as an orator; how, after the collapse of the red republic of Munich, he became a propaganda officer, giving courses to initiate soldiers into civic life. He tells how he made the acquaintance of Gottfried Feder, who furnished him with the elements of his economic program, how he established contacts with a group of comrades who shared in his convictions, how one day he assisted in the organization of a new group called "Deutsche Arbeiter Partei" and took

23

part in the discussion, how willy nilly he was enrolled as number seven in the committee and found himself definitely becoming the animator of a very small party, the treasury of which contained only seven and a half marks—a party which had neither program nor plan of action and which saved itself from ridicule only by "the confused sentiment that there was nothing to hope for from existing organizations for the regeneration of the German nation and the cure of the ills from which she was suffering."

Hitler decided to take this embryonic group in hand. In less than two years he was able, by his activity, to raise it from its insignificant position. On February 24, 1920 he drafted the program of 25 points; he organized the guards of Brown Shirts and Black Shirts (S.A. and S.S.), he gave the party its flag with the swastika, and the party gained ground not only in Munich but also in numerous Bavarian villages. Finally he bought for it, in November, 1920, its newspaper organ, the *Völkischer Beobachter*.

During the first phase of his activity, Hitler's chief concern was to recruit a solid, robust, disciplined, trained and fanatical militia, which would permit him to hold meetings without the danger of obstruction by his better organized and more determined opponents. He considered it necessary to organize shock troops capable of delivering punishment in an efficient manner, of "putting out" opponents during stormy meetings and of holding foes in awe during public demonstrations. The first exploits of the new party were the brawls in various meeting places in Munich (Hofbrauhaus or Zirkus Krone) or in popular demonstrations against the financial measures of the Entente, against the law concerning the protection of the republic or against the insufficiency of passive resistance to the Franco-Belgian invasion of the Ruhr.

After the occupation of the Ruhr, the Hitler troops became more and more quasi-military formations. They planned active resistance and they considered the organization of armed surprise attacks. After Stresemann's decree of September 26, 1923, ordering the cessation of passive resistance in the Rhine valley, the Hitler bands joined in the Bavarian protest movement against this decree. This movement embraced the most disparate elements. There were anti-republican Bavarian particularists who were federalists and hostile to Prussia; there were chiefs of secret societies held responsible for the murder of Rathenau, who were being sought by the police; there were some dissidents from the German Nationalists, Wulle and Graefe, who had founded a violently racial and revolutionary group; there were some local leaders like Streicher of Nuremberg or Dinter in Thuringia; finally there was Ludendorf himself.

All these people, although diverse in origin and tendencies, were in accord on one point: they wished to overthrow by an armed coup the republic and the parliamentary regime first in Munich, then in the Reich, and install the dictatorship of one strong man. In November, 1923, the crisis came to a head. The racialists organized armed bands in Küstrin, in Mecklenburg and in Bavaria. Hitler and Ludendorf were to act in Munich and set the Bavarian government in action against Berlin. At the last minute, however, the Bavarian leaders recoiled before the idea of engaging in a movement of open rebellion against the Reich. The putsch, attempted by Hitler and Ludendorf, ended on the 9th of November in the memorable shooting in the streets of Munich. Hitler and his partisans were thrown into prison; on April 1, 1924 Hitler was condemned to five years' imprisonment and interned in the fortress of Landsberg on the Lech.

The defeat of the Munich putsch could have brought about the total collapse of Hitler's work. His best friends had fled or were in prison. His followers had disbanded. He himself was, for one year, confined in Landsberg and not in any position to exercise direct influence on his followers.

Hitler then came to the conclusion that he had committed

tactical blunders. The first blunder, he felt, was that he had engaged the party in action too soon, before he had sufficient means at his command, while it was associated with doubtful and ill-matched allies. The second blunder was that he placed his hope for success in armed rebellion through conspiracy and extra-legal means. Hitler decided that this, too, was an error. In order to win Germany it was necessary not to deviate from legal means, to win the confidence and the votes of the people and to be chosen by the nation itself as dictator. This was the lesson which Hitler derived from his unsuccessful *coup d'état*. From then on he claimed he would never swerve from legality. But, when the moment came, he would claim power for himself alone.

This brings us to the second phase of the political life of Hitler which includes the five years from 1924 to 1929, in the course of which, the *Führer* reorganized his party and steered it to its first marked triumphs. I have no intention of going into the vicissitudes of this evolution here. The details of this story are still insufficiently known. I wish merely to indicate in broad strokes the general lines of movement and to note the general causes which led to the extraordinary rise of National Socialism.

Among the causes, the personal factor no doubt played an important role. I shall not attempt to decide upon the exact measure of the "genius" of Hitler. But he obviously possesses the strong talents of a demagogue and a statesman. He is, first of all, a popular orator of the first order who knows how to speak to the masses, to excite them and to kindle in them the flame of passion. He has also the undeniable gift of seduction; he knows how to tame men and allure women. He is a man of iron will and tireless activity. And he possesses also the flair of the born politician, that intuition which permits him to sense the confused aspirations of the crowd, to discern how the wind is blowing and to divine what should and can be done at each particular moment. He realized that he had to avoid becoming involved either in a military putsch which would inevitably fail, or in a monarchist plot which had no chance of success. He knew that he could not go far in the direction of socialism without embroiling himself with the nationalists or the bourgeois groups whom he was trying to win over to his side, and that he could not readily align himself with the reactionary right and the industrial magnates without the danger of destroying the popular movement which supported him. He decided that it would be dangerous for him to engage in a violent conflict with Rome. Very deliberately and with all the means at his disposal, he sought to achieve unified command of the party under his own absolute dictatorship.

Thus we see Hitler disassociating himself in due time from Ludendorf, from whom he was separated by profound differences in temperament, from nationalist dissidents who turned toward an ever more fantastic revolutionary racialism, and from the socialist left wing of his own party which, under Otto Strasser, was proceeding along lines very much akin to communism. Hitler was able to maintain his organizations independent of the Reichswehr by always avoiding any irremediable alienation of the military leaders. He knew how to re-establish the unity of his party in Bavaria, how to smooth out the antagonism which threatened to develop between the organizations in southern Germany and those in the north, how to maintain discipline among his troops, removing from his staff the mediocrities, the strongheaded and the blunderers, how to assert his ascendancy over his collaborators and how to maintain agitation in each state without engaging constantly in a death struggle against the government.

If we now attempt to identify the general causes favoring the rise of National Socialism, we may arrive at the following conclusions: When Hitler began his activity, his propaganda was almost identical with that of the German Nationalists. The same causes, therefore, which brought on this wave of

27

nationalism also favored the development of Hitlerism. These consisted in the unanimous revolt of German opinion against the Versailles Peace and its consequences, the irritation produced by the Ruhr invasion and the opposition incited by the policy of fulfilment or *rapprochement*.

To these first causes was added another: the economic collapse of the middle classes brought about by the fall of the mark in 1923. The entire bourgeois class was enveloped in an unprecedented catastrophe. It saw its acquired riches go up in smoke and it was almost completely proletarianized. This collapse was particularly serious among the social strata from which the middle parties, Democrats, People's Party and Centre, were recruited. This entire group was "radicalized" by the disaster which they experienced. But they could not join the Socialists whom they held responsible for Germany's misfortunes, nor could they follow the Communists because of their old prejudices against the "reds." A group of "despairing individuals," therefore, swelled the ranks of the extremists of the right and the secret organizations. Many others were attracted by National Socialism, which took care from the beginning to show special sympathy for the proletarian who lived by his daily work, and to stand aloof from the privileged, the aristocracy and the industrial and financial "profiteers." The university youth, in particular, whose parents had been ruined by inflation, who no longer saw any way of continuing their studies and thus found their situation more and more difficult, furnished an increasing number of adherents to Hitlerism.

The conclusion of the Locarno pacts and the entrance of Germany into the League of Nations in September 1926 marked the culminating point of the policy of *rapprochement* as pursued by Stresemann. Very soon after, however, a period of stagnation set in which continued for more than two years. At the time of the Thoiry conversations, Stresemann as well as Briand was under the illusion that Franco-German differ-

ences were to be definitely regulated. In reality, the sentiments of neither of the ministers were in harmony with those
of their respective countries. In Germany as in France public
opinion was very much more nationalist than the statesmen
thought. Briand had reflected, to Stresemann, the famous "repercussions" of Locarno. Despite the new agreement, however, French opinion, viewing the rapid economic recovery
of Germany, her powerful dynamism and the continuous influence of the factions of the right, was far from believing
that French security was safely assured. This led the French
to consider it inadvisable to give up carelessly the guarantees
of the Versailles Treaty. For these guarantees appeared to
many as the last resource available if, by some concurrence
of troublesome circumstances, their security were threatened.
From the start they did not desire any great haste in accelerat-
ing the rhythm of the Locarno "repercussions." Stresemann
waited in vain for them. On June 23, 1927 he solemnly placed
before the Reichstag the question *"Gallia quo vadis?"* and
demanded to know if the Poincaré government intended to
pursue the Locarno policy or return to that of the Ruhr. This
stagnation furnished the National Socialists, who, unlike the
German Nationalists, had never participated in the government, with an admirable opportunity to denounce the failure
of the policy of *rapprochement* and to insist vociferously that
from the first day it had never been anything but a gross
deception.

In 1929 the development of the world economic crisis
brought added strength to the Nazis.

After a short period of prosperity in 1927, which had been
induced above all by the influx of American credits, symptoms of a crisis began to manifest themselves in the beginning
of 1928 with undeniable signs. American money became
scarce and budgetary difficulties began to show themselves. In
September it was decided to nominate a new committee of
experts to examine the financial situation of Germany. In

1929, the situation was openly serious. The flow of foreign credits stopped, the financial embarrassments of the Reich and the states and municipalities increased, factory orders decreased and trade diminished. In March and April the situation became strained and a loss of confidence shook the Reichsbank itself. Bank failures multiplied. In October the formidable stock-exchange crash in New York City gave the signal for the world crisis which had been developing. Germany, too, felt the consequences of that tremendous catastrophe. By the end of the year it was in complete economic and financial atrophy. Above all, that most serious plague, unemployment, was increasing month by month. During the summer of 1927 which had marked the high point of German prosperity, the curve of unemployment had reached the low point with the number of 540,000 unemployed. In the summer of 1929 the number passed 720,000; during the winter it passed 2 million and from then on it continued to increase until by the beginning of 1933 it had passed the 6 million mark. This army of unemployed drifted toward the forces of the extremist parties and particularly the National Socialists. The latter were the principal beneficiaries of the great wave of discontent which was unloosed by the growing misery of the population affected by this plague.

In the same year 1929, the Young Plan was drawn up. It was signed on June 7 and completed by the Hague agreements of August 29, 1929 and January 20, 1930. These arrangements, however, immediately aroused passionate resistance not only in nationalist circles but also in the world of big industry. During the negotiations one of the German experts, Vögler, had preferred to resign rather than accept responsibility for the proposed agreements. As early as June 15 the offensive of the German nationalists was unloosed against the Young Plan. On July 8, at the meeting of the Langnamverein, big industry in its turn indicated its uncomprising hostility. On July 9 a committee was formed, consisting of

German Nationalists, Stahlhelm and National Socialists, to organize legal resistance by bringing about a plebiscite against the adoption of the Young Plan. The two main arguments adduced against the project were the following: (1) The duration of the payments imposed upon Germany was intolerable: it was not right to charge future generations for fifty-eight years with this crushing burden. (2) The levying of an annual payment of two billion marks necessarily involved in the long run a sort of "loss of substance" for Germany. Little by little Germany would run the risk of losing all real autonomy and of sinking to the state of a kind of "colony," which would work under the control of international capitalism and for foreign masters.

7. *From the Young Plan to the Fall of Brüning*

The Young Plan provided the occasion for the alliance between the German Nationalists and the National Socialists which, in the course of three years, resulted in bringing the Nazis to power. The *rapprochement* between the two groups was not carried through without difficulty. For despite similarities in their aims the two groups also revealed many differences.

From the point of view of social antecedents the Nazis and the German Nationalists differed greatly as to the social classes from which they were derived. The German Nationalists, or rather their leaders, came from the old privileged classes. They were the heirs of the ruling élite of the old regime, the landed and military aristocracy, high dignitaries, university professors and students, big industry and high finance and the liberal professions. Their tendencies, therefore, were in most respects conservative or reactionary. They affirmed their monarchist convictions and their fidelity to the overthrown dynasties. They looked for the re-establishment of the old order by an authoritarian regime which would restore influence and leadership to the traditional ruling groups.

Hitler, on the contrary, was a man of the people. He attracted to himself the masses of "little men" who had suffered from the state of affairs brought about by the revolution of 1918. These included the crowd of disinherited, declassed malcontents, and rebels of all sorts. His propaganda was effective above all among the mass of the bourgeoisie which had been hit by inflation and economic crisis, among workers and artisans demoralized by unemployment, among dismissed salaried employees, among peasants ruined by the burden of debts and the poor market for their products, among great numbers of intellectuals who saw no way out of their distress, and among adventurers who were left without employment after the army had been demobilized. Behind him were organized bands and fanatics. Hitler, therefore, did not for a moment contemplate turning backward and restoring the past. There was not a trace of dynastic enthusiasm in him. The "Third Reich" which he wished to establish in no way resembled the old German Empire. At the head of the "Third Reich" was to be a *Führer* who would be designated neither by birth nor elected by a majority, but who would be accepted by the free choice of the people because of his superiority. The followers who assembled at the rolling of his drum had nothing in common with the old conservative party. It was a revolutionary crowd, disdainful of rank, culture and intelligence. It had nothing to lose in a general upheaval, and was ready for violent action and hazardous adventures in order to achieve its place in the sun and satisfy its grudges.

After the elections of May 20, 1928, when the National Socialists had obtained twelve seats in the Reichstag with about 800,000 votes, the first relations were established between Hitler and Hugenberg, the leader of the German Nationalists and one of the most powerful leaders of heavy industry. The meeting involved many difficulties. Hugenberg was at the moment being taken to task by the socializing wing of the Nazi Party, and Hitler himself only with reluctance decided to renounce the splendid isolation to which he had accustomed his followers. Hitler showed himself little disposed at first to join the plebiscite committee which Hugenberg organized to fight the Young Plan. Upon reflection, however, he decided for it. It is not difficult to see the motives which guided the two contracting parties. Each hoped to make use of the other for its own personal ends. The captains of industry in the camp of the Nationalists believed it good policy to support and finance a movement which aimed to overthrow the position of socialism and which looked like an excellent protection against bolshevist contagion. The Nationalist politicians deluded themselves with the hope of utilizing for their cause the propagandistic genius of the Nazis. They believed they could exercise a directing influence upon the powerful movement which the Nazis had created and use them as an army against communism and the power of the trade unions. The military evidenced a certain sympathy for a party which furnished the Reichswehr with a considerable number of disciplined young men, drilled and hardened by physical training.

Hitler realized the advantages he would possess in being allied with a party which shared many of his ideas, which would furnish him with badly needed money, which would put at his disposal an imposing apparatus of propaganda and publicity, and which, besides, numbered in its ranks men possessing experience in business and in the practice of government.

Hitler soon took a decided turn from the extremist radicalism dear to more than one of his lieutenants. To be sure, he was far from throwing in his lot with the moderates. He publicly proclaimed that on the day of victory he would demand a reckoning from those who had betrayed Germany and that "heads would roll" at that time. But he affirmed with no less emphasis his strong desire to conquer power by legal

33

means and not through mutiny. In addition he agreed to participation with the Nationalists in power and permitted his lieutenant, Frick, to accept the post of Minister of Public Instruction in Thuringia. He took vigorous action against the undisciplined party members who refused to bow to the new tactics. In May 1930 he chased Otto Strasser from the party and in 1931 he suppressed an uprising of mutinous Berlin Storm Troopers under the lead of Stennes.

On March 27, 1930, the cabinet headed by the Socialist Hermann Müller was ousted by a coalition of bourgeois and peasant parties. In forty-eight hours it was replaced by a cabinet headed by the leader of the Centre Party, Dr. Brüning. The new cabinet contained moderates of all shades, including dissident Nationalists who refused to associate themselves with the intransigeant policy of Hugenberg. Brüning did not have a majority in the Reichstag. The extremists on the left and right, the German Nationalists of Hugenberg and the Socialists and Communists, formed in effect a very much greater bloc than the middle parties. On the other hand, Brüning had formidable support at his command. He was favored by President Hindenburg, he had the strong support of the bureaucracy and the army, and he was popular in Centrist circles. Moreover, although he was not supported by the Socialists, he was at least "tolerated" by them since they preferred a Centrist government to a Hugenberg-Hitler regime. For the same reason too, Brüning was favored by the "red and black" Prussian government, which was half Socialist, half Centrist, and which felt itself threatened from the right.

The parliamentary regime, however, had already ceased to function normally. Brüning was incapable of solving the financial problems on account of the quarrels of the parties, each of which, according to the expression of Finance Minister Dietrich, wished "to cook its own soup." When Brüning did not succeed in having the Reichstag vote the necessary reforms, he entered resolutely upon the path of dictatorship. By means of decrees issued under article 48 of the constitution he set up the necessary taxes to obtain a balanced budget. When the Reichstag refused to ratify this measure the President, at the request of the Chancellor decreed the dissolution of the Reichstag and Brüning again, by virtue of article 48, enacted a series of provisional measures which were similar to the financial program repudiated by the Reichstag. On September 14, 1930 the nation was called upon to decide on the differences which had arisen between government and parliament. These elections resulted in an amazing triumph for the Nazis. Hitler succeeded in mobilizing behind him the mass of indifferent citizens who until then had abstained from voting and the strength of his party increased from 12 deputies to 107.

During the two years which his ministry lasted, Brüning maintained himself in power against a hostile parliament only through these dictatorial methods. He would convene the Reichstag for a few days and then adjourn it. He obtained ratification for the measures which he had taken by very small majorities and then only by waving before the Reichstag the threat of dissolution.

During the first period of the Brüning ministry the alliance formed between Hitler and Hugenberg continued in force. On October 11, 1930 at Bad Harzburg, Hitler participated in a grand demonstration of "national opposition" with representatives of the Stahlhelm, of the Landbund, of the Alldeutscher Verband, with the former director of the Reichsbank, Dr. Schacht, and with other personalities. This combination was now ready to unite against Brüning.

The agreement did not last very long, however, and soon the various coalition groups reasserted their independence. There was a rumor at the time that Brüning made an attempt to gain the support of Hitler. It has been said that the Chancellor made the following proposition to him: if Hitler would support Brüning the latter would promise to resign at the end of a year and then propose to Marshal von Hindenburg that Hitler be designated Chancellor. This rumor, however, remains unverified. All that is known is that Hitler made contacts at the time with the President, with whom he had an interview and a political conversation on October 10, 1931, and with Groener and Brüning, whom he met in January, 1932. Brüning was anxious at that time to have the presidential term of von Hindenburg renewed without the procedure of an election but rather by the Reichstag voting a modification of the constitution to that effect. If Hitler would have consented the matter could have been arranged by the support of the National Socialist votes despite the opposition of the right. Negotiations, however, came to naught. Hitler united with Hugenberg in demanding a regular presidential election.

The election campaign was carried on with a great deal of bitterness and ended on April 10, after the second balloting, with the re-election of Marshal von Hindenburg by 19,359,-635 votes against the 13,418,051 votes obtained by Hitler.*

The conflict between Hitler and the Brüning government became more violent. The Prussian government carried out raids in the homes of various Nazi leaders and claimed that it had proof in its hands that the National Socialists were preparing for civil war, and demanded that action for high treason be instituted against the Nazis. On April 13, Minister of Defense Groener proclaimed the dissolution of the Hitler militia. At that moment General Schleicher, who during this period had remained in personal touch with Hitler, made a decisive thrust against the Centrist cabinet. Together with the principal leaders of the Reichswehr he took steps against Groener in the course of which he explained to the minister that in view of the measures he had taken against the Hitler militia, he had lost the confidence of the army. On May 12,

---

* In the first election on March 13, Hindenburg received 18,650,730 votes, Hitler 11,339,285, Thälmann 4,983,197 and Düsterberg 2,558,000. In the second election Thälmann received 3,706,655 votes.—*Ed.*

Groener was dismissed. This was followed very soon by the dismissal of Brüning, who had broken with President Hindenburg on the question of the large feudal estates in East Prussia which he had proposed to consign to internal colonization.

8. The Von Papen Interregnum

The German Nationalists assumed power on June 1, 1932 with the designation of Franz von Papen as Chancellor. The new Chancellor, enjoying the personal affection and absolute confidence of the old President, governed, as did his predecessor, in purely dictatorial fashion. He maintained himself by means of the authority which the illustrious field-marshal still enjoyed in Germany and by the solid support of the Reichswehr and the police. The von Papen cabinet lived from day to day, governing by decrees, after the manner of a committee of public safety, without any parliamentary method and perhaps even without strict legality. But it did not hesitate to make it known that it did not consider itself dependent upon a Reichstag vote and that it would remain at its post as long as its leader, the Marshal, might deem necessary.

The attitude of the von Papen cabinet towards National Socialism was entirely different from that of the Brüning cabinet. The new Chancellor immediately indicated his intention of concentrating all constructive energies and those mindful of public welfare,—in other words, all "national" forces,—on overcoming the crisis through which Germany was passing. This meant, therefore, the Nazis as well as the German Nationalists, the Centre and the middle parties. Brüning had treated the Nazis as subversive revolutionists who were to be ousted from the Reichswehr, whose formations were disbanded and to whom was forbidden the wearing of uniforms and the holding of public demonstrations. This, in the eyes of the new government, was unjust and unwise. Unjust, because one could not deny to the National Socialists a

37

generous idealism and a passionate desire to serve their country; unwise, because the obvious reason for the success of the Nazis was that, having always remained in the opposition, they had thus escaped the unpopularity which inevitably accompanies participation in the government. This was an inadmissible situation. It was necessary to admit the National Socialists to the exercise of power in order to compel them to show the measure of their constructive capacities and to lead them to the consciousness of their responsibilities. Only at this price could a normal regime be established in Germany allowing for the formation of a stable political will.

This was one of the essential tasks which the von Papen cabinet undertook to bring about. It intended no longer to bar the way to National Socialism but to incorporate it into the general stream of German political life as a powerful movement, legitimate in its essential aims and to be reckoned with thereafter. It was simply a question, therefore, of enlisting the Nazis in common action with all the national forces. This obviously presupposed a change of attitude on the part of the public authorities. From then on the Nazis no longer were considered as trouble makers who had to be subdued, but as a party of order whose intemperate language and gestures were to be excused, whose willingness to co-operate in the work of national regeneration was to be taken for granted and who were to be accorded a place in the government to which they were entitled by their numerical importance. Formerly the extremists of the right and the left, Nazis and Communists, had been placed on the same level. Now it was admitted that the National Socialists had been defamed and that they had the right to be vindicated.

Under these conditions the von Papen cabinet, in order to obtain toleration for the Nazis, made two important concessions to them. The first was the dissolution of the Reichstag proclaimed by the President on June 4, 1932. The second was the renewed legalization of the Nazi militia, which had been banned by Groener. The former minister had viewed the existence of a private army of 400,000 eager young men, who were organized in military fashion and subject to the authority of one leader, as a danger to the very existence of the state, whose authority already seemed to him to be dangerously shaken. The move against Groener made by Schleicher and his colleagues proved superabundantly that the Reichswehr circles did not consider this a danger. It was perfectly logical, therefore, that the von Papen cabinet, in which Schleicher was Reichswehr Minister, should rescind this measure and by decree of June 15, suppress the previous ban on the organization of public demonstrations in uniform by the Nazis.

The elections took place on July 31. They brought to Hitler his expected triumph. In the 1930 elections the Nazis had received 6,401,210 votes and elected 107 deputies. They now returned 230 deputies with 13,732,779 votes, or 37 per cent of the total electorate. They thus became "the most powerful party which had ever existed in Germany" although they did not control a majority in the Reichstag. But they represented more than one third of the Reichstag, which meant that no modification of the constitution could be made without their consent, since a majority of two thirds was necessary for such changes. The other parties suffered serious losses. The Social Democrats elected only 133 deputies while the Communists increased their number to 89. The Catholic Centre barely held its own, the German Nationalists lost heavily and the middle parties were wholly wiped out. It was quite evident that the proletarianized bourgeoisie had almost entirely deserted the old parties in favor of the National Socialists.

Following these two concessions Hitler began to manifest a certain tolerance towards the von Papen cabinet. But although he abstained from attacking it, he also refused to make common front with it. Nazi newspapers stressed the transitory

39

character of the von Papen government and they indicated that its main usefulness was to prepare for the advent of integral National Socialism. After a short while, however, this neutral attitude gave way to one of decided hostility.

The measure whereby public demonstrations by Nazi storm troops were again allowed soon had very serious repercussions. Their parades and clamor acted as provocations to the opponents of Hitlerism and they soon showed themselves to be a danger to public peace, inspiring as they did a permanent state of excitement in the populace. Under such conditions some of the states protested against this measure, which threatened to prove disastrous to the maintenance of order and a regrettable interference of the Reich in the internal affairs of the states. In fact, the restoration of permission for the wearing of uniforms was immediately followed by a recrudescence of political crimes. Communists and Hitlerites battled almost daily with knives, with revolvers or with bombs. Everywhere, especially in Altona, Königsberg and in Silesia, there were brawls and ambuscades which resulted in hundreds of dead and wounded. The responsibility for these acts of terrorism was naturally difficult to establish. Each side vehemently affirmed that it had been provoked by the other or that their incriminating acts were reprisals against previous acts of violence. The government inclined more toward blaming the Communists but the impartiality of its statements was not altogether above suspicion. In any case political terrorism raged on, not only up to the day of the voting but even after the elections.

The reds and the browns continued to kill each other despite the political truce decreed by the government. The government, fearing the wrath of the Hitlerites, had hesitated for a long time to enforce severely the suppression of political assassinations. Finally on August 9, however, a decree appeared considerably increasing the penalties for those guilty of acts of terrorism. On August 22, as a result of this decree,

five National Socialists were condemned to death following a
political murder perpetrated at Potempa under particularly
scandalous conditions. This verdict immediately unloosed a
tempest of unprecedented violence among the Nazis, who
brazenly summoned the government to set aside the "bloody
verdict" and threatened more violence if justice was allowed
to follow its course.

It was in such an atmosphere, after the election of July 31,
that the negotiations commenced for a change in the cabinet
which was to bring about the break between Hitler and the
government. A change could easily have been calculated
which would have provided the cabinet with a safe parliamentary majority. This would have been possible if the Catholic Centre had combined its votes with those of the united
right. The Centre was not *a priori* opposed to such a combination. Centrist leaders felt that the National Socialists
would have to undertake official participation in the government or at least consent to give the government open support.
But they could not accept anything but a coalition cabinet in
which no party was to exercise exclusive influence. It was,
however, precisely on this question of the sharing of power
that agreement seemed impossible. Elated by their election
victory, the Nazis declared they were ready to assume governmental responsibility and enter the cabinet, but on the
condition that they were to be the masters and hold the key
positions in their hands. The Centrist leaders, however, were
too wary and too realistic tacticians to allow the Nazis unlimited power. The President, too, was conscious of his responsibilities as Chief of State and he hesitated in giving his
blank signature to a demagogue who had never shown any
proof of constructive political capacities.

Under these conditions the conversations between Hindenburg, von Papen and Hitler ended on August 13, with an interview which, it seemed, was very stormy and from which
Hitler, in any case, went out humiliated and exasperated. Each

41

party, to be sure, threw the responsibility for the failure on the other. One said that Hitler had voluntarily excluded himself from power by pressing his demand for "all or nothing," and that by his intransigeance he had thus failed in his historical mission. The Nazis, on the contrary, claimed that the *Führer* had never demanded "complete power" but only "unequivocal leadership of the government," and that he had quit the negotiations only because they had refused to his party the share of influence to which it was legitimately entitled. Whatever may have caused it, the break was complete. Hitler announced that he would oppose the Chancellor by all legal means. The President, on his side, gave Hitler to understand that he would not tolerate any attempt to change legal order through violence and that in his capacity as chief of the army he had the means wherewith to oppose any such move. The Nazi press gave vent to its disillusionment and anger in most violent terms. They insisted that their *Führer* had been insulted and they demanded public prosecution of "that reactionary clique of aristocrats" which was attempting to impose its will on Germany.

Logically the situation should have ended with a crash. The von Papen cabinet found itself in open conflict with all the parties, those of the left as well as of the right. Only the German Nationalists ranged themselves behind it. The Reichstag was in the position at any moment to vote lack of confidence in the cabinet and force it to resign. The Chancellor, on his side, had in his pocket the authorization of the President to dissolve the Reichstag if it should venture to overthrow the cabinet.

Such a state of affairs could not continue for long. On September 12, indeed, Communists and National Socialists made a sharp attack upon the cabinet. But the Chancellor succeeded in placing the dissolution decree upon the presiding officer's desk before the vote of non-confidence had been made. From that moment the Reichstag was legally dissolved, and it could not therefore carry out any effective vote. The motion by which it expressed its lack of confidence in the Chancellor by 513 votes against 32 and 5 abstentions was no longer of any effective import.

The moral effect, nevertheless, was considerable. It was established that the "cabinet of barons" had 95 per cent of the parliament against it. The authority of the President himself was compromised. The question was raised whether the dissolution of the Reichstag which he had just proclaimed was indeed legal and whether it actually involved an attack upon the constitution he had sworn to respect. It is a significant fact that in such a situation the country did not stir. This goes a long way to illustrate the discredit into which the Reichstag had fallen by reason of the wrangling of the parties and their manifest incapacity to work together for positive action. The old Marshal, the army and the government appeared as the supreme guarantors of order. There was some fear of what would happen on the day the authority of the President disappeared. For his authority seemed the last resource against the coming of chaos.

On September 17 the new elections were fixed for November 6. The situation was not an easy one for Hitler. He had committed several tactical blunders. The telegram in which he had expressed his solidarity with the assassins of Potempa had produced a bad effect. The tone of his polemics against Hindenburg also lacked good taste. Everywhere his words were repeated, "He is 85 years old, I am 45. I can wait." His defeat in the presidential election of August 13 and the way in which he had been dismissed and reprimanded by Hindenburg had brought damage to his reputation of invincibility. But above all the party needed money. The conflicts with the men of the right had stopped the contributions which had been coming from that source. Hitler, therefore, was forced to decrease his bounties and relax his propaganda. Goebbels complains in his diary of the emptiness of the party treasury.

43

This was the time when the streets in all big cities were filled with brown shirts carrying enormous money boxes and making collections for the party. For the first time the party showed a decline. The elections of November 6 gave them only 196 deputies in place of 230 and the state elections which followed showed an equal or even stronger decline.

The cabinet crisis which followed the November elections brought new disillusionment to Hitler. The situation of the Chancellor had become untenable. In open conflict with the Socialists and Communists, rejected as a renegade by the Centrists, absolutely at variance with the National Socialists, von Papen also incurred the opposition of the southern states who were hostile to the absorption of Prussia into the Reich and to the projects of constitutional reform which had been announced by the cabinet. Within the cabinet itself the dissension between agrarians and industrialists was increasing.

Von Papen had no solid backing either in the nation or the Reichstag. In the eyes of the masses he represented the incarnation of a small and thoroughly unpopular clique of aristocrats and industrial magnates who made claims to leadership. This impasse had to be surmounted at any price. To accomplish this it was necessary to get the President to dissolve the Reichstag again and to govern definitely without its co-operation. But in order to get Hindenburg to become a party to such an extreme measure it was necessary to bring him irrefutable proof that party dissensions made impossible the formation of a parliamentary cabinet. In accord with the President, von Papen sounded the ground. He was quickly convinced that outside of his old partisans he would find no one in the Reichstag who would be disposed to favor the formation of a cabinet of concentration under his leadership. On November 17, he therefore offered his resignation to the Marshal and it was accepted. The crisis was brought to a head.

The situation developed according to the customary pat-

44

tern. The President proceeded to consult with party leaders and he received the impression from them that the constitution of a cabinet resting on a parliamentary majority was not to be considered *a priori* impossible. With this settled he charged Hitler, the leader of the largest party, to form a *parliamentary* cabinet. He imposed precise conditions on him however. These were to keep Schleicher in the war ministry, Neurath in the foreign office, not to restore the dualism between Prussia and the Reich, to set up no restrictions upon the presidential prerogatives (article 48) and to formulate a precise economic program.

Hitler at first accepted the offer of the President, but after having consulted his friends he soon saw that there was a contradiction between the task which had been entrusted to him (to form a parliamentary cabinet) and the conditions which they sought to impose on him. Even without engaging in regular consultation with party leaders, he demanded that the President entrust him with the task of forming a *presidential* cabinet with authorization to dissolve the Reichstag if it rebelled. The Marshal's answer was that a presidential cabinet could only be formed if it were outside and above the parties, consequently the task of forming such a cabinet could not be entrusted to a party chief, and what is more, of a party which demanded all the power for itself. A government so constituted, said the President, would really be a dictatorship of one party, and as such, the most dangerous solution of all. In such a solution the President could not conscientiously participate. Hitler thereupon immediately relinquished the task, which he held incapable of execution. For the second time he had demanded for himself and his followers all the power, and not being able to get it, he broke off the conversations.

Again each one threw the blame for the responsibility of the break upon the other. Hitler complained of having been "maneuvered" by the President. In the presidential camp it was stated that Hitler, puffed up with the feeling of his im-

45

portance, dangerously identified his cause with the interests
of the nation and was obstinately pursuing the aim of setting
up the dictatorship of his party. On both sides now the attempt was made to soften the effects of the break. The President assured the leader of the Nazis that his door would
always be open to him and that he did not give up hope of
seeing him co-operate some day in a government of national
union. Hitler, on his part, spoke of the Marshal in respectful
terms. But the break was none the less complete. Hitler announced that he would bring about the fall of every new
cabinet as he had done to von Papen's and he predicted that
before long they would come to seek him out as their saviour.

The impossibility of constituting a parliamentary government was quite evident. Nothing remained for Hindenburg
except to form another presidential cabinet. Von Papen for a
time hoped to re-enter the scene in this way, for he continued
to enjoy the full confidence of the President. But it was quite
evident that von Papen and his "hussar's policy" was thoroughly unpopular and that a revival of his "cabinet of barons"
would unloose a violent opposition throughout the country.
It would have appeared as a veritable defiance to almost the
entire nation, as an insolent attempt of a small feudal caste
under cover of the weakness of parliamentarianism, to arro-
gate unto itself a dictatorship which was not wanted at any
price by the great majority of the German people. Von Papen
himself was forced to admit that certain of his former colleagues had refused to give him further aid.

General Schleicher in particular, sure of the confidence
of the army, thought that it would be unwise to strain matters too far. Schleicher wished rather to make a move to the
left, to stretch out his hand to the powerful trade union
groups and to attempt in this way to assure to the government sufficient support in the country even though there
would be no possibility of organizing a majority for it in the
Reichstag. Under these conditions von Papen, who was a

good-natured gambler, yielded before Schleicher and convinced the Marshal of the need of entrusting the Reichswehr chief with the task of forming a new cabinet. It was thus that Schleicher found himself on December 2, 1932, led to accept, probably most reluctantly, the dangerous post to which Hindenburg called him. The next day the cabinet was formed. On December 6, Schleicher was able to establish contact with the Reichstag without having again to resort to dissolution and new elections, which no one wanted at this time.

9. The Schleicher Interlude

The ministry of General von Schleicher was but a brief interlude which lasted scarcely two months. Schleicher's policy was based on very judicious considerations. Chancellor von Papen had been disturbing and provoking and he had made attempts at innovations. He had waved the threat of a vast reform of the Weimar constitution, which had alarmed every one. In the field of economic policy he had begun some interesting reforms for combating unemployment which had not yet produced their full effect. To Schleicher, on the other hand, it seemed that the safest thing under such circumstances was to refrain from all dangerous innovations in constitutional matters, to gain time to permit the economic crisis to reach its waning point and to allow sufficient time for the measures taken by the last cabinet to develop and mature. For that it was important above all to treat the working classes kindly, and, in that way, to evidence clearly his desire for social peace. In order to carry out this design Schleicher undertook negotiations with the leaders of the Socialist trade unions, Leipart and Otte, with the leader of the Christian trade unions, Stegerwald, and finally with Gregor Strasser, the brother of Otto Strasser, and the representative of the left socializing wing of National Socialism. On January 6

Schleicher arranged a secret interview between Strasser and Hindenburg.

Schleicher's plan was not lacking in resourcefulness but it quickly proved itself completely inoperative. Schleicher compromised the leaders of the trade unions without gaining the confidence of their membership. It was the same with Stegerwald. As regards Strasser, Schleicher had overestimated his influence. Summoned by Hitler to break off his conversations with the Chancellor, Strasser resisted this order without, however, coming out into open revolt against the *Führer*. Hitler imposed a forced leave of absence for several weeks upon him and Strasser was unable to secure any appreciable following. The attempts of Schleicher to come to terms with the Centre Party and his negotiations with Prelate Kaas for changes in the cabinet bore no fruit. No less ineffectual were his efforts, finally, to lead Hugenberg to co-operate with Stegerwald. The socializing tendencies of Schleicher brought upon him the mistrust and even hostility of the bristling leader of the German Nationalist Party and soon Schleicher was being called the "red Chancellor" in all the leading circles.

It was amidst such conditions that, thanks to the intervention of von Papen, the alliance between Hitler and heavy industry was renewed. Hitler, in the course of all the cabinet crises, had always claimed for himself complete power and had always refused to share power with the other party chiefs. He was too shrewd not to understand that the moment was rapidly approaching when he would have a pressing interest in entering a government in order to hold his organizations in line and maintain the enthusiasm of his followers. It was clear that a new dissolution of the Reichstag involved grave dangers for him. Where would he find the necessary money to defray the expenses of the electoral campaign?

This was what prompted the intervention of von Papen. Von Papen had been treated very harshly by Hitler who had called him "the representative of a caste which was destined to disappear." Despite that the ex-Chancellor did not relax his hold. Faithful despite everything to the authoritarian government which had rejected him, he offered to bring together all the nationalist parties against bolshevism. From whom did the initiative come? From von Papen? From Schleicher? From Hitler? Not very much is known. The fact remains that with Schleicher's knowledge and with his consent, Hitler and von Papen met on January 4, 1933 in the home of the rich banker, Schroeder, of Cologne, the representative of the Rhineland financiers who until a short time before had supported Hitler. The interview was to have remained secret. The indiscretion of a photographer, however, whose camera surprised the conspirators when they went out, made the fact known. It is probable that von Papen had lured Hitler into moderation by making him see that he would have to accept a share of power if he was to have money for elections. It has been stated that Hitler had actually offered to subordinate himself to Schleicher upon the condition that he get the Ministries of Reichswehr and Interior as well as the post of Reich Commissar of Prussia. In other words he demanded control over the army and the police. Papen is said to have transmitted these proposals to Schleicher on January 9 but Schleicher did not consider Hitler's demands as a basis for discussion.

At this moment a crisis was provoked by the appearance of the agrarians on the scene. The Reichstag not long before had voted important appropriations for the maintenance of the great landed estates of East Prussia (*Osthilfe*). The distribution of these grants, however, had involved serious abuses in which a number of the large land owners were compromised. The *Osthilfe* was being examined at that time by the Budget Commission of the Reichstag and there was imminent danger of a public scandal. In the face of this eventuality the Landbund arrogantly assumed the offensive and, under the leadership of its heads, voted a resolution which accused the government in terms of unprecedented violence of allowing

49

agriculture to be despoiled in a shameful way by favoring the powerful financial interests of the export industry with its internationalist tendency. On January 11 this resolution was communicated to the press and the result was a break between the Landbund and the government. On January 19 Cabinet Minister von Braun gave his explanations on the *Osthilfe* to the Budget Commission and on the 25th of January the Commission decided, against the votes of the right, to entrust to the Court of Accounts, the task of exercising control over the aid granted by the *Osthilfe*.

This affair proved troublesome for Schleicher. The Junkers had succeeded in aligning the President with their interests by inducing German industry to present to him in 1927 the estate and home at Neudeck. The practical spirit of the donors had been revealed in the slight fact that the gift had been made tax-exempt and, in order to evade inheritance taxes, had been placed in the name of the President's son, Colonel Oskar von Hindenburg. The latter, indeed, pursued with vigor the interests of the agrarians in this *Osthilfe* affair. Brüning had already fallen because he had incurred the hostility of this powerful group. Schleicher, in his turn, fell for the same reasons. Foreseeing that he was to have a minority in the Reichstag, the Chancellor demanded from the President the authorization to dissolve the Reichstag if necessary. Hindenburg, however, refused to accord to the "red Chancellor" these plenary powers which he had so recently and without hesitation granted to von Papen. Schleicher realized that he had been abandoned by everyone. Against him was the hostility of Hugenberg whom he had alarmed by his socializing schemes and the hate of the Junkers whose interests he had placed in jeopardy. Hindenburg, who gave his full sympathy to his "comrade" von Papen, was not well disposed to Schleicher. Schleicher thus fell without being able to offer any resistance. On January 28 he handed in his resignation. Forty-eight hours later the new cabinet was formed with

Hitler as Chancellor, flanked by Hugenberg, von Papen and the Stahlhelm.

The agreement was apparently not realized without difficulty but its conclusion was hastened by the threats coming from the side of the Reichswehr. Rumors, which have found an echo in the foreign press, have it that Schleicher, outraged at having been treated in this fashion, had, with the aid of his intimate associate, General von Bredow, prepared for the intervention of the Reichswehr on January 30 with the arrest of Hitler and von Papen, with a general strike proclaimed by the trade unions and with the proclamation of a military dictatorship. President Hindenburg would have been presented with a *fait accompli*. It was in order to prevent the execution of this plan that the new ministry was constituted with such unusual haste. Emil Ludwig describes these days of treachery at length in his book on Hindenburg (1935). No one can say how much the information on which this story is based is worth. The fact simply remains that General von Bredow was dismissed the day following the advent of the new cabinet and that General Schleicher was assassinated by Hitler's order on June 30, 1934, indicating the deep resentment and distrust which the demagogue felt for the former Chancellor.

BOOK II

National Socialism in Power

II. *National Socialism in Power*

1. The Consolidation of Power

AS SOON as the nationalist government was organized it issued a call to the German people, which was a violent declaration of war against Socialists and Communists. The "Marxist parties," said the declaration, had been given fourteen years in which to show what they could do. During these fourteen years, however, they had destroyed the spiritual unity of the country, ruined the peasant class and brought upon the industrial workers the terrible scourge of unemployment. Behind socialism loomed the red specter of communism: one year of bolshevism would bring Germany to chaos and make it a field of ruins. The new government undertook within four years to save the peasant, to overcome unemployment, to put an end to the egotistic struggle between classes, to bring the finances of the Reich, the states and the municipalities into a healthy condition and to bar the way to communism—in short to heal all the wounds which the Marxists, in fourteen years of incapacity, had brought to Germany.

The government began its work immediately. In view of the unalterable opposition of the Socialists and the coolness of the Centrists, the formation of a government majority in the Reichstag appeared impossible. Hitler then obtained without difficulty from President Hindenburg a decree dissolving the Reichstag on February 1, in order to give the country the opportunity to declare itself towards the nationalist government which had just been formed.

Where did the actual authority in this new nationalist

coalition government reside? At first sight it seemed that everything had been calculated in order to assure undisputed preponderance to the German Nationalists. Vice-Chancellor von Papen, who at the same time also headed the Prussian cabinet, was given the right to be present at all interviews between Hitler and the President of the Reich. Hugenberg combined in his person the direction of the important Ministries of Agriculture and Economics for both the Reich and Prussia. Foreign affairs and finances remained in the hands of the previous cabinet ministers, Herr von Neurath and Count Schwerin-Krosigk, who were simon-pure conservatives. Herr Seldte, leader of the Stahlhelm, who received the post of Minister of Labor, was also a conservative. The Reichswehr was entrusted to General von Blomberg who passed for a safe officer. The Nazis held the posts of Reich Minister of Interior (Frick), Prussian Minister of Interior (Göring), of the Air Ministry (Göring) and also that of Propaganda (Goebbels). It thus seemed at first that fate had not been so kind to the Nazis. It is true that they had at their disposal the police, the aerial forces and above all the formidable apparatus of press and radio, which was an instrument of the first order in the hands of a man expert in using it. On the whole, however, it looked as if the conservative influence in the cabinet was large and safely assured.

This, however, was but appearance. In reality the conservatives never existed for the Nazis. They were a handful of aristocrats and specialists, often intelligent and experienced, it is true, but they had no one behind them, their voices brought no echo in the country and they were lacking in any dynamic power. The Nazis, on the contrary, were a band of fanatics, led by a demagogue who was endowed with an iron will and capable of prodigious activity and irresistible eloquence. His power rested on the support of a staff of robust lieutenants ready for anything and imbued with absolute devotion; on a party solidly organized, consisting at the time of thirteen to fourteen million voters; and on a powerful army of brown and black militia. Each word the *Führer* uttered re-sounded throughout the entire country and every act of his was re-enforced by the street agitation which he directed at his will. From the start Hitler was not a chancellor of a cabinet of concentration obliged to deal gently with his associates, but rather the master whose will prevailed over all and who exercised an ever increasing fascination even on the President of the Reich.

An entirely new tone was thus immediately introduced into German public life. National Socialism addressed itself deliberately to the masses. The masses needed simple words and elementary ideas which were adapted to their level of culture. They were taken not by reasoning and proofs but by the appeal to the heart and by an infusion of love and above all hate. The *Führer* set about his tremendous undertaking in a large-scale way. It was necessary to inculcate a new faith into the German people who had been misled and unbalanced by the uninterrupted succession of calamities which had befallen them since 1918. This new faith was to be made up of nationalist fanaticism and racialist fervor. It was necessary to stir up in them a healthy hate of all the evil elements which were held responsible for Germany's woes and near collapse, in particular communism and Marxism. It was necessary also to arouse in the masses an enthusiasm for the "Third Reich," for a Germany rid of the pitiful rivalries between states jealous of their sovereignty, and freed of the strife between classes which had become hardened in the defense of their egotistic interests. They had to be won over to the idea of a totalitarian state which would fashion out of all these elements one organism united by indissoluble bonds of solidarity in which the citizen no longer thought of "I" but of "we," and in which the great principle of general welfare before individual welfare was to be realized. In such a com-

munity social justice would be realized far more than in the
past.

These few very simple sentiments had to be drummed into
the heads of the crowd, and the people were to be given the
feeling that they were marching in irresistible tempo towards
a better future. In order to attain this end it was necessary to
speak to the people with "intolerance" and with "fanaticism,"
just as one speaks to "sweepers, to locksmiths or to sewer-
men." Political propaganda, Hitler held, is valuable only for
the effect it exercises on such frustrated spirits, and not by
the logical cogency it might have for a group of superior intelligence. If refined people find propaganda made in this
fashion trivial and vulgar it is so much the worse for them.
It simply proves that they have no understanding of the
problems which have to be solved. Hitler finds no term too
contemptuous for those whom he disdainfully calls *"Intelligenz-
ler,"*—for the conscientious individuals with their scientific
scruples, their worries over objectivity and their desire to be
tolerant—and even more for those refined individuals who
take pride in their superior culture and treat with contempt
the more elementary homilies of Nazi propaganda. Hitler did
not seek the approbation of this élite class. He wished to conquer the hearts of the masses and he chose the suitable means
to do it: means which were simple, direct and brutal. All the
worse for those fastidious people who curl up their lips in
scorn! They would soon see the vanity of their puerile
disdain.

Less than eight days before the election day and in the
midst of the election period, aid of inestimable value was
brought to the National Socialist campaign by the burning of
the Reichstag which was set on fire during the night of February 27 and 28 by the Dutch communist, Van der Lubbe.

Let us first take a realistic view of the political struggle as
it appeared at the time. The Nazis had just denounced communism as the principal enemy. Here, at precisely the right

time, an attempt, as sensational as it was stupid, and without any possible practical advantage, comes to furnish Hitler with astounding confirmation of his diagnosis. At the same time it provides an admirable pretext for putting opponents using such means "outside the law." The consequences of this power were of tremendous importance. Up to that time the Marxist block in the Reichstag had, as we have seen, formed a group equivalent in numbers to that of the National Socialists. They were thus in a position to prevent any changes in the constitution. The instant Hitler was able, under the pretext of guarding against the communist peril, not only to suspend a party from its constitutional guarantees and throw into prison the greater part of the communist leaders, but also to exclude from the Reichstag the representatives of communism who, despite the formidable pressure against them, still received 4,848,058 votes in the elections of March 5, 1933, it became clear that the parliamentary strength and power of resistance of the Marxists would be dangerously diminished. The Socialists naturally not only vigorously repudiated any connection with the attempt of Van der Lubbe but categorically maintained that the burning of the Reichstag was really an act directed against the parliamentary regime as a whole. International opinion, also, for the most part, received the news of the fire with decided skepticism. There is a strong suspicion that the Nazis were not altogether strangers to this attempt which gave force to their propaganda in such unhoped for fashion.*

German opinion, on the other hand, seemed disposed to accept the official version of the Reichstag fire which was given the day after the event. In the first place the Germans were more inclined to admit the reality of the communist danger. Conservatives and bourgeoisie had feared the spread

---

* For the extremely critical view of the Reichstag fire and the trial, see Reed, Douglas, *The Burning of the Reichstag* (New York 1934) and *Dimitroff contra Göring* (New York 1934).—*Ed.*

and Gunther's *Inside Europe*

of bolshevism in Germany since the revolution of 1918. Even after the bloody suppression of the extremist elements in 1919 this apprehension still remained alive. Foreign observers seemed generally convinced that in a country as disciplined and cultivated as Germany and as highly industrialized as it continued to be after the shocks of the war and post-war period, the chances for a bolshevist movement were very meager.

In some German circles, however, and particularly in the official world, the view was widespread that revolutionary troubles always remained a disturbing possibility. They insisted that there was danger in the underground propaganda of communist "cells" and in the dangerous power of the "Red Front," which they represented as an army of almost a million armed men. The appearance of bolshevist troops near the German frontier, they maintained, would risk provoking a general mobilization of all the revolutionary forces and they stressed the fact that the regular army was numerically not sufficient to cope with an eventuality of such a nature. Hence they urged the necessity of setting up a military force, alongside the Reichswehr, to maintain order and suppress any attempt at civil war.

This argument was not very convincing to foreigners, for they had always suspected the German government of "playing up" the bolshevist danger in order to justify the existence of large semi-military organizations, which were so often represented abroad as an illegal army. There is no doubt, however, that this argument did make an impression in Germany, particularly in Bavaria, Saxony, Thuringia and Hamburg, which had been the scenes of more or less violent revolutionary movements. This impression was further strengthened by the acts of terrorism perpetrated by the "reds" during the period preceding the Nazi accession to power. It found objective justification in the steady increase in the number of Communist deputies in the Reichstag beginning with 1924.

At that time they had 45; in 1928 they had 54, in 1930, 77, on July 31, 1932, 89, and finally in November 1932, 100, elected by almost six million voters.

When Goebbels, therefore, in his speech of September 14, 1933, cited the book *Bewaffneter Aufstand* as significant proof of insurrectionary tendencies manifested in January and February; when he asserted that the country was at that time in the process of sinking toward chaos; when Nazi propaganda represented the flaming Reichstag as the signal which was to call to arms all the soldiers of the revolution for the final struggle—let us not hasten to look upon those declarations as invectives which deceived no one and which were laughed at by the initiated. A mass of people, still haunted by the anguishing memory of the crisis of 1918-1919 and made uneasy by the nocturnal warfare raging for months between Communists and Nazis, believed in the reality of a bolshevist danger more sincerely than foreigners can imagine. Moreover they swallowed with much less skepticism than foreigners did the tremendous uproar which filled the Nazi press on the day following the attempt. They approved of the rigorous measures immediately taken by the government. Without the need of too much pressure they also admitted the importance of the "victory" which Goebbels emphasized several months later in September, when he said "that from that time on there could no longer be any question of a communist danger," but that the Nazis had arrived just in time to save Germany from an imminent catastrophe. He concluded his speech of October 21 with the following words: "We are convinced that posterity will be more just to us and admit that we preserved Germany, and consequently Europe, from bolshevism."

The elections for the Reichstag were held on March 5. They gave Hitler an overwhelming victory. His party won 288 seats, the German Nationalists 52, while the Socialists elected only 120 deputies and the Centre Party 73. Neverthe-

61

less the government coalition with its 340 deputies out of a total of 647 seats did not command the two-thirds majority necessary to amend the constitution. Hitler had resolved to overthrow the Weimar regime and in his declaration of policy to the Reichstag he summoned the deputies to choose between peace or war with the nationalist government. He was ready for one or the other alternative, he declared. Parliament could have and should have determined on war had it retained faith in itself and in the Republic. The opposition, however, had been cut down by the exclusion of the Communists and demoralized by repeated defeats. It had been abandoned by the Centrists who, putting their trust in the apparent moderation of the Chancellor's declarations and despite their scruples, agreed to rally to the majority. Hitler thus succeeded on March 23 in squeezing through the law which conferred upon the government the plenary powers which it demanded, i.e., the power to promulgate and immediately enforce new laws without the approval of the Reichstag, even in cases where they did not conform to the constitution. Thus Hitler now held in his hands the legal means whereby he could exercise uncontrolled power in Germany and overthrow the social and political regime of the country without being obliged to defer to a Reichstag which from that day on assumed only an ornamental role.

In fact, Hitler was to exercise this dictatorial power alone. His associates of the right were either eliminated or subdued. The ambitious Hugenberg laid down his duties on June 27, 1933; the same day the German Nationalist party voluntarily dissolved; a few days before (June 21) the Stahlhelm had agreed to become absorbed by the Nazi organizations. The other conservative ministers confined themselves each to his specialty and left the general direction of affairs to the Chancellor. Hitler did not dare break with them. He was intelligent enough to understand that he could not dispense with the technical capacities which he found in the ranks of the old conservatives or of big industry. He voluntarily retained them in the functions which they exercised and in the administrative posts which they occupied. Supreme authority, however, rested with him and to him alone was reserved the power to make decisions on all important matters. No one was deceived in this either. All effective power was in the hands of Hitler and his aides.

2. The Main Features of Nazi Policy

Without losing an instant, Hitler, as soon as he was installed in power, yoked himself with energy and prodigious activity to the task of completely remodeling all institutions in Germany which he considered indispensable. He took care, however, not to proceed in the manner of a dogmatic revolutionary. After having vanquished his opponents and having obtained unlimited powers, he did not immediately proceed to reform the constitution and to issue a new legal code to govern regenerated Germany. The Weimar constitution had in fact been abrogated on the day the law of plenary powers had been voted and on the day the Reichstag had been stripped of its right of control and of its legislative functions. But Hitler refrained from abolishing it through any official decision or replacing it by a new code. Through additions and successive modifications, however, he brought about an almost complete refashioning of the Reich organization without ever expressly having abrogated the old constitution. "Following his accession to power," declared Secretary of State Stuckart at the beginning of 1936,* "the *Führer* consciously refused to give the Third Reich a written constitution. He believed that the essential thing was not what constitution a country possesses, but rather under what constitution it lives, i.e., under what conditions of internal unity and order the nation lives. He, therefore, allowed the Ger-

* Special number of the *Völkischer Beobachter*, Jan. 30, 1936.

man unified, authoritarian and people's state to develop
through organic and legal evolution, adapted to the general
situation and to the needs of the moment. The Third Reich
thus already has a new constitution in the sense that there is
a political organization of the German people in the Third
Reich. This does not find its expression, however, in a constitutional charter but in a series of fundamental laws and
above all in the fundamental concepts of National Socialism
in the field of public law. These concepts have already acquired the force of customary law."

In proceeding in this way Hitler gave heed to the profoundly realistic instinct which he possesses. He placed no
trust in the virtue of a code which had been elaborated in the
abstract, and he did not wish to allow himself to be held in
check by the paragraphs of a written charter. It was essential,
he believed, to allow the revolution sufficient time to develop
gradually all its inherent potentialities. Moreover, in place of
creating new institutions all of one pattern, he thought it
would be better to allow them to develop in successive stages
so as to profit by the lessons of experience and, by a series of
additions and modifications, to bring into being an organism
likely to endure. He was guided above all by a principle
which lay at the very basis of his conception of the National
Socialist revolution: his conception of the necessary dualism
between state and party.

National Socialism for Hitler rested fundamentally on a
Weltanschauung. "The National Socialist idea," he said, "has
its organizing base in the party." The party "represents the
political conscience, the political conception, and the political
will of the nation." It is the party which has placed the state
at the service of the National Socialist *Weltanschauung* and
it is the party which ought to set the final goals in all domains
of life and harmonize public life with national duty.* The

* In the Law for the Guarantee of the Unity of the Party and the State
of December 1, 1933, article 1 expressly states: "After the victory of the

64

Führer is the party and the party is the *Führer*. The party is the agency which exercises supreme control and makes the final decisions. It gathers into it the elements most suitable for the exercise of power. "It should be established in principle that all Germans are to be formed by the ideological principles of National Socialism, that the better National Socialists are to become members of the party and that, finally, the better members of the party are to assume direction of the state."

For Hitler the party was not merely a temporary organization which was eventually to be merged into the state. He retained the party and its organization intact alongside the state and its administrative divisions. For although National Socialism has seized the key positions in the state it has allowed many of the older functionaries to keep their positions. These officials had certain technical capacities but the fervor of their National Socialism was doubtful. The party organization thus covers the entire country with its immense network (at the Nuremberg Congress of 1933, 160,000 party "functionaries" filed by Hitler) and Hitler plainly indicated in his long proclamation of September 12 at the 1935 Congress that if, during the course of a struggle against the internal enemies of the Reich, the bureaucracy shows itself impotent, the party itself would be called upon to intervene and make up for the insufficiency of the administration. In addition to the state and its agencies, therefore, Hitler has kept the party and the brown shirts, who represent the protective organ of the party. The brown shirts are, for Hitler, the element which preserves the active revolutionary spirit in the nation and which ultimately stimulates the benumbed energies of the state agencies.

National Socialist Revolution, the National Socialist German Labor Party has become the incarnation of the very idea of the state and it is indissolubly united to the state. It is a corporation of public law (*eine Körperschaft des öffentlichen Rechtes*)." (This law further provided that the Deputy to the Leader, Hess, and the chief of the S.A., at that time Röhm, were to be members of the cabinet. Since June 1934, however, when Röhm was executed, the S.A. chief of staff has not been a member of the cabinet. —*Ed.*)

It is, therefore, understandable that under these conditions, Hitler avoided tying down an organization which he desired to keep elastic by the rigorous prescriptions of a new charter.

With this in mind, let us try to indicate what the essential aspects are of the revolutionary task into which Hitler and his followers launched headlong with that extraordinary dynamism which animates their movement.

(1) In accordance with the program formulated in the proclamation of February 1, Hitler immediately proceeded to organize the "subsistence battle," (*Ernährungsschlacht*) and the "employment battle" (*Arbeitsschlacht*); these he undertook to win in four years. In other words he embarked, on the one hand, on the plan to reorganize completely the German peasantry for whom he provided a solid foundation of existence and upon whom he depended to feed the German people in as autonomous a fashion as possible and without recourse to foreign imports. On the other hand, in order to combat the scourge of unemployment, he completely refashioned the whole organization of labor. In place of the many employers' and workers' organizations always fighting one another, he substituted a single *Arbeitsfront* where employers and workers in one organization together administered the large German industrial system. Finally, by bold credit expansion he set in motion again the machinery of German economy and in that manner created, if not immediate material prosperity, at least an era of renewed activity and improved economic conditions. We shall devote two special chapters later to a more detailed study of this aspect of the Nazi revolution. We shall therefore not stress the point here and we shall confine ourselves merely to stating that after four years of rule the Nazis pride themselves on having attained, if not definite, at least highly encouraging results. They claim that they saved the peasant class from ruin, bettered and rationalized agricultural production, insured the feeding of the German people, abolished the struggles of classes, provided some work

for four and a half million unemployed and galvanized economic production into new life.

(2) National Socialism also aims to make of Germany a nation founded on the fact of race. Blood and race are, in its conception, the eternal regenerating sources of the life of a people. The preservation of the purity of blood and national health are absolute postulates for the existence of the German nation and state. Only those who are German by race and those related to them by blood are able to co-operate in the determination of the German destiny and future. We shall deal separately with this doctrine of race and its corollaries, —antisemitism, sterilization laws, the encouragement of births, and the Spartan form of education for the molding of the youth.

(3) The National Socialist Reich is a state founded on the principle of authority (*Führerstaat*). It is distinguished from the democratic state in that authority comes from above and not from below. The leader is not elected by any parliament or by an electoral body or economic group and he is not responsible, as in a democracy, to his subordinates, but only to his superiors. As far as the supreme *Führer* is concerned he is responsible to no one but God and his own conscience. The qualifications for leadership, at all stages of the hierarchy, are gained by the confidence inspired freely in those who are to be commanded and by the superiority of "achievement" (*Leistung*) which gains the spontaneous respect of the masses.

This led, first of all, to the disappearance or the transformation of the old institutions. The Reichstag, stripped of all effective influence, deprived of its right of control and of its legislative powers, is no longer convened except on rare occasions. It is awaiting the day when it will disappear completely. The old organized parties, whose wrangling had led Germany to the brink of ruin, were dissolved one after another.* Only

* The Socialist Party was dissolved on June 22, 1933; on June 27 came the turn of the German Nationalists; on July 4 the People's Party and the Bavarian People's Party disappeared; on July 5 finally, the Centre Party.

the one National Socialist Party remained and it identified itself with the entire nation. In the same way the trade unions, by which the struggle of classes had been organized in the old Germany, disappeared on May 2, 1933. Nothing remained, as we shall see later, but a single large corporate organization which embraced within itself all social aspects and all classes. Even the cabinet of ministers which governed the Reich changed its nature. Under the old system it was a collegial assembly in which the Chancellor was but *primus inter pares*, and, at least in theory, he could be outvoted by his colleagues. Under the National Socialist regime the cabinet became but a council of leaders (*Führerrat*) which the *Führer* gathers round him in order to be informed of what is happening in the major departments of the state and to take their advice on the problems which arise. He alone, however, is master and he reserves for himself the entire power of decision and full responsibility. All power thus is concentrated in the hands of one leader, Hitler, who, at the death of Marshal von Hindenburg on August 2, 1934, combined in himself the functions of Chancellor and President of the Reich under the title of *Führer* and *Reichskanzler*.

The *Führer*, moreover, the National Socialists are very careful to point out, is not like a Caesar or an autocrat. He was freely chosen by the nation and imposed himself upon their choice by the superiority of his endowments and by his prestige. They insist on the fact that he came to power by legal vote and not by force, *coup d'état* or uprising; that he had been raised to supreme power by an immense popular wave of confidence and enthusiasm; that the people and the government are in full accord; that the plebiscite of November 12, 1933, following Germany's exit from the League of Nations, had given the National Socialist Government 93.5 per cent of the German votes and that the plebiscite of August 19, 1934, after the death of Hindenburg, had indicated the personal confidence of the Germans in Hitler by the casting of over 38 million affirmative votes against only 4,294,654 negative votes with 872,296 blank ballots and 2 million not voting.*

The Hitler regime, therefore, had not been established by violence nor imposed by terror. The National Socialists pride themselves that their revolution was "bloodless" and resulted in much less violence than, for example, the Revolution of 1789 or the Commune of 1871. They maintain that it was the people who chose Hitler spontaneously as their leader, who lifted him on their shield and who support his political activity. But, continue the Nazis, even though the people have the right to choose the leader whom they invest with power, they do not, on the other hand, themselves desire to govern. They voluntarily entrust this task to the leader whom they have chosen. Authority, from the start, is exercised by him and the group of men who supported him during the period of struggle and who possess his confidence. Hitler holds a mandate from the people which confers upon him sovereign power. He exercises this power through a hierarchy in which each individual at each stage is responsible to his superior (and not to his subordinates as in a democracy) and where everything culminates in the *Führer* who is responsible only to his conscience and to God. The entire nation, in this way, is organized into one cluster around the *Führer*, who was chosen by the people and invested by them with unlimited authority.

This system, the Nazis admit, has possible disadvantages. The hierarchy must not be converted into a rigid bureaucracy and it is necessary above all to prevent the development of a gulf between the *Führer* and the people, as was the case during the time of William II. The series of large party Congresses held at Nuremberg every year indicate the means whereby Hitler preserves contact between the group of lead-

* The August plebiscite gave to Hitler only 88.1% of the votes cast. In the plebiscite on German foreign policy on March 29, 1936, Hitler was credited with 44,409,523 votes out of 44,952,476 votes cast. This represented 98.5% of the eligible voters.—*Ed.*

ers, the corps of party functionaries, the army of militants who protect the regime, the *Wehrmacht*, since 1935 converted into the national army, and the masses of the people. The new Council of State established in Prussia and convened for the first time on December 15, 1933, under the presidency of the Prussian Prime Minister Göring, was also specifically meant to institute and maintain a regular and active collaboration between government representatives and those personalities who occupy distinguished places and exercise a directing influence in various domains of national life. In these ways, the Chancellor declared, he was convinced the bond established between the supreme authority and the people was a solid one, and the nation would never again fall under the pernicious influence of those forces of dissolution and discord which had brought Germany to the brink of chaos.

(4) The Reich is a unified state. There is but one single sovereign authority in the Reich and there are only citizens or subjects of the Reich. This implies the abandonment of the conception of the Reich as a federation of autonomous states.

On this point National Socialism is merely pursuing to its ultimate conclusions the evolution which had already been started by the von Papen cabinet. Chancellor von Papen had desired to destroy the dualism between Prussia and the Reich by bringing about the fusion of the two governments. In order to attain this end it was necessary to bring about the overthrow of the Braun-Severing cabinet in Prussia. This cabinet, which was the product of the coalition of Socialists and Centrists, had governed Prussia for a long time and appeared to be the principal focus of resistance in Germany to nationalist and fascist power.

The nationalist groups had counted on the Prussian Landtag elections of April 24, 1932 to bring about the overthrow of this regime. But their calculations were foiled. The National Socialists had indeed achieved a startling success at the expense of the middle parties but the Socialists and Centrists had just about held their own. The Braun-Severing cabinet found itself in a minority and tendered its resignation. The Landtag chose as its presiding officer the National Socialist, Kerrl. Because of the continuous disagreement between the Centrists and the Nazis, however, the designation of a new Prime Minister was impossible since no candidate was able to gather an *absolute* majority of the votes, as required by law.*

The Braun cabinet, although having resigned, continued nevertheless to direct affairs while waiting for the parties to agree on the naming of a new Prime Minister. The parties of the right were exasperated at the indefinite prolongation of this paradoxical situation. Following the fall of Brüning they redoubled their violence. The German Nationalists urged the appointment of a Reich Commissar for Prussia and the Speaker of the Landtag, Kerrl, protested "in the name of the will of the people" against the continuance in office of a Socialist ministry in Prussia and summoned the Reich cabinet to put an end to this scandal. Chancellor von Papen willingly yielded to this pressure. He was of the opinion that the Prussian government, in placing extremists of the right and the left on the same footing, had viewed the red peril with too great indulgence and that, therefore, it had proved itself incapable of maintaining order in Prussia. Under these circumstances he made up his mind to move swiftly. On July 20, 1932 he designated himself as Reich Commissar in Prussia. He proclaimed a state of emergency in Prussia for several days and with the aid of the Reichswehr he succeeded in ousting the Prussian cabinet.

This *coup d'état*, which was feebly justified by a supposed collusion between the Prussian government and the communists, aroused the displeasure of the anti-fascists and also stirred up a lively opposition among the states of the south.

* The law requiring an *absolute* majority for the designation of a Prime Minister in Prussia was passed by the old Landtag a few days before the elections, in order to meet just such a condition as developed. This change was violently denounced by the rightist circles.—*Ed.*

They looked with concern at von Papen combining in his person, after the example of Bismarck, the double office of Chancellor of the Reich and Prime Minister of Prussia. They were fearful as to what would happen to the autonomy of the states after such intervention of the Reich into their internal affairs. To those faithful to the federal idea this attack upon the Prussian government seemed to be a grave violation of one of the fundamental principles of the Weimar constitution.

On July 21, the matter was brought before the Supreme Court at Leipzig by the ousted Prussian ministers, who wished to have the court establish the illegality of the measures which had been taken against them. On the same day they were joined by the governments of Bavaria, Würtemberg, Baden and Hesse. Every one felt that it would be difficult to obtain any definite condemnation from the state tribunal of so important a political act by the executive power. The court proceedings were concluded on October 25 with a paradoxical verdict. The Supreme Court declared that the decree of July 20 was legal and that the Reich Commissar consequently had the right to dismiss and to appoint officials in Prussia. It stated, on the other hand, however, that no proof had been established that the Prussian state or its ministers had failed in the carrying out of their duties towards the Reich. Under these conditions it declared that the Prussian cabinet could not be ousted and they therefore continued legally to be ministers. There were, then, *two* regular governments in Prussia: one was simply temporary but it held the effective power since it carried on the administrative machinery (the Reich Commissar); the other remained in office without any time limit and retained the right to issue instructions to the Prussian representatives to the Reichsrat, but it was deprived of any direction of Prussian affairs so long as the Commissar governed. Such was the paradoxical situation which confronted Hitler when he assumed power.

Hitler's feelings on the matter of federalism are not uncertain. He had already declared himself in favor of the unified state in his *Mein Kampf* (p. 633 ff.). In his speech to the Nuremberg Congress in September 1933, he set forth his views in clear terms. In the course of the history of Germany, he said, the centrifugal development of the different German tribes had brought about the constitution of states which were jealous of their political and spiritual autonomy. Their narrow particularism had often endangered German national unity. Hitler was convinced that these gifts of the past should not be preserved. The old Reich had been organized, theoretically at least, as a federation of states or *Länder*. This, however, was a narrow conception which was bound to disappear. "A people who speak one language, who possess the same culture and whose destinies were worked out in the course of a common history, can do nothing else but strive toward a unified political leadership. The new German Reich ought not to be erected on the foundation of the states any more than on the basis of the German tribes, but rather on the entire nation and on the National Socialist Party, which comprises and unites within itself the entire German nation."

Hitler's action along these lines was swift and determined. On February 6, 1933 a decree, issued by President von Hindenburg, by virtue of article 48 of the constitution, put an end to the dual government in Prussia and transferred to the Reich Commissar all the powers of the Prussian ministry. The same day the Prussian Landtag was dissolved. After a vain attempt at protest the members of the Prussian cabinet recognized the futility of their resistance and on March 27 declared that they had resigned their functions. Hitler in the same way quickly disposed of particularist resistance in the southern states. On March 8, 1933 General von Epp was named Reich Commissar in Bavaria and was accepted without difficulty by the population. Two days later National Socialist governments were set up in Saxony, Baden and Würtemberg, then also in Hesse. On April 7, 1933 the administrative autonomy of the states was practically eliminated by the law concerning the *Statthalter*. The latter officials were named by the President at the suggestion of the Chancellor and were installed by the central government alongside of the local authorities. The *Statthalter* are appointed for the duration of a Landtag term and may be dismissed by the government at will. They have the right to appoint or dismiss the Prime Minister of the state, to dissolve the Landtag and to appoint and dismiss all officials and judges of the particular state. In the name of the Reich they exercise complete authority in the various states. It is also significant that when elections were set for the Reichstag on November 12, 1933, it was specified that the state diets were not to be re-elected, indicating clearly that it was the intention of the Nazi leaders to suppress the institution of local diets in the future.

It is probable that in the very near future the state divisions will disappear entirely and will be replaced by a rational division of the Reich into a certain number of provinces or regions. In any case there was a set of legislative measures which paved the way for this transformation. There was, first of all, the law of January 30, 1934 on the reorganization of the Reich. Article 1 sanctioned the disappearance of popular representation in the states and article 2 provided that "the rights of sovereignty of the states pass to the Reich" and that "the state governments are subordinate to the government of the Reich." The specific intention of the law was expressed in the following declaration by Hitler: "The German tribes are those elements out of which God constituted our people. They are a part of its substance and shall continue to exist so long as there is a German people. But political structures of particular states are the products of action of men of the past. They are partly good, but also partly very bad. As human products they are perishable. We are *one* people and we wish to live in *one* Reich!"

There was also the law of February 14, which did away with the Reichsrat as well as with separate diplomatic representatives of the states in the Reich. On May 1, 1934 the post of Reich Minister of Science, Public Instruction and Popular Education was created. On June 16 and December 5, 1934 the administration of justice was unified and the Reich minister assumed direction of affairs first in Prussia, then in the other states of the Reich. The laws of January 30, 1935 specified anew the powers of the *Statthalter*, and reorganized municipal administration according to the principle of autonomy which had been proclaimed by Baron vom Stein.

Finally, there was a group of measures whereby a number of state ministries were suppressed either by being merged with corresponding ministries of the Reich or by their direction being entrusted to the *Statthalter* of the state. As a result of these measures there is only one local minister in Prussia today, the Minister of Finance; in Bavaria there are two, in Würtemberg three, while in Saxony and Hesse they have all disappeared. It is obvious that the government has up to the present aimed to avoid aggravating whatever particularist sentiment still remains in Germany by too precipitate a constitutional reform. In fact, however, the administrative unification of Germany has already been realized.

(5) Since March 13, 1935, one may say that the Reich has become a military state. For in the eyes of Hitler the party and the army are the two fundamental pillars, indissolubly united, on which the structure of the Reich rests. "The party gives to the army the people, and the people give to the army the soldiers, and both together give to the German Reich the security of internal peace and the power which permits it to assert itself." Hitler is at once the party leader, supreme commander of the army and the chief of state. We shall point out in subsequent pages the major educational function which Hitler assigns to the army in the Third Reich.

75

3. *The Organization of Victory*

If we now attempt to draw a general time curve of National Socialist evolution we first notice a revolutionary phase. During this period Hitler, at the head of his party, took possession of the newly conquered positions, systematically destroyed communism, disciplined the states by installing Nazi governments there, inaugurated his racialist policy of eliminating the Jewish element, assured himself of secure positions in the different government services by ousting his most outspoken opponents, eliminating the Jews and placing trusted followers in important key positions. He destroyed the old class and party organizations, suppressed groups like the *Reichsbanner*, the *Stahlhelm*, the *Jungdeutschen Orden* and even the *Waffenring*, which seemed to him suspect or superfluous. It was a somewhat tumultuous period in which direct action by militant Nazis made itself strongly felt without the *Führer* ever allowing the agitation to degenerate into anarchy.

This phase was ended at the beginning of the summer of 1933. On July 6, Hitler declared: "The revolution is not a permanent state, it ought not to degenerate into a lasting state." On July 11, Frick asserted emphatically: "The German revolution is terminated." From the beginning the *Führer* warned his followers against "individual actions." He insisted that they respect discipline, that they observe legality and that the local groups abstain from all unconsidered initiative. The era of conquest was closed. The first grand party reunion in Nuremberg in September 1933 was a huge cry of triumph. Germany, which for so many years had exhibited to the stranger an appearance of distress and anguish, underwent a complete metamorphosis. All those who visited the country at that time or who heard the comments of tourists, those who surveyed the papers and illustrated magazines, or who heard the echo of the great public demonstrations and inter-

76

minable harangues of propaganda speakers on the radio, all received the impression that a large part of the Germans—in any case those whom they saw and heard—had once again found courage and new hope.

It seemed that the Germans marched with joy under their brown shirts, that they participated enthusiastically in the innumerable demonstrations which the government, with its sure sense of the psychology of the masses, had organized. They acclaimed the *Führer* and his aides with spontaneous enthusiasm; they seemed filled with a mystic faith in the national regeneration and they borrowed from this faith a new energy to bear the burdens of a period of transition, affirming very strongly their determination to triumph over the obstacles which stood in their way. The depressing feeling of the "end of a world" or of the "decline of the West" seemed to give way to the fervent hope of a resurrection and of a regeneration of a "Third Reich." Give this sentiment whatever name you please, call it euphoria, mystical exaltation, group delirium or hysterical folly—the name matters little—the sentiment was there. Those who viewed Germany at this time from abroad and who had been impressed by the stories of émigrés around them, might have had the feeling that the country was subjected to a regime of dictatorship, of constraint and of terror. But looking at what went on in the streets, and becoming impregnated with the spirit of the crowds, the dominant impression was something quite different. It then appeared that the Nazis and those who had rallied to Hitlerism had now received the regime which they desired and that they gladly followed the leader whom they had chosen. Far from considering themselves oppressed they felt released, liberated from the constraints which had hindered them, free in a word—infinitely more free than they had felt under the so-called regime of democratic liberty through which they had just passed.

When, in the autumn of 1933, the first results of the "employment battle" began to be felt and when the number of unemployed in October 1933 had decreased by 2½ millions; when, above all, on October 14, Hitler staged his first grand play in foreign affairs and announced, without any harm resulting to the country thereby, that Germany had left the League of Nations, the confidence in the *Führer* was general. On November 12, the German people approved the attitude taken by the government by 40,609,247 votes against two million.

There was obviously something a bit artificial about this apparent unanimity of opinion and about the appearance of cheerfulness which the German people exhibited at that time. It seemed impossible to suppose that millions of Germans who on March 5, 1933 had still voted for the bourgeois parties, the Centre, the Socialists and even for Communists, would instantly become converted to National Socialism. Many, no doubt, had scrambled onto the victorious bandwagon. Others had adapted themselves to the new situation either because of a prudent desire to preserve their positions and their means of livelihood, or else simply because of that instinct of discipline which makes a German voluntarily subordinate himself to strong authority. But a considerable number of the former opponents of the Nazis were moved by sentiments which had nothing in common with those of the Nazis.

Alongside the official Germany which cries "Heil Hitler" there is another Germany which has hidden itself and remains silent or which for practical reasons pretends adherence to the regime. It is impossible to estimate the importance of the number of malcontents, for they are reduced to silence and are practically non-existent for the outside world. But they are there all the same. Alongside the "old guard," which has participated in the movement from its inception, alongside the converts who one by one joined the earlier nucleus, alongside those resigned individuals who at the very least betray some desire to understand or to tolerate National Socialism, there is—Hitler himself knows it well and has referred to it many times—a residue of recalcitrants who still retain their decided hostility. According to Hitler they consist of Jews and Marxists, impenitent reactionaries who are always ready for intrigue, surly individuals who continually indulge in criticism, and conspirators who are plotting secretly in the dark. Hitler has severely admonished them on various occasions. He despises the prudent who keep quiet, but he issues a warning that he will attack pitilessly any one who shall show his opposition by either word or deed.

Towards the spring of 1934 this group of malcontents began to raise their heads more boldly. In his speech of May 11, Goebbels sounded a very clear warning to them. In June the warnings became more specific and earnest. On June 18, Göring served notice that he would destroy without mercy any imprudent persons who thought that the moment had come to attempt a "second revolution" without the express consent and the order of the *Führer*. On June 25, Rudolf Hess cautioned the "credulous idealists" against the "provocateurs" and the "visionaries with blinkers" who wished to start the game of revolution all over again in Germany. On the other hand on March 17, Vice Chancellor von Papen had delivered a speech at Marburg—reflecting, it is said, certain sentiments of Hindenburg himself—which was taken to be the program of a cabal of the right. It was immediately taken by Hitler as an act of treason and banned by the censor. It was under these conditions that on June 30, 1934, of sinister memory, Hitler undertook that terrible series of executions which mowed down the chief of staff of the Brown Militia, Röhm, and a long list of storm troop leaders, together with several direct collaborators of Herr von Papen and a list of famous members of the high German aristocracy, ending finally with General von Schleicher and his wife.*

* The total number of people killed as a result of this purge is still unknown. Hitler in his speech to the Reichstag on July 13, 1934 put the

We have only an imperfect notion as yet regarding the meaning of this mournful tragedy. Some have said that Hitler believed it his duty to drown in blood the danger of a kind of revolt of Janissaries in his own camp which might have been accompanied by the insurrection of aristocratic *frondeurs* and perhaps by shady intrigues with a foreign power. Nothing definite is known. Hitler's holiday was rudely interrupted by this bloody interlude, which resounded through Germany like a sudden peal of thunder. No one in the government fell, however, and no reaction was produced in any quarter. On July 3 the Reichstag voted a law justifying the measures carried out on June 30 and July 1 and 2 as legitimate acts of defense of the state (*Staatsnotwehr*) and as the suppression of an attempt at high treason. President Hindenburg, on July 2, sent his Chancellor a telegram in which he thanked him for having saved the German people from a great danger. Thanks to his decision and courage, the President said, Hitler had nipped in the bud all attempts against the safety of the state. Vice Chancellor von Papen provisionally remained in his post. On July 13, Hitler himself offered an apology before the Reichstag for his acts. And everything went on in Germany as if nothing had happened.

For a year the evolution of the Reich went on. After the death of Hindenburg on August 2, 1934, Hitler became sole master of Germany. His additional successes further increased

---

total at 77. Other conservative estimates have put it at 109. Among those more important people executed were the S.A. leaders Ernst Röhm, Edmund Heines, Karl Ernst, Peter von Heydebreck, Ritter von Krauser and Wilhelm Schmidt; personal enemies of Hitler like von Kahr, Dr. Stützl and Dr. Georg Heim; political opponents like General and Frau von Schleicher, General von Bredow, Gregor Strasser, Lieutenant Scheringer and Dr. Morsbach; Catholic leaders like Dr. Erich Klausener, head of the German Catholic Action, Dr. Beck, leader of the Munich Catholic Action, and von Bose and Dr. E. Jung, two close collaborators of von Papen. The events of June 30 have been described in a most dramatic fashion in Otto Strasser's *Die deutsche Bartholomäusnacht* (Zurich 1935). Strasser is not wholly reliable but more than any other of the émigré writers he still has intimate contacts with the inner doings of the Nazi party.—*Ed.*

his prestige. Unemployment continued to decrease. The corporate organization of the country was developed. The Saar plebiscite on January 13, 1935 resulted in an immense majority for the return to Germany. The re-establishment of compulsory military service on March 15, 1935 through Germany's unilateral decision was carried out without provoking any dangerous reaction in Europe. The agreement with England of June 18, 1935, allowed for Germany's naval rearmament.

The opponents of the regime, however, were not entirely silenced. Denunciation was now directed by the Nazis against the "insolence" of the Jews in raising their heads again. It was necessary, they insisted, to tame them by rigorous measures. They declaimed also against the revival of the "political clergy" who were engaged in unbridled propaganda against the very principles of National Socialism. At the Nuremberg Congress of September 1935, Hitler raised his voice against bolshevism as well as against the little group of reactionaries who, he said, had learned nothing. He also attacked the maneuvres of the Jews and the revival of an aggressive clericalism whose political agitation, he held, threatened to bring about a new *Kulturkampf*. The Reichstag was convoked in order to declare the flag with the swastika as the national symbol for the country and the army, and to vote the law which deprived the Jews of German citizenship and forbade mixed marriages between Aryans and non-Aryans.

On March 7, 1936, finally, Hitler proceeded, in violation of the Treaty of Versailles and the Locarno agreements, to reoccupy the demilitarized zone of the Rhineland by German troops. Again the nation was called upon to declare itself in a plebiscite on this step which raised a great stir all over Europe. On March 29, 1936 out of 45½ million registered voters, 45 millions, i.e. 99 per cent, took part in the vote and close to 44½ million voted for Hitler. Once more the entire nation placed itself behind its *Führer*.

BOOK III

Foreign Policy

III. *Foreign Policy*

1. The Bellicose Ideology of Mein Kampf

AS LONG as the National Socialists had constituted an opposition party, the tactics of the *Führer* were very simple. The chief aim which Hitler had pursued during this time was to hammer away at the governments which had ruled Germany after the conclusion of peace. These governments, for better or for worse, had pursued a policy of fulfilment, of *rapprochement* with France and of European co-operation. They endeavored thereby to permit Germany to refashion itself, to recoup its strength, to repair its industrial condition and little by little to regain its position in Europe. Hitler exploited to his advantage and against those who had assumed the ungrateful task of directing German policy during the hard post-war years, all the rancor and hate which had accumulated within vanquished Germany in the course of a long period of humiliation, privation, deceit and distress of all sorts. If one observes the writings and speeches of Hitler, particularly his *Mein Kampf*, one sees how in these texts a political ideology was evolved which was plainly threatening to the peace of Europe and of special menace to the position of France.

The Treaty of Versailles is represented by Hitler as a glaring violation of every species of right and as the source of all the evils of Germany as well as of Europe. It had enslaved Germany and converted it into an exploited colony. Germany had lost its territorial sovereignty and if it pleased France to occupy the Ruhr region even in peace time, she was able to do so without meeting a shadow of resistance. In the same way, said Hitler, the Czechs, the Poles or the Danes were free to invade Germany at their will and with impunity. In accepting the armistice conditions, unilateral disarmaments, commissions of control, foreign interference in the administration of Germany's finances, customs and railroads, Germany had practically surrendered all her independence. She had delivered herself to the arbitrary will of her enemies.

It is not a disaster for a healthy people to lose a war, taught Hitler. Defeat and its resulting evils may be the ransom for errors committed and may force the nation to salutary self-assertion. One condition, however, was necessary. The nation must immediately grit its teeth and prepare with all its energy to battle for future regeneration. What National Socialists never pardoned their Jewish, Marxist or bourgeois enemies, said Hitler, was that, by their policy of resignation and compromise, these elements did their utmost to check the self-assertion of the German people. They propagated revolutionary or pacifist ideas, defamed the war and preached reconciliation and universal fraternity. Such an attitude was, in the eyes of Hitler, unexpiable treason towards the German race and fatherland. In order to repair this evil, it was necessary to eradicate the internal enemy, to re-establish the sound state of the nation, to revive in it the vengeful passions and sacred flame of patriotism and military spirit, the courage to say "no" to its oppressors and to oppose them with not only passive but also active resistance—in a word, to prepare the people for a "war of liberation."

France, in the eyes of Hitler, represented Germany's principal enemy and France was the first to be vanquished. According to Hitler, the instinct of national preservation inevitably pushes France towards the dismemberment of Germany. All French governments, Hitler declared, whether Bourbon or Jacobin, Bonapartist or reactionary, clerical or socialist, endeavored to gain the left bank of the Rhine and to break up

86

German unity. In order to insure success all means were considered fair. France did not even recoil before the crime *par excellence*, the crime against race, when it sent the colonial troops across the Rhine to contaminate German blood. French policy thus appeared to Hitler as an attack upon the white race. Contaminated by contact with inferior races which it has called to its aid, the French people, said Hitler, are destined to inevitable decay and are approximating more and more the cultural level of negroes. In a few more centuries, Hitler declared, a negroid France will constitute a vast semi-African and semi-European state, stretching from the Rhine to the Congo. In this state the degenerate descendants of the ancient Franks will have been overwhelmed by the flood of inferior races and their defense will be secured by an army consisting more of colonial elements than of European.

In order to break down the world hegemony to which France had raised herself by the Versailles Treaty, Germany must create allies in her turn. Such allies she will find in Italy and in England. After 1870, England felt that her traditional naval and commercial supremacy was being threatened by the tremendous economic upswing of Germany and she entered the war in 1914 in order to bar the way to the inordinate ambitions of the pan-Germans. She had gained nothing from this move, however. The World War, by bringing about the total collapse of Germany, had made France the first military power in the world and thus brought about a new break in the European equilibrium. England, although victorious, really had lost the war. She should, therefore, by the very force of circumstances, ally herself with vanquished Germany against France, who in order to perpetuate her artificial hegemony, wished to eliminate Germany as a Great Power and for all time bar the way to German regeneration.

The second ally for Germany was to be found in fascist Italy. Italy now free of her hereditary enemy, Austria-Hungary, would inevitably align herself against France who is opposed to Italian colonial expansion and to Italian ambitions in the Mediterranean.

The alliance thus formed with England and Italy would first be directed towards France and the breaking down of French military supremacy. Germany would then turn against Russia. This very obviously presented a break not only with Bismarck's doctrine, but also with the traditional policy of German diplomacy since the signing of the Rapallo agreements. It was, however, strongly dictated by circumstances. A Russo-German alliance, in the first place, would inevitably result in an Anglo-French counter attack. This would involve incalculable damage for Germany, which would necessarily become the battlefield of the conflicting forces. Besides, how could National Socialist Germany, after having posed as the deadly enemy of Marxist communism, conclude an alliance with the band of Jewish revolutionists who had bolshevized Russia and who were preparing with all their energy for world revolution and the advent of international Jewish despotism? Finally, Germany was in need of land in order to carry out any extensive agrarian policy and in order to supply her race with the additional territory necessary for subsistence. Such territory, however, could only be found in Russia. It was, therefore, necessary to renounce all expansion towards the south and west and take up the tradition, interrupted for several centuries, of expansion towards the east. Germany would again proceed against the Slavs, as the Knights of the Teutonic Order had done in the past, and conquer new lands. The sword would precede the plow.

The National Socialist program appeared as a possible danger to peace from still another point of view. One of the important articles of the Nazi program is "the reunion of all Germans into one Great Germany." Beside the sixty-seven million inhabitants of the Reich, the Nazis continue to count as Germans the thirty odd millions spread throughout the entire world who speak a German dialect or who did so at some time in their history. When the National Socialist ideology was formed the Nazis expressly admitted that their aim was not to restore the frontiers of 1914 but to reconquer all the territories lost to Germanism. They would act accordingly, even against the will of the inhabitants, if the independence and the political needs of the mother country demanded it. They held that frontiers were nothing sacred or eternal, that they were the work of man and of chance, that it was the duty of each nation to defend its territory and that Germany was obligated to give to the German race the territory which it needed in order to preserve itself from a miserable end.

Thus German policy deliberately aimed to maintain the feeling of community of race and culture among the inhabitants of the Reich as well as among the Germans abroad. The consequences drawn from this fact are immediately apparent. They were enunciated with perfect clarity by the former chief of staff of the S.A., Ernst Röhm: "If the French are said to number about 36 millions, the Italians barely a few million more, the Poles only 16 to 17 million, the Czechs a million, one can see what influence our people of 100 million can exert in the balance of world politics!"

This aspiration towards a Great Germany, moreover, is not merely platonic. It rests upon an imposing organization, consisting of numerous institutes, associations, centers of study, all of which aim—with the more or less express aid of Reich authorities—to propagate the knowledge of Germanism abroad, to support it in all possible ways, to foster its cultural, administrative and economic development and to draw closer its ties with the Reich.*

* The N.S.D.A.P. maintained a special division for Nazi groups in foreign countries. The head of this organization was Ernst Wilhelm Bohle, a German educated in South Africa. At the end of 1936 a new department was created in the Ministry of Foreign Affairs called the "Foreign Organization in the Foreign Office" and Herr Bohle was put at the head of this division. For this entire subject consult the well-documented work of Paul Lévy, *La Germanisme a l'étranger* published in 1933 by the Alsatian

The Third Reich

What is the practical bearing of this propaganda? It is almost impossible to say precisely. France is also interested in Frenchmen abroad. She too works for the diffusion of French culture throughout the world and maintains French activities abroad. No one would suspect, for an instant, however, that France wishes to annex Brussels, Geneva, or Quebec or that she pretends to intervene in the internal affairs of Belgium, Switzerland or Canada. Do we have the same guarantee with regard to Germany? It is doubtful. In the case of the Reich, the purely linguistic and cultural propaganda very often develops into political propaganda. Representatives of German "minorities" in foreign countries appear more or less openly as advance guards of the German "idea," and certain parties even claim the right to pave the way for reunion to Germany. This is where the danger begins. For the complete realization of a Great Germany of 100 million inhabitants, even though carried out in gradual stages, would necessarily imply a new European war, the prospect of which Hitler, at the time he wrote his autobiography, did not seem to spurn.

Finally for those who seek to avoid the horrors of another great European war, there is nothing reassuring in the combative realism which the author of *Mein Kampf* arrogantly proclaims on every occasion. His unlimited contempt for pacifism and for those who oppose war as a means of regulating differences between nations is well known. Hitler cares nothing for what "scribblers" recognize as the so called "rights" which a population has to the territory it inhabits and cultivates. There is no human law, according to Hitler, which is strong enough to resist the law of nature, and the law of nature condemns the weak. A nation should defend its possessions if it is capable of so doing. If it is not capable or if it does not possess the necessary courage or energy—well, let it emigrate, disappear or allow itself to be

Committee of Studies and Information, and the *Brown Network* (London 1935).—*Ed.*

subdued. There is a sort of right of expropriation which Hitler expressly proclaims as belonging to the superior and stronger peoples. "A nation that wishes to be great has the right to all the land which may be necessary for it. This right is transformed into a duty when the extension of its territory becomes a necessary condition for its existence."

It is in terms of this *Weltanschauung* that Hitler envisaged the foreign policy which he prescribed for Germany. Germany after 1918 found herself in the situation of a people of 100 million inhabitants, only a portion of whom enjoyed relative independence. What should the Germany which remained free do? It goes without saying that she could not hurl herself against her enemy in order to recover her lost possessions. She did not have the necessary force for that. But, said Hitler, she should prepare for the restoration of the German power, which alone could regain for Germany that which belongs to her. She should "forge the sword," which will liberate Germany from the state of oppression in which she finds herself. Germany's foreign policy should aim to give the country security during the period of transition in which she would prepare her rearmament and find her "companions in arms" to aid her in the hour of danger. Hitler's greatest dream, set down in very expressive form in the political testament at the end of *Mein Kampf*, was to secure for Germany a sort of monopoly of military power in Europe. "Never allow two continental powers to emerge in Europe. Look upon every attempt to organize a second military power on the borders of Germany, even though it be only in the form of a potential military state, as an assault against Germany and view it not only as your *right* but as your *duty* to use all means, not barring force of arms, to prevent the emergence of such a state and to overthrow it if such a state already exists." (p. 754)

It will readily be seen that such principles are not likely to

inspire in Germany's neighbors an unlimited confidence in her
desire for peace.

2. Chancellor Hitler Talks of Peace

When Hitler came to power and began to feel his responsibility for the destiny of his country weighing down upon
him, the problems of international politics no longer presented themselves in so simple a form. As long as the Nazis
were in opposition their denunciation of the treason of Marxists and pacifists, their demand for a war of liberation and their
call for a crusade against bolshevism all served as admirable
subjects for propaganda and as such they were exceptionally
effective. The perspective changed as soon as it became necessary to go from theory to practice. It became exceedingly
dangerous for a chief of state to adhere completely to a program of foreign policy such as had been outlined in *Mein
Kampf.*

A change in Hitler's own evolution had already become
evident soon after the elections of 1930. At that time the Nazi
party for the first time emerged as a potential ruling party.
In his interviews to journalists and particularly in his conversations with Lord Rothermere, Hitler developed a program in which he expressed himself with very much more
moderation toward France. When, in the fall of 1930, Gus-
tave Hervé, exponent of reconciliation between French and
German nationalists, submitted his "conditions of peace" to
the leaders of the German parties of the right, Hitler replied
in the *Völkischer Beobachter* of October 26, 1930, that National Socialists have "a very strong desire for an amicable
understanding with other nations." He felt that world peace
would be assured "the moment that France and Germany arrived at a genuine understanding based on reciprocal equality
of their natural rights." Hitler was not tempted, however, by
the proposal for a military alliance which the French jour-

nalist had suggested. Against whom would this alliance be directed, asked Hitler. He concluded that it would be better to work for the disarmament of France rather than for the rearmament of Germany.

The "moderation" of the National Socialists was still more accentuated when Hitler assumed power in January, 1933. This was due to various reasons. The first reason was that National Socialism was and claimed to be essentially a movement of internal national regeneration. The purification of the German nation, the struggle against the internal enemy, the entire reorganization of the unified nation, the battle against unemployment, the economic and social reconstruction of the country—these were the immediate tasks of National Socialism. It strove to realize these tasks with feverish haste. Hitler did not fail to see that this internal regeneration occupied the chief place in the interests of the German people. This is what truly interested them; this is what stimulated their minds and inspired their hearts. The resumption of *Weltpolitik* was a matter of only secondary interest to them.

The second reason for the moderation of the Nazis was that they perceived that too radical "activism" in foreign policy might possibly bring on catastrophe. No one could abandon himself to the illusion that preparations for the "war of liberation" would be an easy thing. Every one was aware of the enormous risks which would be involved for Germany in a war with France under the existing state of armaments. On this point every one agreed, from Ludendorf to the Nationalists and the Nazis. Thus, whereas the preaching of a "war of liberation" had been Hitler's *leitmotiv* during his agitation, the reiteration of Germany's "desire for peace" became one of the constant themes of Nazi politics from the moment the *Führer* assumed power. In practice the Nazis were not able to do very much else but to continue, without any appreciable differences, the policy of their predecessors. This was visibly manifested in the fact that the direction of foreign

93

affairs did not change hands. Wilhelmstrasse continued to be guided by a diplomat of the old style, Herr von Neurath, who retained practically all his collaborators. In spite of the alterations which had been carried out in almost all phases of political life, foreign affairs remained what they had been and militant National Socialists did not as yet assume any important diplomatic posts.*

Under these conditions, the first official Nazi manifestations in foreign policy were of exemplary moderation. The program issued by the National government on February 2, 1933, immediately following its assumption of power, confined itself to explaining in a brief sentence that the new cabinet was conscious of the duty incumbent upon it "to work for the maintenance and consolidation of peace, which the world needs more than ever." Hitler, too, in his speech before the Reichstag on March 21, 1933 declared: "We wish to show ourselves as sincere friends of a peace destined to heal, once and for all, the wounds from which all are still bleeding."

The declaration of policy which Hitler made before the Reichstag on May 17, 1933 was more explicit and detailed. He astonished the world by his conciliatory tone. Hitler declared himself a partisan of international co-operation and of the maintenance of peace. Of course, he attacked the Treaty of Versailles which he considered a creation of passion and he demanded that it be revised. He demanded equal rights for all nations and general disarmament. He maintained that the National Socialist militias were not military organizations but only served the ends of domestic policy. He also gave assurance that the auxiliary police forces would be dissolved before the end of the year. Germany, he declared, was ready to provide all the guarantees for security which might be desired,

---

* There was, however, a special section for foreign affairs in the N.S.D.A.P., under the leadership of Alfred Rosenberg, which was of considerable influence. Later too, Joachim von Ribbentrop, an ardent disciple of Hitler, became Hitler's ambassador-at-large in foreign affairs and finally German ambassador to London.—*Ed.*

but only in the same measure as other nations. He accepted the disarmament plan drawn up by Ramsay MacDonald and even consented to the dissolution of the Reichswehr under the sole condition that they would accept a period of transition of five years. Germany would even agree to renounce the use of so-called "offensive" arms and would not refuse to submit its physical training organizations to the inspection of an international commission of control for the survey of all phases of disarmament. Hitler rallied to the suggestion of a four power pact proposed by Mussolini. He insisted, however, on the necessity for Germany of immediate equality of rights (*Gleichberechtigung*) with the other nations in the matter of armaments—equality which was not merely theoretical and purely formal but straight-forward and effective. He let it be clearly understood, however, that if this condition were not met, it would be difficult for Germany to remain in the League of Nations. These declarations, exempt of all discussion and criticism, received the unanimous approval of the Reichstag.

They were followed by other declarations of a similar tendency. In the speech of June 1, 1933, for example, Hitler reiterated in solemn fashion his desire for peace. "No new European war," he said, "could bring anything better than the unsatisfactory situation of today. . . . Another outbreak of such a crisis of madness would necessarily involve the destruction of society and public order." In an interview on June 28, 1933, granted to the correspondent of the *Petit Journal*, the Minister of Propaganda, Goebbels, echoed these sentiments. He assured the correspondent that a government of young men, who have known war and are conscious of their responsibilities, will, more than any other government, be animated by a sincere desire for peace. From that he deduced that the Nazi regime offered France more stability than any other regime, for the Nazis possessed the sense of reality and knew how to measure the weight of their responsibilities. "On the day on which we shall have signed an agreement, you can feel confident that we will keep it." Goebbels concluded by emphasizing the usefulness of direct conversations between the two governments whose co-operation, better than any other combination, would assure peace and prosperity for Europe. It would be easy to multiply quotations in which the same tendency was revealed. Those which we have given are sufficient to testify to the care which Nazi leaders took to show Europe their conciliatory dispositions and their desire for peace.

It is not astonishing therefore that the first important act of the Nazi government in foreign affairs was a conciliatory gesture towards Poland. No democratic regime would ever have been able to allow itself such a gesture without unloosing in the entire rightist press a hue and cry of indignant clamor and charges of high treason.

3. German-Polish Relations

During the entire period which preceded the advent of National Socialism the German attitude towards Poland was very clear. It was well summarized in the book by Werner von Rheinbaben, *Von Versailles zur Freiheit* (Hamburg, Hanseatische Verlagsanstalt, 1927). After the Locarno agreements Germany was able to provide Poland with a guarantee of non-aggression but she could not go beyond that and she was forced to refuse any guarantee of the existing frontiers of Poland. Germany recognized the revival of the Polish state. As a matter of fact she had called such a state back to life in 1916 and she was ready to give Poland all the necessary guarantees for an outlet to the sea for its products and for Polish participation in all primary affairs relating to Upper Silesia. But she could not recognize as definitive either the creation of the Polish corridor, which isolated East Prussia from the rest of the Reich, or the division of Upper Silesia, which arbitrarily split up an economic region better left as one indivisible whole. "God and history shall decide," concluded Herr von Rheinbaben, quoting the work of a Polish writer who had recently studied ways of *rapprochement* between Poland and Germany. There was no reason to doubt the sincerity of the promise repeatedly made by Germany not to resort to force of arms in order to settle her dispute with Poland, but the situation between the two countries remained none the less critical. Germany, citing article 19 of the Peace of Versailles, asserted that she had the right, without lessening her respect for the treaty, to hope for and to demand a partial readjustment of the European situation. Poland, on her side, remained free to look for support wherewith to resist German pressure. This simply implied that given an irritating word by Germany or a foolish step by Poland, war between the two countries would be inevitable. It was clear, therefore, to all who followed Polish-German relations that there was a permanent state of tension which was both political and economic. Von Rheinbaben very properly remarked that it would be most unwise to underestimate the seriousness of this situation.

When Hitler became Chancellor and Colonel Beck became Polish Foreign Minister, this state of affairs began to undergo an appreciable change. A series of interesting articles by Friedrich Sieburg in the *Frankfurter Zeitung* from November 26 to December 31, 1933 revealed the new German orientation in Polish policy. Poland certainly did not think of breaking her ties with France. These had been re-enforced by the visit of Colonel Beck to Paris in September 1933. The French guarantee was always looked upon by the Poles as their greatest asset in case of serious danger. But they were perfectly aware that it also presented a serious contingency, namely: to what extent would French public opinion allow French armed intervention in behalf of Poland, if such should be necessary? Moreover the Poles also aspired to be something more than a satellite of French policy. They aimed to become independent and to assure their security by their own means. This accounts for the non-aggression pact with Russia which they signed on July 25, 1932. This also accounts for their desire for a *rapprochement* with Germany. This *rapprochement* began in May 1933 by an exchange of declarations between the Chancellor and the Polish ambassador in Berlin on the one side, and the Polish Foreign Minister and the German ambassador in Warsaw on the other. It was carried on in the conversations between Hitler and the new Polish ambassador Lipski on November 16, and culminated on January 26, 1934 in an agreement which established cordial co-operation between Germany and Poland. On the surface, the new treaty did not change the existing situation very much. It provided no solution of the territorial differences between Germany and Poland. The fact that the two countries agreed "under no circumstances to resort to force in order to regulate differences which might arise between them" was nothing new. But the conclusion of this agreement created an atmosphere of trust between the two nations which facilitated the regulation of all conflicts and which gives some basis for the hope that after years of eternal conflict, the political, economic and cultural problems which separate Germany and Poland might proceed henceforth toward positive solution.

On March 7, 1934 a commercial agreement put an end to the state of economic war which had existed for a long time between the two nations. Congratulations were exchanged on both sides for having avoided a conflict which might have brought on new disasters. In his speech of January 30, 1934 to the Reichstag, Hitler expressly stated: "Whatever might be the differences which shall arise in the future between the two countries, all attempts at solving them by military action would involve calamities the effect of which would be far out of proportion to the importance of possible gain."

Foreign Policy

4. Nazi Activities in Austria and Central Europe

The situation created by the rise of National Socialism was much less reassuring with respect to Austria. There was a definite reaction in Austria against the triumph of Hitlerism. This reaction was personified in Chancellor Dollfuss. Whereas until now *Anschluss* to Germany had been desired by practically all Austrian groups, there was now a resurrection of "Austrianism." This movement was not at all opposed to the Germanism of the old culture and in fact considered itself as the heir of this tradition. But it did set itself definitely against Prussianism; against the Nordic barbarism which, in their eyes, Hitlerism represented. "We others, Austrians, are Germans," declared an official representative of this tendency at the Salzburg Congress of May 19, 1933. "We are fully conscious of the solidarity of destiny which binds all the branches of the German race. Austria, the *Ostmark*, has always been an important agency of the German mission in Europe. It remains so in our own day and it may be said that this special mission of the *Ostmark* has a particularly real and profound meaning today—today when blind national chauvinism, savage methods of violence and centralization by force, are all bent upon isolating Germany politically and culturally from the rest of the world." An "Austrian front" was formed under the vigorous leadership of Dollfuss, having as its basis the Christian Socialist Party and the Heimwehr. It mercilessly combatted the dictatorship of the reds as well as of the browns, turned its back resolutely on the democratic regime, which it accused of having demoralized and dechristianized the country and of having made it into a heap of material and moral ruin. It expressed its preference for an authoritarian regime steering Austria with a firm hand mid-way between the bolshevism of the left and that of the right. During the bloody days of February 1934, Dollfuss smashed the Austrian

Socialists without pity. He turned with equal energy against the furious assaults which came from the National Socialists.

The German press portrayed the action of Dollfuss as the futile attempt of a dictatorial government, which had no majority either in the country or in parliament, to govern by decree, to maintain itself by the force of bayonets and to prevent, by violence, the Austrian Nazis from pursuing a campaign which would have brought about the pacification of Austria just as Hitler's triumph had put an end to the chaos which had been raging in Germany during the last days of the parliamentary regime. Abroad, particularly in Italy and in France, it was never doubted that there was actually a local National Socialist party in Austria and that this party numbered perhaps one third of the population. But every one believed that the German Nazis had a share of responsibility for the behavior of the Austrian Nazis. It is probable that the Nazis hoped that the same sort of operations would succeed in Austria as had been effective in Bavaria. The Nazis had gained the upper hand over the Bavarian particularists despite the boast of the latter that they would throw into prison the first Reich Commissar who dared to pass the Bavarian border. The Nazis were very much disappointed, however, when they met the resistance of the Austrian government to this maneuver and they were outraged by the resolute attitude of Chancellor Dollfuss who declared categorically at the Congress of Salzburg in May 1934: "Whoever, in order to achieve their domestic political aims, shall make use of aid *from abroad* (in this case the Nazis of Germany) against the government, will be guilty of high treason."

When a terrorist campaign, directed by the Austrian Nazis against the regular government, developed in Austria, every one believed that the German government was guilty of either direct or indirect responsibility for this violence. From all evidence the German Nazis indulged in propaganda against the Dollfuss government which the authorities of the Reich could not ignore. It was from Munich, through the official broadcasting station, that Habicht, the direct agent of Hitler, launched his furious tirades against the Austrian government, his incitements to civil war and his threats to those in Vienna who defended the independence of their country. It was in Bavaria that the fugitive Nazis, who had been organized into an armed legion ready to attempt a coup in Austrian territory, found refuge.

The rude methods of propaganda used by Germany which were of more than doubtful propriety, the obstinacy with which she clung to her proceedings, caused alarm not only in Austria, France and the little Entente, but also in England. There was ground for suspicion that she was preparing for a secret *Anschluss*, whereby a Nazi government would be set up in Austria which would then be entirely bound to a unified Reich. The powers issued a solemn warning to Germany that Austrian independence would have to be maintained. Even Italy, despite the friendly relations which she enjoyed at the time with the Reich, participated in the various diplomatic actions taken to stop the German campaign against Austria. It seems certain that, at the time of Hitler's visit to Italy, Mussolini did not fail to advise prudence and that he manifested some bitterness at the continuation of Nazi acts of terrorism. Mussolini indicated this by arranging a most cordial reception for Dollfuss in Rome, by encouraging Austrian resistance to German pressure, and by granting to Austria all the economic advantages that he was able to concede without endangering Italian interests. The murder of Chancellor Dollfuss on July 25, 1934 almost set the spark to Europe. If the Nazi putsch had triumphed in Vienna at that moment it would have meant the certain intervention of the Italian regiments massed at the Brenner with all the unforeseen consequences which this step could have involved.

With the advent of Schuschnigg as Austrian Prime Minister, the tension diminished. On July 11, 1936 an arrangement was signed between Austria and Germany which guaranteed the complete sovereignty of the Vienna government and expressly stipulated that the question of National Socialism in Austria was an exclusively Austrian problem in which Germany promised not to meddle. On the other hand this agreement stressed the strong bonds which united the two countries. Austria proclaimed herself a "German state" and announced her intention of making her political policy conform to this fact. It is too soon as yet to say to what extent Austrian independence has been guaranteed by this accord. *Anschluss* to Germany was not officially proclaimed and everything leads to the belief that it will not be carried out for some time. But it is hard not to believe that Austria has become more or less enmeshed in the wake of German policy.

Vienna still remains the "nerve center" of Europe. The Socialists no longer exist as an organized force but they have not pardoned the government for its brutality and they are silently biding their time. The Austrian Nazis have become less virulent but they have not disarmed, and informed observers claim that their propaganda continues to make progress among the middle classes and intellectuals. The restoration of the Hapsburgs which might be popular in Austria and which would probably create an effective bar to *Anschluss* is rendered impossible by the absolute veto maintained by the Czechs and the little Entente.* The German attitude has become more reserved. No one can tell, however, if this is because Germany has really renounced *Anschluss* or because she thinks that time is working in her favor and that by the progressive diffusion of the National Socialist virus, Austria will sooner or later have to join the Hitlerites, if not

* This view of monarchism as a bar to Nazi *Anschluss* has been advocated by the third vice-mayor of Vienna, Dr Ernst Karl Winter. Winter elaborated his views in a brochure, *Monarchie und Arbeiterschaft* (Vienna 1936) in which he advocated union with the Socialist workers on such a platform. The brochure was confiscated by the government and the author was forced to take a leave of absence on October 23, 1936.—*Ed.*

de jure, at least in fact. The prospects for the future, under these conditions, remain uncertain and no one knows how long the precarious equilibrium, maintained for better or worse at present, can last.

The German press also stressed the fact that as a result of this Austro-German accord as well as of the protocols signed by Italy with Austria and Hungary and, thanks to the Italo-German collaboration, a new order of affairs will be established in South-Eastern Europe, in which also those Balkan countries, previously under Russian and French influence, would participate. It is quite obvious, therefore, that Germany together with Italy is making a strong effort to withdraw Danubian Europe from French and Russian influences. The dismissal of Titulesco in Rumania and the peace concluded between Bulgaria and Jugo-Slavia were looked upon by the German press as Nazi diplomatic gains. The results of this diplomatic campaign are still uncertain. The situation is, however, most disturbing to Czechoslovakia, who is tied to France and Russia by military and political agreements and who might thus find herself isolated from her neighbors. Czechoslovakia also contains a very active German minority. She is thus exposed to pressure which might become very disturbing at any moment. It was very disquieting for this reason to note that in the speech of January 30, 1937 Hitler failed completely to mention Czechoslovakia in his discussion of foreign policy.

5. Nazi Rearmament

On October 14, 1933, Germany notified Europe that she was withdrawing from the Disarmament Commission and leaving the League of Nations. This step evidently was not unexpected. For a long time Germany had manifested her growing impatience with the lack of any tangible results from the Geneva negotiations. When, on July 23, 1932, after six months of laborious and confused discussions, the Disarmament Conference finally finished the "first phase" of its work and adopted a resolution whereby the signatory powers were exhorted to carry out the first decisive step towards "a substantial reduction of armaments," the chief of the German delegation delivered an important declaration in behalf of his government. He indicated that a necessary condition for the ultimate participation of Germany in the work of the conference would be "the clear and specific recognition of the equality of rights for all nations." He added: "It would not be compatible with the sentiments of honor and international justice if the conference, desiring to set up rules and principles for the disarmament of states, would at the same time exclude Germany or other states from these general rules and principles and subject a particular state to discriminatory exception." The German delegate also declared that the principle of equal rights had not yet been accepted by all the governments and he concluded by saying that Germany would not be able to continue her collaboration at the conference if a satisfactory solution of this decisive question had not been reached when the work of the conference was resumed. The German government thus plainly threatened to withdraw from the conference if it did not obtain satisfaction on the question of the principle of equal rights, which it considered so essential. After thorny negotiations a formula was finally agreed upon on December 11, which was signed by the five participating powers. The agreement recognized Germany's demand for equal rights and thus allowed her to resume participation at Geneva.

After ten months of negotiation, however, no tangible results were achieved. Germany as a result withdrew from the conference. At the same time she published her reasons and they were convincing in every way for German public opinion. Imbued with the conviction that she was not responsible for the war and that she had amply fulfilled the obligation of disarmament imposed upon her by the Treaty of Versailles, Germany was offended by the delay in carrying out the promise of equality of armaments which had been made to her. She refused to allow herself any longer to be treated with suspicion and as a country of inferior rights. She therefore withdrew from Geneva. By her protestations of peace, by her offer of direct conversations with France and by her formal declaration promising to respect existing treaties, however, Germany took pains to indicate that her withdrawal did not imply any kind of break or threat to anyone. A commission had been established at Geneva which had been sitting for years without ever having achieved any positive results. Germany refused to continue these palavers which seemed more barren every day. Germany felt that she had fulfilled to the letter all obligations imposed upon her by the treaty. The other nations were delaying in carrying out the obligations which they had assumed. It was their affair. But Germany thought that under such conditions it was not in keeping with her dignity to continue to participate in an assembly in which she did not enjoy a position of equality with other nations. She therefore left. The others were at liberty to continue their discussions until they agreed. Germany waits, ready to resume discussions on the day when her partners will have recognized that they cannot treat Germany as a second-rank nation and will consent to negotiate with her as equal to equal. While waiting, Germany staged a plebiscite which was to show the world that on this question which touched her honor the entire nation was as one man behind the *Führer*.

This interpretation seems entirely plausible at first. Unfortunately, upon deeper analysis, it becomes evident that the German argument was convincing only to those who accept the German "legend" concerning the origins of the war, concerning German responsibilities and concerning the reality of German disarmament. It does not take into account the fact,

which no one can suppress, that there is no universally accepted "truth" regarding these controversial issues but that
opinion varies from country to country and each nation clings
to its own position. As soon as one becomes willing, however,
to take this fact into account, the matter becomes singularly
complicated. If, despite these fundamental differences, there
are to be any practical results in the question of disarmament,
and if this problem, which is of such infinite delicacy, is to be
solved, it is necessary to find a compromise which will allow
the nations with their widely divergent points of view on
important questions, to unite on a compromise solution which
each is able to accept after making certain sacrifices.

The German gesture was justified as an attitude of offended
dignity. The inequality of rights in respect to military matters, which was imposed unilaterally by the treaty, was considered to be a permanent humiliation and offense to German
national sentiment. This argument proved to be a very powerful one. It seemed entirely convincing to Italian opinion
and to some circles of British and American opinion. In
France, too, it was not ignored. As the war recedes in point
of time, it becomes more and more difficult to maintain any
absolute right to an arrangement whereby a distinction is
made between peoples who have a right to arm and those who
have not. No one in France entertained the idea of keeping
Germany as a second-rate power or of treating her as a pariah.
All were agreed in their desire to have realized in Europe,
with as brief a delay as possible, a state of affairs where, in
principle as well as in fact, the equality of all nations in military affairs would be achieved without contest, and where
national security would be assured not only for France but
for all peoples, particularly for the Germans who were com-
plaining of being exposed without defense to possible attacks
by their neighbors. The difficulty which had to be solved was,
therefore, not a matter of principle. Everybody wanted equal
rights and security for all. The problem was to find how to

realize *in fact* this equality and security which all wanted in theory. Arguments without end immediately arose regarding this question.

In the negotiations, divergences arose endlessly between the French and German experts with reference to the actual extent of armament or rearmament of their respective countries. There were endless debates on the irritating question of Germany's "secret armaments," on the comparison of French and German military budgets, on the estimation of the military value of police forces, sport associations and brown militia, and on the evaluation of the "potential war strength" of the two nations. There was no agreement on the possibility of setting up an international force capable of guaranteeing security to all, nor on the possibility of definitely determining in all cases who was the aggressor, on the extent of the obligations of members of the League of Nations against a recognized aggressor, nor on the right of neutrality. There was also no accord on the appraisal of the "moral" dispositions of the nations in view. The Frenchman, who had the feeling of being "sated," of not having anything to demand from anyone and not asking for anything except to cultivate his garden, shrugged his shoulders when they accused him of aspiring towards the hegemony of Europe and of being intent on perpetuating his artificial domination on the continent or above all of planning a preventive war. The German on his side, however, refused to admit that there was any legitimate ground for concern regarding the cause of peace from either the establishment of a regime of uncontrolled dictatorship, from the renaissance of a nationalist and militarist spirit in the youth across the Rhine, or from the official measures taken to develop and organize physical training and the combative spirit. Germany was indignant when they suspected that in order to give more weight to her demands regarding state frontiers she had voluntarily resorted if not to force of arms at least to the ways of intimidation familiar to the German diplomacy of the old regime.

Amidst this sea of contradictions and disputes, the simple layman had long given up hope of understanding the problem and he inclined more or less to place his trust in the experts. He understood that the problem which confronted the leaders of European politics was something quite other than a question of principle. The practical realization of this equality of rights to which all agreed in theory, presupposed an evaluation of the concrete or moral forces, and agreement regarding these was far from being realized. The average Frenchman, moreover, felt that this investigation ought to be all the more thorough because France, who in 1914 had been the victim of aggression (according to the "legend" accepted in France), should not unwittingly deprive herself of the provisions of the Treaty of 1918 which constituted the material guarantee of her security.

Under these conditions French opinion had little understanding of what seemed to be merely an excess of untimely impatience on the part of Germany. The French representatives at Geneva had already come to believe—at least that is the way it appeared in Paris—that the goal, pursued for such a long time in vain, had finally been attained and that the compromise formula would soon be found. It was precisely at that moment that the Germans chose to break off negotiations and withdraw to their tents. From then on practically all Frenchmen—and not only Frenchmen—believed that by this departure, accompanied by much ado, Germany had gone back to the policy of banging her fist on the table, which her diplomats had pursued before the war and which had brought such disastrous results.

From then on the question was raised as to how valuable were the reassuring declarations which Hitler had directed toward France in his speech of October 14, 1933, and which had been broadcast by radio throughout the entire world.

Hitler had solemnly declared, in the name of his people, that Germany was imbued with the desire to put an end to a hostility which might lead both nations to sacrifices out of all proportion to the possible benefits to be derived. He had announced that after the question of the Saar was regulated there was no other territorial dispute between the two peoples. He thus implicitly accepted the renunciation of Alsace-Lorraine already made at Locarno. He declared: "The German people are convinced that their military honor has remained intact in the course of the thousand battles and struggles of the Great War. At the same time we look upon the French soldier as our old and glorious opponent. We, and with us all the German people, would be happy at the idea that our children and our infants would be spared the tragic sufferings which we, men of honor, saw around us and ourselves experienced." These were certainly important declarations. It was a new and even moving note in the mouth of Hitler. If this call for reconciliation did not meet with the same response which it might have met under other circumstances, it was obviously due to the fact that the very moment when the Chancellor was proposing direct conversations to France, he was, by his precipitate and very showy gesture of breaking away from the League of Nations, strengthening the French spirit of mistrust and insecurity which had always made Franco-German relations so difficult. The French Prime Minister, Daladier, well expressed the general sentiment of France when, in his speech to parliament, he addressed this sober and measured reply to Hitler: "We are not deaf to any appeal. But we are not blind to any act. If there is a desire for an understanding why begin by a rupture?"

From all appearances Germany's exit from the League was but a preliminary step in preparation for German rearmament in case the Entente powers would not agree to disarm. This step obviously involved risks since it constituted a direct violation of the Treaty of Versailles. Hitler, therefore, waited patiently until the thorny question of the Saar was regulated before he proceeded. As soon as the plebiscite, set for January 13, 1935, had given an overwhelming majority in favor of the return to Germany and when on March 1, the Saar administration had officially been restored to German authorities, the Reich leaders believed that the moment had arrived for public announcement of the measures which they had secretly prepared at least six months before. On March 16, 1935 Hitler, throwing off by unilateral action all the obligations which the Treaty of Versailles had imposed upon Germany, officially re-established compulsory military service for all men from eighteen to forty-five and fixed at his will the strength of the army which he considered necessary to assure the security of the Reich. In place of the 100,000 men in the Reichswehr, Germany would from now on have an army of 12 army corps and 36 divisions, corresponding to a strength of about 550,000 men, and supplied with all the arms used in other countries.

Once again Germany, weary of discussion, had acted. Adroitly exploiting the unpardonable delays of diplomacy and the tactical errors and disagreements of the signatory powers of the Treaty of Versailles, Germany had boldly proclaimed to Europe her will to consider abrogated the stipulations regarding disarmament. She thus confronted the powers with the alternative of either taking up arms in order to enforce respect for the treaty or else woefully accepting the *fait accompli*.

The *Führer's* calculations proved to be correct. Europe, and France in particular, recoiled from the idea of provoking a war and they took note of the German step without any serious resistance. Some few reservations were made, some platonic protests, censure marked by all the diplomatic cautions was expressed by the League of Nations, and that was all. German public opinion was jubilant. The restoration of the German military forces was in their eyes a satisfaction of their self-respect and the wiping out of a grievous humiliation resented for many years; it also brought to the nation the security which it had lacked until then. Strange as it may seem to those who have even a slight acquaintance with the dispositions of France, many Germans, even among the better informed leaders, appeared up to a recent date, to have actually entertained genuine fears of the possibility of a preventive war undertaken by France. German armament had dissipated that uncertainty. Now, they say, it is too late to attempt any operations of this kind and they emphasize the point that from now on an invasion of Germany would be something much more than an easy military promenade. They jeer at the French for their lack of realistic sense in having allowed the moment to go by when such an attempt might have met with no serious resistance. The *Führer* was thus acclaimed by the entire nation for having *dared*, at the opportune moment, to take a step which no government before him had risked.

Naval rearmament immediately followed land rearmament. England in its turn was confronted by Germany's determined and irrevocable decision. The danger this time was serious. The repudiation of the military clauses of the Versailles Treaty had particularly affected France. French pacific intentions were only too well known and Germany thought she could face the inevitable bad feeling without fear of any serious reprisals. But it should be remembered that the foreign policy which Hitler had advocated called for a conciliatory attitude towards England. Every one knew that England was not to be trifled with in the matter of naval armaments. One of the major causes for the English attitude in 1914 had been the fact that England sensed in the ambitious programs of naval construction of William II, a threat to her supremacy on the sea. There was room for fear that Germany, by proclaiming her will to restore her navy, might again arouse British mistrust and enmity, provoking dangerous consequences for Germany. Hitler, in any case, risked finding himself more isolated than ever and confronted by a "united front" of the old allies, who would be resolved to call a halt to the rising ambitions of an aggressive pan-Germanism.

Berlin gossip has it, that the naval conversations with England were the work of the *Führer* and his personal aide, von Ribbentrop, and were undertaken against the advice of the leading officials of German politics. In any case there was a persistent rumor in the month of June, 1935 of a shake-up of high officials in Wilhelmstrasse. This did not take place, however. The step which Hitler took on this point undoubtedly was a dangerous one. The success which crowned it was tremendous. Confronted by the German desire for naval rearmament, England, after a brief suggestion of displeasure, quickly decided to come to terms. British leaders believed that the best way to safeguard this primary English interest would be to circumscribe the fire and conclude a direct and separate agreement with Germany which would set a maximum limit to German armaments acceptable to both countries. In agreeing to this transaction Germany not only received the right to inaugurate, with English consent, an important program of naval construction, but she also sowed the seeds of further discord among the signatories of the Versailles Treaty.

The conclusion of the naval agreement signed in London on June 18, 1935 between England and Germany aroused a great stir in France. It was the occasion for polemics in the press and for diplomatic maneuvers intended to mitigate the disagreement which had unexpectedly developed between the two allied nations, and to hold together the Entente which was considered valuable for the peace of the world. In general it was nevertheless obvious that by his bold initiative in the question of disarmament Hitler had scored an amazing success which also solidified his prestige in Germany. He had won the right to rearm officially both on land and on sea and this was accomplished without a violent break with France and without provoking any dangerous resentment on the part of England.

6. General Orientation of Nazi Policy

The long speech which Hitler delivered before the Reichstag on May 21, 1935 was a justification of his conduct in the past; it was also an eloquent declaration of the general guiding principles of his intentions, an exposition of his views on European policy and a summary of suggestions for the future.

The Chancellor once more solemnly proclaimed his absolute disavowal of any imperialist designs. Germany has no ambitions of conquest, she desires no expansion at the expense of any other nation and she repudiates any idea of "Germanization." Her rearmament, he declared, is of no warlike significance. Germany decided to fix the size of her army by herself only when it appeared certain that the signatories of the Versailles Treaty either could not or would not carry out the promise of general disarmament which had been the counterpart of the initial German disarmament. It is not Germany, therefore, who has violated the treaty. Her step was nothing but the necessary reply to the violation of the treaty by the other powers. This step, however, implied no threat to anyone. It merely re-established the equilibrium of armaments which had been destroyed for many years, to the disadvantage of Germany, by the continuous insincerity of the Entente powers in the matter of disarmament. Germany was convinced that war would never succeed in procuring advantages for any country in proportion to the destruction it would cause. Germany wanted peace in all sincerity and with all her heart and for a very elementary reason, because she knew that a new war, far from alleviating the general distress in Europe, would only increase it.

As for the general orientation of German policy, Hitler as well as his aides insisted repeatedly upon the absolute antagonism between National Socialist Germany and Russia. It was an antagonism of ideas and of principles as well as an emotional antipathy. No conciliation was possible between Soviet communism and German corporatism. For Hitler, Russia has nothing to do with Europe; she is a permanent source of danger to European culture as well as to the social equilibrium of our age. The Chancellor would never think of attacking Russia. He leaves each one free to seek salvation in his own fashion. He desires to maintain correct relations with Russia and he will allow the continuation of the Berlin agreement.* But he is the implacable enemy of bolshevism as soon as it seeks to spread beyond its own frontiers. At no price will he enter into any agreement which might lead him to intervene *in favor* of Russia. This accounts for his antagonism to the eastern pact which France persistently urged him to join.†

As for France, Hitler, his aides and his press were unanimous in the affirmation of their desire to bring about better relations between the two nations. They asked France to wipe away all old and recent grievances, admit the sincerity of their words of peace and accept the loyal co-operation which they offer France on a plane of equality. France, they said, must give up viewing Germany as a menace to the peace of the world and lining up against her a complicated system of alliances. The supposed aim of these alliances was to make Germany incapable of disturbing the peace by her appetite for conquest and domination. Germany, however, does not have such designs and she has solemnly repudiated all such intentions. Again Hitler declared that since the restoration of the Saar there were no more territorial differences between the two countries. He expressly declared that Germany re-

* An agreement for the extension of German-Soviet trade was signed in Berlin on April 29, 1936.—*Ed.*

† The high point of anti-Russian propaganda was reached at the Nuremberg Congress of 1936. The fight against bolshevism was the slogan of the Congress and bitter denunciations of the Soviet Union were made by Hitler, Goebbels and Alfred Rosenberg. This was soon followed by the German-Japanese agreement. For this see p. 121 and Appendix.—*Ed.*

nounced all pretenses to Alsace-Lorraine, for which she had not long ago made war. He is willing to make a concession to the French need of security even though it is painful to the pride of the Germans, namely to respect the clause pertaining to the demilitarisation of the left bank of the Rhine. He would require, however, that France give him her confidence in exchange. He remained thoroughly skeptical of the eastern pact or the Danubian pact whereby France expected to guard against imaginary dangers. He did not believe in the efficacy of the French policy which strives for the collective organization of European security by a complicated system of general arrangements. Above all he held that the alliance which France concluded with bolshevism was contrary to all French traditions, to the interests of civilized Europe and even incompatible, so it seemed to him, with the Locarno agreements. He wanted France to accept in good grace the hand which he extended to her. The English barrier has been surmounted, said the *Frankfurter Zeitung* in an important editorial: England has made her peace with the new Germany, since Germany has frankly declared that she accepts in all sincerity the undisputed naval supremacy of England and promises to maintain her navy at 35 per cent of the British navy. It would be necessary also to clear the French stage and bring French opinion to the same degree of comprehension to which English public opinion had been raised.

As for Austria, Germany proclaimed her entire disinterest. She wished neither to annex Austria nor to interfere into her internal affairs. There was one condition, however, namely that other powers likewise abstain from all intervention and leave Austria free to organize her government as she likes. The same attitude was taken concerning the Baltic countries. Germany was ready to sign non-aggression pacts with all her neighbors in the East. She was happy to see her frontiers partially protected by a group of smaller independent states. If she makes an exception of Lithuania it is only because

Lithuania has undertaken a bitter persecution of the 140,000 Germans living under her rule: "As long as it will not be possible for the powers that have guaranteed the status of Memel to bring Lithuania to the observation of the elementary rules of international law, we shall, on our side, not be able to conclude any kind of treaty with this state." For the future, finally, Germany declared herself ready to co-operate in the organization of security and of lasting peace in Europe. She was, in principle, ready to sign non-aggression pacts with all her neighbors. She agreed to conclude a "Locarno of the air," a pact which would limit the construction of military airplanes. She was also ready to avoid an armament race, and examine the question of a limitation or even gradual decrease of land armaments on the condition, of course, that these sacrifices were agreed to by *all* the powers and that all would renounce simultaneously the use of particular types of armaments such as poison gas, heavy tanks, heavy artillery, etc.

It followed from Hitler's speech that he would agree to re-enter the League of Nations on two conditions, which he clearly indicated. The first was that the Covenant of the League be made distinctly separate from the Versailles Treaty and the second that its terms include a clause which would permit at given times the peaceful revision of arrangements which had become outworn or judged dangerous to the maintenance of peace. The Nazi press underscored the fact that nowhere had the demand for the restitution of colonies or the granting of colonial mandates been presented as a condition *sine qua non* of Germany's return to the League.

The German press further emphasized the capital importance of Hitler's speech from the point of view of the maintenance of peace. It cited the words of Baldwin to the Commons: "I believe that even in the eleventh hour we may yet within our own life time banish from the world the most fearful terror and the most dastardly prostitution of man's invention ever known." The Nazis felt that they had suc-

ceeded in banishing the specter of war and they pointed to
the fact that even in Paris, where many were wary of taking
a firm position towards the suggestions of the Chancellor, a
strong impression had been produced. The clouds had not all
been dispersed but the Nazis believed that an important step
had been made on the road to conciliation.

The Italo-Abyssinian conflict was followed by the German
press with prudent reserve often blended with irony. Germany scrupulously avoided becoming involved in the affair.
She was not at all alarmed by the colonial ambitions and
imperialist activity of Italy. She refrained from showing any
tenderness for the cause of the "liberty" of Abyssinia and she
had no such feeling. She pointed to the Pharisaism in the
righteous indignation of certain pacifists who wished to bar
Italy from acts which all colonizing people had permitted
themselves a hundred times, and who were calling for "sanctions" against Italy. She was not sorry to state that even in
the simple case of the Italo-Abyssinian conflict, where there
was no doubt as to who was the aggressor, the mechanism of
sanctions had operated very poorly. The French system of
"alliances," on the other hand, in the case of French obligations towards Italy, had strongly hindered the normal functioning of the defensive apparatus of the League of Nations.
At the same time it constituted a measure of the seriousness of
the problem which confronted England. Already menaced in
her insular security by the progress of military aviation, the
development of Italian imperialism now appeared as a menace
to English domination in the Mediterranean as well as in the
valley of the Nile. If France were to range herself beside Italy
the Mediterranean would then become a Latin lake. The
stakes of the game being played in Abyssinia were enormous
for British imperialism. The Germans were therefore not at
all amazed at the earnest attitude which the English displayed
in this affair and the vigor with which they pursued their
policy of naval and aerial rearmament. They noted, on the

other hand, the difficult situation in which France found herself. France was called upon to serve as mediator between two nations which she had hoped to unite in common action against the German "danger," although she wished above all to displease neither one nor the other.

Germany obviously had no interest in seeing the crisis aggravated into a conflagration, the extent of which it was difficult to foresee. It was also evident that Germany measured the advantages that accrued to her out of this capital event of world politics which set Mussolinian and British imperialism against each other. Now it was no longer pan-Germanism which appeared as the sower of discord and the trouble maker of European peace. The French policy of "security" directed against Germany, was meeting with growing opposition. The common front of Italy, England and France, created at Stresa, threatened to break or was actually broken. The League of Nations, from which Germany had withdrawn, was faced with new difficulties. The Italo-Abyssinian episode thus served to postpone for Germany a series of embarrassing problems and threatened to break up the group of powers who had resolved to block the way against the ultimate ambitions of pan-Germanism. Out of this fact German diplomacy acquired new freedom of movement.

Germany's intentions, moreover, were wrapt in mystery. There was scarcely any doubt that her policy was clearly oriented against Russia. The persistent opposition which she showed to the ratification of the alliance between France and the Soviet Union was sufficient indication of this antagonism and this was stressed continually in the speeches of Nazi leaders. But on what powers did she count for organizing an anti-Soviet bloc? It seemed that she envisaged a *rapprochement* with Japan. No one knew as yet what definite direction Italian policy would take. But it seemed clear that after a period of marked hostility Italy would again attempt a *rapprochement* with Germany. Did Nazi diplomacy entertain any hope of turning France away from the Russian "alliance" and assuring herself at least of French neutrality in the event of war with Russia? Who could tell! The same absolute uncertainty existed as to the *immediate* aims envisaged by German diplomacy: abolition of the clause of the demilitarization of the Rhine? Possession of colonies or colonial mandates? Extension of German influence in Jugo-Slavia and Rumania? No one knew.

Whatever it may have been, it was clear that the step whereby Germany officially proclaimed her rearmament and the energy with which she pushed her military preparations in the economic field, despite the financial difficulties with which she was grappling, revived mistrust everywhere, despite the reassuring pronouncements with which Hitler had surrounded his acts. Germany heard Baldwin declare that "the frontier of England was on the Rhine" and that English rearmament was necessitated not only by the Italian danger but also by the concern which the future ambitions of Germany inspired in British statesmen. Relations with France continued to bear the stamp of definite reserve on the part of both nations. Even Holland betrayed the fears which she felt for her security by the vote of large credits for the building of fortifications.

7. *Repudiation of Locarno*

The speech of March 7, 1936, in which Hitler repudiated the Locarno treaties and announced the entry of German troops into the demilitarized zone of the Rhine, crowned the state of international tension in which Europe found itself. What was the significance and portent of this move? Hitler declared that it should be viewed as the culmination of the long effort of Germany to recover her full power as a free nation. Threatened in her security by the French pact with Soviet Russia, she had freed herself from this last clause, which was an injury to Germany's national dignity. In possession once again of her full sovereign rights over the entire extent of her territory, she was now ready to bury the hatchet of war and conclude non-aggression pacts with her neighbors for twenty-five years, re-enter the League of Nations, sign a convention limiting air forces, and negotiate a disarmament agreement and a project for the Franco-German demilitarization of the Rhine frontier. In France, on the other hand, the re-entry of German troops into the Rhineland aroused considerable emotion. It was not the fact of military reoccupation which disturbed the French so much. It had not been difficult to foresee that Germany, after having rearmed, would also claim the right to bring troops again into the demilitarized zone. This was an eventuality which everyone foresaw. What alarmed and offended France was the way in which Hitler proceeded and the way in which he justified his *modus operandi*.

If Hitler truly believed that the pact concluded by France with Soviet Russia was a violation of the Locarno treaty and constituted a grave danger for Germany, if he refused to accept the explanations which France gave him and which appeared convincing to European opinion, he could have appealed to the World Court, whose arbitration France had accepted in advance. Or even more, he could have entered into negotiations with the signatory powers of the Locarno treaty. The whole world waited for such a move and France certainly did not shun it. But in place of negotiation, the *Führer*, in order to avoid the delays and weariness of discussion, once more confronted France with a *fait accompli*. This time he violated not only the Treaty of Versailles but also the Locarno pact, which had been freely signed by Germany and which he himself had explicitly recognized as binding. The *Führer*, by his move, thus placed before France the alternative of either parrying on her part with a similar move—for example the occupation of the bridge-heads of the Rhine—

which would have led directly to war, or of accepting, though under protest, this deliberately hostile move which he used to impose his will on France by a unilateral decision.

This move offended France in the first place because it was impossible to see in it anything but a gratuitous challenge. Or better, it was a test, a trial of resistance, to which the Germans subjected France because they thought that by reason of the well known pacific aims of France they could risk this step without exposing themselves to dangerous retaliation. They thought they were sufficiently strong and France sufficiently weak and "debilitated" so that the test would involve only a minimum of danger for them.

But it was more. The German step showed itself to be a grave threat to the very principles of international order, as Mr. Eden declared with great force: "The abrogation of the Locarno treaty and the occupation of the demilitarized zone have profoundly shaken confidence in any engagement into which the government of Germany may, in the future, enter. . . . It strikes a severe blow at the principle of sanctity of treaties which underlies the whole structure of international relations." Nothing was more correct. Among the French, in any case, Germany's move no doubt increased considerably their mistrust of *any* convention entered into with Germany. What real security could France find in a "scrap of paper" likely to be torn up one fine day in just the same arbitrary way as the Locarno treaty? Even admitting that France had been too "negative" in the past and that by reason of French legalistic pedantry or pessimistic skepticism she had allowed many an auspicious occasion for making peace with Germany to pass by, it remains true that Hitler did everything at this time to strengthen French conviction that, as far as Germany was concerned, the French could rely on nothing for their security except the power of their arms, their alliances and the promises of aid by their friends in case of unjustified aggression.

This accounts also for the skepticism with which French opinion greeted the positive suggestions contained in Hitler's speech of March 7. He offers France peace. But what does that mean? Hitler knows very well that in an age like ours, in which *all* peoples have a horror of war and where it is certain that a great war cannot be undertaken without the enthusiastic support of the entire nation, it becomes impossible to *declare* war without the support of public opinion. In practice, therefore, a war is not possible except when each of the peoples concerned is convinced—as was the case in 1914—that it is defending its own life and is fighting for its independence. Under these conditions Hitler knows very well that he will refrain from engaging with France in any war which is avowedly one of revenge or of conquest. He is able to give public assurance of this in all sincerity because if war does break out it will be, in his opinion, as well as in that of his people, *an imposed and defensive war*. A well-engineered propaganda would under any condition be able to persuade the Germans that they were not the aggressors but the victims, in just the same way as they are being told today that it was not they but France who had really violated the Locarno treaty. When, therefore, Hitler promises not to attack France for twenty-five years he guarantees her against an act which he has decided well in advance not to commit, since it would constitute the worst kind of imprudence on his part.

The crisis was therefore brought to a head. It is certainly one of the most serious which has arisen since 1919. No one wishes to assume responsibility for war, neither Hitler nor the German General Staff, nor France nor Europe. But everyone feels that this war, which no one wants, might break out unexpectedly and at the slightest imprudence of language or tactics. How can it be averted? How can European security be placed on a more solid basis? Diplomacy is occupied in trying to solve this problem and to reconcile the divergent points of view of the parties concerned—of Germany, a prisoner of her policies who definitely does not wish to give the impression that she is retreating—of France, who refuses to negotiate under threat and demands the re-establishment of the violated right as a prerequisite for all conversations—of England who, anxious above all to ward off the present danger, inclines to accept the *fait accompli* and to give heed to the better part of the concrete offers made by Germany—of neutrals who hesitate to enter into any agreements which might involve them at any given moment in a general conflict.

8. The Fourth Year

The fourth year of Nazi rule concluded without the political atmosphere in any way having been clarified and without any success on the part of the political leaders in arriving at anything resembling European equilibrium. The German press proposed the following formula to characterize the perplexities which were haunting the diplomats in the present situation: "Who should guarantee whom against what?" Let us examine the principal aspects of the situation which continues to harass the world.

The Ethiopian adventure is practically liquidated. On May 5, 1936 Mussolini announced to the world the complete victory of fascist arms and the annexation of Ethiopia. On May 9 he proclaimed from the balcony of the Palazzo Venetia that the Italian king would henceforth also be known as Emperor of Ethiopia. On July 15 the economic sanctions taken against Italy were lifted, although the powers did not yet decide to recognize the annexation of Abyssinia nor to strike the name of this nation from the list of members of the League of Nations. The *rapprochement* between Germany and Italy which had been developing for some time became more marked. It took on definite shape with the visit to Berlin of the Italian Foreign Minister, Count Ciano, and culminated on October 24 in Germany's recognition of the Italian king as

the Emperor of Ethiopia. In a speech on November 1, Mussolini emphasized the significance of the sympathetic relations
which had been established between Rome and Berlin. "The
meetings at Berlin," he said, "had as a result an understanding
between the two countries on definite problems, some of
which are particularly troublesome these days. . . . This
Berlin-Rome protocol is not a barrier. It is rather an axis
around which all European states animated by a desire for
peace may collaborate on troubles."

Little by little the situation with respect to England was
also eased. On January 2, 1937 England signed a gentlemen's
agreement with Italy, which although not a concrete treaty
on all questions pending between the two nations, nevertheless re-established harmony, eliminated the possibility of a
Mediterranean conflict and proclaimed Italian disinterestedness with regard to Spain and particularly in the Balearic
Islands. It was generally felt that the re-establishment of good
relations with France would soon follow and permit the
resumption of negotiations for the conclusion of an agreement
to take the place of the Locarno arrangements.

On July 18, 1936 civil war broke out in Spain. General
Franco, at the head of his Moroccan troops, began his march
on Madrid. German leaders lost no time in sensing what was
for them the true meaning of this event. In their eyes this
war unquestionably set "red" Spain and "white" Spain against
each other. But the most important fact was that the "reds"
were inspired, supported and surrounded by bolshevists from
Moscow. The Germans held that a handful of red revolutionists had been able to launch a movement provoking the opposition of all genuine Spanish elements only because affairs had
been managed as early as 1931, and more especially in 1936,
by foreigners who were completely indifferent to the interests of Spain and who merely used Spain to further their goal
of world revolution. For the leaders of the Reich the Spanish
revolution marked a new effort on the part of bolshevism to

extend the red wave through Western Europe and to set up a communist citadel in Barcelona which would serve them as a base of operations for later campaigns.

This resulted in an intensification of Nazi animosity against bolshevism, revealed in the violent tone of their speeches at the 1936 Congress at Nuremberg. This also accounted for their determination from the start not to tolerate at any cost either the complete triumph of the "reds" over all of Spain or the setting up of what they called a "Soviet colony" in Catalonia. This, they said, would be a menace not only to Portugal, which has been struggling for many years against the contagion of the bolshevist pest, but also to England and France. They believed that their views were shared not only by Fascist nations like Italy but also by all other Western nations, in so far as they were not themselves contaminated by Moscow communism. Suspicions have often been put forward that Hitler had other more practical aims apart from these ideological concerns, such as the creation of a German naval base in the Mediterranean or ultimate access to the rich mines of Spain and Spanish Morocco. The Nazis, however, have always loudly proclaimed their disinterestedness in these matters.

The Germans took cognizance of the danger presented for Europe in the Spanish civil war and of the urgency of preventing the conflict between Spanish "reds" and "whites" from degenerating into an ideological war, in which the two rival faiths of fascism and democracy, with Italy and Germany on one side and France and Russia on the other, would fight it out on the fields of Spain. The proposal for neutrality in which France took the initiative, none the less immediately aroused a good deal of mistrust among the Germans. They detected in this proposal an attempt to "create an alibi" by means of setting up a system whereby the French government would be free of any suspicion of favoring the loyalists but would in practice allow the Russians and the followers of the

French popular front secretly to come to the aid of the Spanish *frente popular* with munitions, money and volunteers. Subsequent events indicated that the German suspicions were in a large measure well founded. Neutrality has most patently been only a fiction, useful perhaps only in so far as it prevented direct and possibly dangerous intervention by the governments themselves, but none the less a fiction which has been abundantly violated by every one. In both Spanish camps there is a profusion of foreign elements, and their intervention has largely contributed to prolonging a conflict which might have long since been concluded had the Spaniards been allowed to fight it out themselves. Will the non-intervention pact initiated by France and England on December 27, 1936 be any more effective? Germany did not dare to reject this proposal but she stipulated that it would have to produce real results and this appeared doubtful to her. In the meantime the Nazis adopted an increasingly hostile attitude towards the loyalist government. On November 18 they recognized the Franco rebel government and accredited their diplomatic representative to it.

The Spanish Moroccan incident of January, 1937 indicated in an alarming way the degree of nervousness of public opinion. On the basis of alarmist reports, which were either false or at any rate premature, the French authorities in Morocco and wide circles in France believed that Germany had initiated a movement of infiltration into Spanish Morocco and that she had already dispatched large contingents of engineers and soldiers. Immediately there was a violent campaign in the French press to urge the government to oppose this new violation of treaties by force if necessary. The Germans retaliated in their turn by attacks upon France which were no less vehement. France, they claimed, was seeking a pretext to seize Spanish Morocco, strike at General Franco from the rear and thus contravene the measures proposed by Great Britain for preventing the influx of foreign volunteers into

Spain. Fortunately, the interview between Hitler and the French ambassador, François-Poncet, on January 11, 1937 put an end to this agitation. An official communique was issued which stated that Germany would continue to respect Spanish territorial integrity and its colonial domains and that France on her side affirmed her intention to conform strictly to the Spanish-Moroccan statute. The situation was immediately relaxed but the alarm had been heated and the tone of the press polemics had once more demonstrated the dangerous international tension in Europe.

Germany's *rapprochement* with Japan which had been under way for some time was officially sealed by the convention signed in Berlin on November 25, 1936. The purpose of this agreement, as announced by the contracting parties, was to organize common defense against "the interference of the Communist International in the internal affairs of the nations," an interference which constituted a menace to the peace and prosperity of these states as well as to world peace. It was agreed that competent authorities of both parties would collaborate in the exchange of information regarding the activity of the Comintern and that a "permanent commission" would be instituted for the purpose of taking the necessary measures for defense against the bolshevist peril.

It is hardly astonishing that this action aroused misgivings not only in Russia, who felt herself directly threatened, but also in France, England and in the United States. They looked upon this treaty as a camouflage for a secret military alliance between Japan and Germany and an indication of imperialist ambitions in the Philippines, in China, in the Pacific and in the Dutch Indies. The German press naturally discounted these interpretations and emphasized that the vigorous propaganda of the Soviet Union throughout the world and particularly in China was a sufficient explanation for the conclusion of a pact the motive of which was merely to combat the dangerous effects of the activities of the Comintern.

The Third Reich

The question of the restitution of the German colonies, which had never ceased to figure among the demands of the Reich, was posed in an urgent manner in a speech by Dr. Schacht at Frankfort on December 9, 1936, also in an article by Schacht very soon after in the American journal, *Foreign Affairs*, and in Hitler's speech of January 30, 1937. Germany, they maintained, needs colonies not for military or imperialistic reasons, but for economic reasons. She is engaged in a serious struggle to get sufficient foodstuffs and raw materials and she, therefore, claims the colonies of which she had been deprived for motives which were not valid in the first place.

There are many persons in England as well as in France who are of the opinion that it might have been better in 1918 not to have deprived Germany of her colonies. These colonies, they feel, had acted as a sort of safety valve for German dynamism. This thesis was recently supported in England by Lord Lothian in a speech which was extensively exploited by Nazi propaganda. Such considerations may seem sensible at first but, unfortunately, it is extremely difficult to agree about what should be done. Neither England and her dominions nor France seem willing to abandon the colonial mandates which had been distributed to them or to allow Germany to carve out for herself a new colonial empire at the expense of Spain, Portugal and Holland. Under such conditions I confess that I cannot see any basis for discussion between Germany and the countries holding colonies. I am afraid that this question will develop in the same way as did the problem of German disarmament. Everyone knew well that it would be difficult to prevent Germany from rearming. But the difficulty in finding an acceptable arrangement was such that the discussions were prolonged without end. The matter was finally settled by unilateral decision on the part of Germany, a move which constituted a serious defeat for French diplomacy and actually damaged French prestige. There is obviously the danger that in the matter of colonies, Germany might confront the world one fine day with a *fait acquis*. This accounts for the public excitement in connection with the Spanish-Moroccan incident. Will the diplomats know how to meet such a danger? We should like to believe that they will, but we are not daring enough to be certain.

There is, finally, the major question left by the breakdown of the Locarno agreement on March 7, 1936. This has not yet been replaced by any new convention. The tension between Germany and France on this point remains in force. The advent of a popular front government in France on June 4, 1936 was not of a nature to facilitate such an agreement, since from an ideological point of view at least, the divergence between the two countries now became greater than before.

In principle the German point of view on the problem of a *rapprochement* with France has not changed. In a review at the end of the year 1936, the *Frankfurter Zeitung* summarized the situation in the following terms: "The two countries have not yet agreed to face each other without bringing in any outside influences. The man of the street, the man who will have to hold a trench or charge through a barrage of fire, knows that neither the event of March 7 nor the desire on the part of Germany to be armed as other nations, can constitute a motive for war between our two countries. If the French and the Germans get together by themselves, there is no motive for war. Our two peoples feel deeply the community of their destiny, and the age of imperialism has passed. The consciousness of this fact has contributed in no small way in the year which has just passed to the possible solution of the serious Franco-German crisis. To this first declaration there might be added in time a second one, namely that it is absurd to regard each other with hostility, and remain armed to the teeth when neither one wishes to attack the other." German public opinion accused France of having disturbed the European equilibrium by her alliance with Russia and Czechoslovakia, which put at her disposal such formidable military power. She hopes, however, that it will not be impossible at some future date to take up again the vital question of arms limitation on a new basis.

Over Great Britain, the Germans did not conceal their disillusionment; they believed that England did not know how to profit from the chances for peace given by the declarations of Hitler on March 7. England, they believed, had assumed an impossible role. This role consisted, on the one hand, of offering to act as arbiter of the differences between France and Germany and, on the other, in revealing a decided partiality toward France while making numerous disobliging gestures against Germany, such as sending the now famous questionnaire and making offensive declarations. British action, moreover, was paralyzed first by troubles with Italy and then by the decision to carry out a great armament program. This the Germans found natural and justifiable but it was obviously not of a nature to facilitate negotiations for disarmament. Moreover, British action was also retarded by the domestic crisis culminating in the abdication of Edward VIII, which for a time paralyzed all British diplomatic activity. The only result achieved under these conditions was the British guarantee against aggression given to France by Minister Eden in his speech of November 20, 1936 at Leamington and the corresponding guarantee given to England by the French Foreign Minister Yvon Delbos, on December 4. The Germans, however, feel that these agreements are "of doubtful value" and that their significance has been greatly shaken by "the return of Belgium to a policy of neutrality." The French, moreover, they feel, will find it necessary to give up their alliances in eastern Europe if they want the English guarantee to retain its value. For they will inspire mistrust among the English, who are unwilling to become involved in any eastern complications through their arrangements with France. The Germans, therefore, underline the fact that under such conditions Anglo-French friendship offers no dangers for them.

Recently the discussions have taken another turn: a great deal of attention has been given by Germany to an article in the London *Times* of December 20, 1936 which was entitled "The German Choice." The main idea in this article was to offer Germany certain economic advantages in return for a limitation of armaments and in general to substitute an economic for a political point of view. It was suggested that in this way practical co-operation could be established between the European nations through economic conferences. This would also be the only way, the writer believed, of solving the problem of Russia: i.e., by a defensive economic campaign against communism. This would be the best way to regulate the problems of eastern Europe. For France's eastern alliances would lose all importance as soon as the practical effects of economic co-operation began to be felt. Similarly the problem of colonies would also be solved of its own accord in this way. The *Frankfurter Zeitung*, while strongly protesting against any interpretation of events which tended to hold Germany alone responsible for the present state of affairs, nevertheless, agreed that the return to economic reason would be most desirable. The rearmament of Germany, the four year plan and the colonial demands were not ends in themselves, said the German paper, and although Germany would never accept a bargain which would lead her to renounce the security which rearmament offers in return for economic concessions, yet she was favorably disposed to join in negotiations for the economic pacification of Europe.

Is it possible then under such conditions to hope for the speedy re-establishment of a political equilibrium on the European continent? It is no doubt true that the state of high tension has been considerably eased. Almost all observers are agreed that the greater part of the German people desire nothing but to be able to continue to work in peace and that they dread war. We have also been assured from good sources that the German army leaders are not at all bellicose. They do not think they are ready as yet and they have no desire to rush prematurely into any dangerous adventure. Moreover there is no pressing need for the *Führer* to precipitate a crisis which would be a leap in the dark for the entire world and for Germany in particular. Hitler's speech of January 30, 1937 was not that of a man who was preparing a brusque attack after a short delay. He made no inordinate demands and he declared that the time for "surprises" had passed. He manifested his good will for European co-operation. "As a state with equal rights Germany, conscious of her European task, will collaborate loyally towards a solution of the problems which touch us as well as the other nations." He insisted that he saw no subject of dispute humanly possible between Germany and France. He prided himself that in the Moroccan incident they had been able to clear up the matter "thanks to a foreign diplomat and his government." He gave assurances to Belgium and to the Netherlands that he was ready to recognize the inviolable neutrality of these states. The German press pointed to the moderate tone of Hitler's speech and to the fact that he left the door open for all negotiations and that he kept himself strictly on the plane of reality.

The economic and financial situation in Germany, as we shall show later, is no longer of the kind to drive the government to desperate measures. Such being the case, there is the feeling that there is really no reason to believe that an explosion is imminent. The friendship between England and France, moreover, seems stronger today than ever. English mistrust of Nazi Germany is attested by numerous signs and Germany, therefore, in case of aggression would most likely find England on the side of France.

Having said this, we must not delude ourselves that the golden age has arrived. There are facts which cannot be interpreted as anything but dangerous symptoms. On August 24,

1936 Germany re-established the period of two year service in the army. On November 14 she abrogated by unilateral decision the clauses of the Versailles Treaty concerning international control of Germany's main rivers. She indicated her haste in completing the list of officers by shortening the term of secondary schools by one year (December). We have also seen that no solution has as yet been provided for the series of problems connected with Spain and Catalonia, the Danubian states and Czechoslovakia. The question of the return of the colonies which Germany has put forward may furnish a pretext, on a day when the occasion will be favorable, for making territorial demands which will be difficult to satisfy.

As for Soviet Russia, the situation seems almost hopeless. Hitler's point of view is that no new treaty of alliance with the Russians would have any value for Germany. It would be inconceivable for National Socialist Germany to find herself in a situation where she would have to provide assistance to a bolshevist state, and on her own side Germany does not wish in any way to receive the aid of a Soviet power. This kind of approach obviously tends to exclude the Soviet Union from the European community and thus makes it almost impossible to establish any general arrangements within the framework of collective security and on the basis of mutual assistance. The possibility of establishing an accord which would take the place of the Locarno agreement likewise still remains very doubtful. Taking everything into account we still continue to live in a dangerous situation, although I sincerely believe that the year 1937 will be a year of "truce" in which no one will dare to push things to the extreme and so provoke a resort to force.

BOOK IV

The Myth of Race

IV. The Myth of Race

1. The Primacy of Race over State

HITLER has always stressed the fact that National Socialism is not based on material interests but on an ideology and a *Weltanschauung*. In his *Mein Kampf* he develops at length the idea that man is not guided by interests, or to speak symbolically, by gold, and that man's fundamental aspiration is not to live well and in comfort with happiness, riches or even power. Man is great only when he is guided by a great idea for which he is ready to make all sacrifices and even give up his life. It was faith in an idea which provided the impetus for the French Revolution of 1789, for the Russian Revolution and for Italian fascism. A social or political movement which does not rest on an idea, says Hitler, is inevitably condemned to impotence for it lacks the necessary militancy to attain the goal for which it strives. "The conviction that one has the right to make use of even the most brutal force is always bound up with a fanatical faith in the necessary triumph of a new order on this earth. A movement which does not fight for the highest goals and ideals will therefore never resort to the final test of arms."*

The idea which provides such inner strength to the National Socialist movement is the myth of race. The Nazi religion of race is not in any sense to be confounded with the cult of the state as it had been honored by Hegel and others, and as it had been developed in Prussia and in the German Empire. Hitler is very specific on this point in his *Mein*

* *Mein Kampf*, p. 597.

Kampf. In Hitler's eyes the state is not an end but a means. It is an indispensable condition for the formation of a superior human culture but it is not the cause of this culture. The cause is found exclusively in the existence of a race which is capable of creating a culture. The state in itself is not the creator of the culture and cannot guarantee the development and survival of a people. All the state can do is preserve and maintain the creative race in its purity. The aim of the state is "the preservation and furthering of a community of living beings of the same physical and spiritual essence." But the state is not the creator. The creative genius rests in the *blood.* It is the task of the racialist state to conserve and to develop these primordial elements which are the generators of all beauty and all human grandeur. The "perfection" of a state resides not in its development of civilization nor in the material power which it embodies but only in the successful way in which it acquits itself of the work of preservation and conservation of what is its essential function. If it allows this creative element to perish or to degenerate the state is evil and is destined for destruction, no matter how great the renown of its civilization or the extent of its empire at a given moment.

The primacy of race over state helps us understand what distinguishes Nazi ideology from the imperialist ideologies of the German Nationalists. The latter placed their emphasis on the state and on its instrument of power, the army. The conservative of the Prussian type makes a cult of the army. It is for him the great school in which the nation is trained in the primary virtues of discipline, self-denial, devotion to the common good, honor and patriotism—virtues which are essential for the greatness of a people. He has nothing but scorn for pacifism and considers perpetual peace not only an unrealizable utopia but also enervating and contemptible. Prussian conservatism aspires toward the continued expansion of German power. During the war it showed itself deliberately annexationist with respect to the west as well as to the east.

The Myth of Race

In Spengler, for example, these ideas take on a paradoxical form and often are offensive in design. He says that "man is an animal of prey," that the normal condition of humanity is war and that the state of peace is only an interlude between two wars. The half century of relative tranquillity which Europe enjoyed between 1870 and 1914 had created for humanity the dangerous illusion that we are made to live in peace. For Spengler, the state, like an athlete, must always be "in form" and ready to strike. It must carry on a perpetual struggle for its existence and for its growth. The philosopher of the *Decline of the West* believed that humanity had entered upon the dangerous era of a struggle for world hegemony. He predicted that the winner of this struggle will be a leader with a will of steel who, at the head of an army of perfectly equipped and entirely devoted mercenaries, will defeat all his opponents and, amidst the indifference of peoples wearied by the din of arms and the furious struggle of rival ambitions, will triumph in the final struggle by his sword. Spengler posed the question of whether Germany, incapable today of raising a new Goethe, might not give the world a second Caesar.

Such conceptions are not identical, however, with those of the National Socialists. To be sure these militaristic and activist tendencies are found also among the Nazis. But they are tempered by the fact that National Socialism is a movement of a people who, after the terrible trials they have come through, aspire to peace and work and who, by virtue of their racialist ideology, reject on principle any kind of conquest and annexation. They expressly repudiate any aggressive tendency, and proclaim very loudly that even a victorious war would bring about the ruin of both the victor and the vanquished. Hitlerism particularly rejects the Caesarist ambitions found in Spengler. It does not aspire to world leadership and is indifferent to the mission of the "white man" or to the uni-

fication of Europe.* What interests the Nazis most is the
destiny of their *race*. They work for the practical regeneration of a Germany ruined by the ravages of war and the trials
of the post-war period.

National Socialism prides itself on its solid scientific foundation. It holds that it is based on the most recent findings of
biology, anthropology, and prehistory, and it endeavors to
develop the teaching of the knowledge of racial science in all
its stages. However, we shall not attempt to present Nazi
ideology here under its "scientific" aspect.† The disciplines
upon which it rests are highly problematic and the layman
who attempts to orient himself in these problems finds himself
confronted by a frightening variety of contradictory theories
about which he is unable to come to any decision. We shall
not risk undertaking this task and shall confine ourselves
merely to indicating briefly the conclusions arrived at regarding the German "race" by the Nazi specialists, and in particular by Professor Hans Günther, who is regarded by the
Nazis as a great authority on this question.‡

These views may be summarized as follows. (1) The Germans are not a pure race but are the result of a complex mixture of "primitive" races—*homo alpinus*, Celts, Teutons,
Slavs, Romans, Prussians, Huns, Avars, Lithuanians, Wends,
Magyars, and Jews. All these in turn are the results of complex mixtures. (2) Out of all these elements has resulted a
group in which Günther discerns five "races" or "character-

* These differences between Spengler and the Nazis were clearly brought
out in Spengler's *Jahre der Entscheidung* (Munich 1933), translated into
English as *Years of Decision* (New York 1934). This was the only attempt at a bold criticism of the Nazi policies published inside Germany.
The Nazi answer to Spengler is found in the little pamphlet by Johann
von Leers, *Spenglers weltpolitisches System und der Nationalsozialismus*
(Berlin 1934).—*Ed.*

† For a recent authoritative study of this question see the volume by
two distinguished British scientists, A. C. Haddon and Julian Huxley, *We
Europeans* (New York 1936).—*Ed.*

‡ For a critical evaluation of Günther's work see Hertz, Friedrich, *Hans
Günther als Rassenforscher*, 2nd ed. (Berlin, Philo Verlag, 1930).—*Ed.*

istic types" (*Merkmalrassen*). These are the Nordic, Westic or Mediterranean, Ostic or Alpine, Dinaric and Baltic races. They are scattered all over Germany but found in relative purity only in the little islets situated between the Elbe and the Weser, i.e., in the territory into which neither Celts nor Slavs ever penetrated and where the Nordic type has remained relatively intact. Elsewhere, however, and particularly in the large cities, there was a degeneration which bordered almost on "racial chaos." From these elementary statements it is very

y general philosophy of life. The racial rest primarily on intuition and faith.

course far antedates Hitler and National t intend to trace here the evolution of ny.* Let us merely point out that the ce," having its basis in the metaphysical , was already developed at length by *s to the German Nation*. It is found later eau and in his celebrated theory of the races. From Gobineau it passed on to above all to Houston Stewart Chamber- d tableau of the racialist legend in his th *Century*. It reappeared in the works f the *Alldeutscher Verband* and in con- , who incorporated antisemitism into his In this way it appears in Hitler's *Mein* fred Rosenberg's *Mythus des XX. Jahr-* nes of Rosenberg's work were conceived finished in 1925, published in Munich es reprinted since then. This work is of because it presents the racial theory in a expressive form, even though, as its

author is at pains to emphasize, it is not official and involves no one else's responsibility but his own. It is certain, never-

* For a historical treatment of this subject see Hertz, Friedrich, *Race and Culture* (New York 1928).—*Ed.*

theless, that it conforms to the National Socialist spirit. Rosenberg, moreover, belongs to the circle of intimates of Hitler and on January 24, 1934 he was officially designated as his confidential adviser on all matters pertaining to *Weltanschauung*. We shall, therefore, attempt to give an exposition of the general lines of this myth of race.

Each race, teaches Rosenberg, has its particular soul, its own religion. In this is expressed the most intimate being of the race and in it too are manifested all the special virtues which are considered to be specific qualities of its very blood. "Soul means race viewed from the interior; and inversely race is the external aspect of soul." To evoke the soul of a race means to discern the value which the race places at the head of its table of values, to know the hierarchy of values which it embraces and the respective importance of these values in state, art and religion. It is one of the fundamental convictions of racialism that the unity of the human species is an absurd hypothesis and a simple abstraction. In reality there is the greatest plurality of races, resting in the final analysis on differences in the hereditary composition of the blood. Each race has its scale of values, its particular conception of beauty and morality and its own religion. Everything such as the unity of the human species, the idea of a universal religion or of a universal morality or of beauty valid for all peoples, is a sorry illusion which has cost humanity oceans of blood.

Human races are not only diverse; they are also of unequal value. For Rosenberg, the superior race, the creative race *par excellence*, is the Nordic race. Its cradle was perhaps in the mythical Atlantis, and its branches are to be recognized in the Amorites of Egypt, in the Aryans of India, in the Greeks of the early period, in the ancient Romans and finally, above all, in all the Germanic peoples, who were the creators of the states of the West and whose supreme representatives are the Germans. The highest value which they recognize is honor.

The Myth of Race

The spirit of this race is personified in the grandiose type of the god Wotan, who embodied the spiritual energies innate in the men of the North—honor and heroism, the art of song, the protection of right, and the eternal striving for wisdom. "Wotan learns that through the fault of the gods and as a result of the breach of contract with the builder of Valhalla, the race of gods is to perish. Conscious of inevitable disaster, he nevertheless orders Heimdall to sound his horn and call the gods for a decisive combat. Eternally dissatisfied and ever searching, the god traverses the universe in order to fathom the mystery of life's destiny and essence. He sacrifices one of his eyes in order to share in this profound wisdom. As a ceaseless wanderer he is the symbol of the Nordic soul, in its endless striving and its eternal becoming, never self-satisfied and never falling back upon Jehovah or upon his representative" (p. 664).

The same spirit reveals itself also among the Ostrogoths of Ulfilas, in the chivalry of the middle ages, in Western mysticism, particularly in the writings of Meister Eckart, in the Albigensian and the Waldensian heresies, in Luther and Coligny, in Frederick the Great, in the old cantor of St. Thomas, Johann Sebastian Bach, and finally in the creator of *Faust*, Goethe. This means that a heroic legend of the ancient Teutons, a sermon of Eckart, a Prussian military march, a fugue of Bach and a monologue of Faust are all the expression of one and the same soul and are the creations of one and the same will, which was manifested for the first time in the world in the traits of the god Wotan and was revealed in modern times in the persons of Frederick II and Bismarck. This will and soul, moreover, is what it is by virtue of blood, the principal creator of all culture.

One can readily see what Rosenberg considers to be the danger which menaces the superior race in all periods of universal history. This danger is contamination with inferior races and the mixing of its blood with blood of inferior qual-

143

ity. The progressive alteration of the Nordic soul and the specifically Nordic values inevitably result from such degeneration. A long series of peoples descended from the noble race of Atlantis have already succumbed through this process of racial degeneration. India, Persia, Greece, and Rome, after flourishing periods of glory, also passed through long periods of decadence which brought them to destruction. In the same way most nations sprung from the Germanic invasions also succumbed when the noble blood of the Germans was vitiated and defiled by contact with the inferior races whom they had subjected.

The same danger threatened and continues to threaten Germany. Germany nearly succumbed under the assault of the Roman Catholic Church and under the influence of a religion of love and of human pity, which was mortal to the Germanic virtues of heroism and honor. For the idea of universal religion of *Catholicism* is in reality foreign to the Nordic race. It springs from the Oriental races, from Syria and Judea, who place at the head of their scale of values love and pity. This Catholicism of Oriental origin has sought to impose itself on the Western world which is founded on another racial basis and on another scale of values. The conflict between Papacy and empire, the wars of religion, the struggle against heresy, the movement of the Counter-Reformation are all characteristic symptoms of this conflict.* Later in the 18th century, Free-Masonry took over in another form this universalist dream. The Free Masons attempted to create a religion of humanity; they aspired to a "humanisation of mankind," which was to culminate finally in a universal ideal in which the synthesis and fusion of all ethnic and national ideas

---

* The Catholic Church prepared a detailed and scholarly analysis of Rosenberg's work under the title of *Studien zum Mythus des XX. Jahrhunderts* (Berlin 1935) and it was issued as an official publication of the Berlin diocese. A Protestant critique of Rosenberg is found in Künneth, Walter, *Antwort auf den Mythus* (Berlin 1935).—*Ed.*

would be realized. Thus the spirit of the Age of Enlightenment was also a peril to the authentic German spirit.

Later still the German spirit was almost contaminated by egalitarian communism, by the spirit of Jewish love of lucre, by the intellectualism which posits the existence of universal truth and by estheticism which believes in a universally valid ideal of beauty. Everywhere and at all times racial purity has been threatened by union with alien races and in particular by union with the Jewish race. The effect of this contamination has been frightful. It brought Germany to the very brink of an abyss. In the cataclysm of the World War of 1914-1918 the Nordic race almost completely disappeared. But the original Nordic myth was still alive among the people as well as among the élite, and it had sufficient vitality to influence thousands and millions of Germans to accept the idea of dying for honor and for fatherland. The qualities of blood showed themselves in the heroic devotion of the German soldier under his gray uniform and helmet of steel. The two million Germans who died for the honor of the German name are the martyrs of the old Germanic myth which is now striving to renew itself, to cast out all the impure elements which have soiled it and to revive under a new form. These martyrs have stirred up in their train millions of enthusiasts who under the sign of the swastika—and not the universalist Catholic cross—are struggling today to make sure that the blood of these victims shall not have been shed in vain and that the "Third Reich," in which the Germanic soul will once again be manifested, shall finally arise.

2. Racial Antisemitism

What were the practical consequences which Hitler drew from this myth of race? He knew very well that the German people have no unity of race, for the various ethnic types of which it is composed were not fused into one unique whole but formed a variety of combinations.. This represents a disadvantage in one sense, since by very reason of this diversity the German lacks the herd instinct which, at the hour of danger, makes for a common and spontaneous front against an aggressor. German hyperindividualism thus tends to scatter itself in all directions. From another point of view, however, this constitutes a superiority. The fusion of several different races, say the Nazis, always results in a lower mean than the level of the highest race. We have seen, however, that this fusion was never accomplished in Germany and that here and there in Germany are still intact islets of the superior racial element, i.e., the Nordic element. It is this advantage which Hitler seeks to turn into account. The aim which Hitler assigns to the state and to the National Socialist Party is to preserve from contamination and to develop as far as possible this precious Nordic element and assure to it a leading role within the community. "Universal history," he says, "is made by minorities, when that minority in numbers comes to personify a majority of will and determination." The highest mission of the state, therefore, is to bring about a racial selection within the German masses and to call to the posts of leadership the survivors of this superior race. Upon them the qualities of their very blood confer the innate capacity for the highest tasks of culture. This process of selection is without doubt a most delicate one but Hitler believes it is possible and that it will lead to fruitful results.

Alongside this positive task the state also has a negative task which is no less important. It must also react with all its strength against contamination of the German race by inferior races and especially by the Semitic race.

Antisemitism has existed at all times in Germany. It developed with special sharpness in the 19th century, however, because of the important role played by the Jews in the

history of capitalism.* Towards the middle of the century, in
1847 when the Jews of Prussia were acquiring civil equality
and the right to hold office, Baron von Thadden-Trieglaff
declared in the Prussian diet and with the full approval of
Bismarck that the true problem was to find out "how the
Christians could be emancipated from the Jews."† In the
course of the second half of the century hostility increased
still more and in the 80's Pastor Stöcker officially introduced
antisemitism into the program of the Conservative Party.
At that time, however, it had not yet acquired the viru-
lence which it displays today. Hitler himself relates that at
the time when he commenced to preoccupy himself with the
Jewish question, the antisemite was still a person without any
great political importance. He was often lightly ridiculed, his
writings enjoyed very little attention and he was accused of
deliberate bad taste and eccentricities of language.

The revolution of 1918 broke down the last barriers which
had separated the Jews from the rest of the population. It led
to a large and sudden increase of Jewish influence in Germany
and, by way of reaction, to a marked recrudescence of hostility against the Jews. With the advent of Hitlerism this flood of
antisemitic passion assumed enormous dimensions. The race
myth denounced the Jew as the "evil principle" *par excellence*. He was the chief enemy of Germany, who in every
epoch has trammelled the free development of the Nordic
race. It was the Oriental and Semitic influences which had
led Christianity to develop into a universal Catholicism. The
Jews have always been a parasitic people living off the substance of the other peoples amidst whom they implanted
themselves. The Jews have been the principal organizers of

* For a narrative account of the Jews in Germany see Lowenthal, Marvin,
The Jews in Germany (New York 1936). An excellent treatment of the
German-Jewish problem is that of Anton van Miller, *Deutsche und Juden*
(Vienna, Soziologische Verlagsanstalt, 1936).—*Ed.*

† The same problem and the identical phrase is found in Karl Marx's
early articles, *Zur Judenfrage*, in 1843.—*Ed.*

Marxist communism and of world revolution. The Jews supplied the leaders for German socialism as well as for Russian bolshevism.

The Jew, said the Nazis, is, moreover, dangerous for another reason. While on his side he practices a rigorous racial exclusivism—a Jewish man will never marry a Christian woman—he nevertheless seeks to implant himself among the "goyim" by favoring the union of Jewish women with Christian men and thus creating a class of mongrels among whom racial purity has disappeared and who thus lend themselves more easily to Semitic influences. The Jews are largely responsible for the crisis of modern culture, for the decline of the West, and for that "decadence" which Nietzsche had already proclaimed as the great peril to the modern world.

If we are to believe the Nazi propagandists, the Jews were on the way to become the masters of the Weimar republic. They had control of the press, the literature, theater, and cinema. In large cities like Berlin they furnished three-fourths of the doctors, lawyers and jurists. They overran the universities and institutions of public instruction; they created public opinion at their will; they exercised a decisive influence on the exchange; they dominated finance and held in tutelage parliament and the parties. The Nazis thus considered them to be the heinous enemies of the German fatherland. They accused them of having demoralized the nation by their pacifist preaching and of having administered the notorious "dagger thrust in the back" to the victorious German army. They held them responsible for the Peace of Versailles, for the policy of fulfilment and *rapprochement* and for the sixty years' tribute imposed upon Germany by the Young Plan. An added peril was the support given by the Nordic of good race to this infiltration of the Semite or the orientalized German into the important domains of modern culture.

Once having come to power, Hitlerism did not lose any time in undertaking the practical battle against Semitic influence. They accused Jewish circles of having organized, particularly in Great Britain and in America, the propaganda against the "atrocities" of the Nazi revolution. They staged on April 1, 1933 a general boycott against all Jewish enterprises. This lasted four days but passed off without any serious troubles. After this the government undertook a series of measures to oust the Jews from the positions in which they had succeeded in establishing themselves. The law of April 7, 1933 contained for the first time the famous article 3, or Aryan paragraph, which stipulated that all German office-holders must be of Aryan race and thus excluded Jews from all public offices. Not only Israelites proper, but any Christian who had one Jewish grandfather or one Jewish grandmother was considered non-Aryan. From this it followed that every official had to furnish documentary evidence of the purity of his blood three generations back. The law of June 30, 1933 forbade any official from marrying a Jewess and excluded from state offices all those married to Jewesses. Finally, there was a series of regulations whereby Jews were ousted from the liberal professions, chiefly law and medicine, and were prevented from participating in the cultural life of Germany as writers, critics, artists, musicians, orchestra leaders, film directors, actors and producers.*

The Nazis declared that in taking these measures they merely obeyed the irresistible pressure of public opinion. They claimed that they had proceeded in the most humane and honorable way. They had taken, they said, the legal method to regulate the Jewish question and develop a new statute which would henceforth make encroachments by these dangerous guests impossible. If regrettable acts had been committed here and there by uncontrollable elements, they said, these were merely the inevitable concomitants of

---

* A detailed account of the place of Jews in German culture is found in the symposium "L'Apport des Juifs d'Allemagne à la civilisation allemande," published as no. 5-6 of *Cahiers Juifs* (Paris 1933), with a preface by Albert Einstein.—*Ed.*

any revolutionary movement. Goebbels compared these to youthful maladies which every organism in the process of development necessarily experiences and declared that it was necessary to guard against taking them too seriously. He stated that in proceeding as they had, the Nazis had at least avoided pogroms as well as disorderly outbreaks of popular wrath. They had proceeded without bloodshed, without unnecessary violence and with commendable discretion.

The Jews were thus deprived of that dangerous hegemony which they had exercised over the German spirit. The Nazis were careful to emphasize the moderation with which they had acted. At the Nuremberg Congress of September, 1933 Rosenberg declared that the party never intended to preach race hatred. He showed the capital importance for a people of what is called "the racial dominant" and he considered it legitimate for the new government to bring about a "renaissance of Germanism." But, said he, they did not aim to rouse the Germans against the Jews. On the contrary they desired that the different races should maintain their relative purity and learn to have regard for each other. "We recognize that the Jewish race has its own laws and we desire that within its proper domain it should develop a culture corresponding to its racial soul; we refuse to Europeanize the blacks and we wish to assure them the preservation of their ethnic originality under the domination of the white man. But we are stoutly opposed to miscegenation between disparate races. Natural laws such as operate in the life of plants and animals are also valid for the human species. The mixture of races breeds not a nation but an ethnic chaos." National Socialism, therefore, he said, aims to prevent the contamination of races and particularly to maintain a clear line of demarcation between Germans and Semites. It expressly repudiates racial pride and it forbears preparing a crusade against the Jews. It refuses to assimilate them but it tolerates them. Those who remain in Germany know that they can be tolerated guests as long as they remain in the place reserved for them according to their numerical proportion but they remain as strangers, living apart from the rest of the nation and exposing themselves to pitiless suppression if they make the slightest attempt to step beyond the limits set to their activity. This suppression, the Nazis feel, had to be carried out with some severity in order that it be effective. It has involved some suffering and individual injustices which could not be avoided; it has also raised formidable hostility against Germany, which entails, at least temporarily, appreciable difficulties for Germany. But a successful operation has been performed, they say, and the scars will soon disappear. The National Socialists are convinced that the development of an autochthonous German culture, not deformed by exotic leaven, will show how salutary was this suppression which raised such factitious indignation abroad.*

The Nazis thus maintained that they did not want to drive the Jews from Germany. The statistics of June 16, 1933 indicate that there were about 500,000 Jews in Germany, which is about 65,000 less than there were in the census of 1925.† In the beginning they were tolerated in the economic field and were able to work freely and participate in trade, indus-

---

* Among the many Jews ousted from German cultural life are such distinguished names as the following: the physicists, Albert Einstein and James Frank; the distinguished chemist, Fritz Haber; the painters, Max Liebermann and Karl Hofer; the musicians, Bruno Walter, Otto Klemperer, Arnold Schönberg, Ernst Toch, Kurt Weill, Artur Schnabel, Carl Flesch and Emanuel Feuermann; the stage directors, Max Reinhardt and Leopold Jessner; the university professors, Hans Kelsen and Ernst Cassirer; the editors, Theodor Wolff and Georg Bernhard and the writers, Alfred Döblin, Lion Feuchtwanger, Bruno Frank, Alfred Kerr, Alfred and Robert Neumann, Jakob Wassermann, Franz Werfel, Arnold Zweig and Stefan Zweig. In addition to these there were many who were married to Jewesses or whose contacts were with Jews, who were also ousted from German cultural life. Among these are Thomas Mann, Paul Hindemith and Adolf Busch.—*Ed.*

† According to the report for 1936 of the German Jewish Central Committee for Aid and Reconstruction, the total number of Jews who left Germany from 1933 to April 1, 1936, amounted to about 90,000. This leaves a total of 409,000 Jews still in Germany.—*Ed.*

try, banking and finance. But the ghetto, although not restored in theory, was nevertheless an established fact. The Jews now lived *by themselves* and separated from the rest of the nation by an invisible but effective wall.*

The measures against the Jews raised considerable feeling abroad and particularly among the co-religionists of the victims of antisemitism. No doubt the émigré Jews also had a considerable part in the anti-Hitler propaganda, or as the Nazis say, in the "campaign of calumnies" against the Reich. The Nazis, therefore, held the Jews partly responsible for the unpopularity of National Socialism abroad. It is also likely that some of the Jews remaining in the Reich showed lack of prudence and drew upon themselves in some way or other the attention of the malevolent Nazis. So that whereas the "moderates" among the Nazis, affected by the bad impression created abroad by German persecution of the Jews, insisted that the antisemitic measures be mitigated, the more radical elements and above all the local and regional authorities, betrayed a renewed hostility towards the Jews which revealed itself in many cases of "individual actions" of a severe nature.†
These were not always approved by the government but they

---

* For the effects of Nazi rule on the internal life of the Jews see Pinson, Koppel S., "The Jewish Spirit in Nazi Germany," in the *Menorah Journal*, vol. xxiv (1936), pp. 228-54.—*Ed.*

† The leader in this violent antisemitic propaganda is Julius Streicher, local Nazi potentate in Nuremberg, and one of the old associates of Adolf Hitler. Streicher publishes the violent antisemitic paper called *Der Stürmer*, which indulges in gross caricatures of Jews and in lewd stories about them. The *Stürmer* is posted in special cases, known as *Stürmerkasten*, and is thus displayed in public squares in all towns and cities of Germany. Among the *Stürmer's* educational activities was also the publication, in 1936, of a Nazi *Mother Goose Book* by a young kindergarten teacher, Elvira Bauer. According to the description of the correspondent of the *London Observer* "The idea is simply, graphically conveyed that the Jew is a new sort of monster, combining all classic qualities of the Old Witch, the bogy man, the Big Bad Wolf, and the wicked ogre. In every illustration the Jew is pictured with parrot-beaked nose, puffy pig eyes, unshaven jowls and thick lascivious lips. His face, never clean, is consistently depicted screwed up in either a snarl or a leer." (See *The New York Times*, January 10, 1937).
—*Ed.*

nevertheless brought on an increasing antisemitic agitation in the country. Jewish stores were boycotted, injurious placards or inscriptions were affixed to Jewish stores, a ban was placed on Jews frequenting public baths and swimming pools, and many hotels and restaurants as well as certain baths and country places were closed to Jews. There was also the continual denunciation of Jewish crimes of "race defilement" committed between Jews and Christians of opposite sexes. The most violent manifestation of this anti-Jewish spirit was the brawl on Kurfürstendam in Berlin, which occurred in July, 1935.*

It was plain that the Chancellor could not very conveniently allow such a state of affairs to continue indefinitely. It was necessary to take a stand one way or the other, either with the moderates or with the radicals. At the Nuremberg Congress of 1935 Hitler adopted the views of the intransigeants and gave his consent to those who thought it useful to continue the antisemitic campaign with redoubled energy. The law voted by the Reichstag on September 15, 1935 withdrew from the Jews the rights of German citizenship and reduced them to the status of mere subjects. Marriages between Christians and Jews were forbidden. Jews were eliminated from the artistic and intellectual life of Germany. Even access to schools and educational institutions where Christian children were instructed was closed to them. The right of acquiring land and real property was practically forbidden them. It has been suggested that National Socialism was really proceeding in the direction of a general expropriation of Jewish property —expropriation without indemnity, since the Jew who is

* This violent wave of anti-Jewish activity in July, 1935 was initiated by the speech of Dr. Goebbels on Tempelhof Field in Berlin on June 30, 1935. Dr. Goebbels said: "Does one believe that we have buttons instead of eyes not to see how certain counter movements in the capital city are once again attempting to spread out? (Applause) And how the bourgeois intellectuals once again are ready to give them brotherly aid with that stupid and inane phrase that the Jew is also a human being. True he is, but what kind of human being! A flea is also an animal, yet not a very pleasing animal. We do not want the Jew any more! He has no place any longer in the German community!" (*Berliner Tageblatt*, July 1, 1935).—*Ed.*

placed in the position of being unable to earn his livelihood in Germany, does not have the right to take his belongings with him out of Germany. It is difficult to predict just where the Nazis will end on the path of antisemitism. It is beyond doubt, however, that they are entering upon a new era of persecution. Even such branches of the government service as foreign affairs and finance where a certain tolerance of the Jew had hitherto been practiced, are now purged of Jewish officials.*

3. The Campaign for Racial Improvement

National Socialism was concerned not only with "purifying" the German race by the systematic elimination of the Jewish element; it also directed its attention to the betterment of the race from the standpoint of quantity as well as of quality. The Nazis have attempted to assure the survival and increasing development of Germanism by encouraging increased child-bearing and by preparing more healthy and robust generations through the prevention of continued propagation by certain types of diseased individuals.

At the time the Nazis came to power there were certain legitimate apprehensions regarding the future of the race. A crisis loomed with respect to births and marriages.

For a long time the birth rate among the German people had been very satisfactory. As far back as 1901, Germany with a population of 56 millions was giving birth to more than 2 million babies a year. But now the German people had been

* A detailed and well-documented analysis of the measures taken by Nazi Germany against the Jews is found in *The Yellow Spot* (London 1936). See also *The Jews in Nazi Germany* (New York 1935) published by the American Jewish Committee and the Annex to the *Letter of Resignation* of James G. McDonald, High Commissioner for German Refugees, addressed to the League of Nations. The latter document was published as a supplement to the issue of January 15, 1936 of *The Christian Century*. A special analysis of the economic measures is found in *Der wirtschaftliche Vernichtungskampf gegen die Juden im dritten Reich* (Paris 1937) published by the World Jewish Congress.—Ed.

rudely seized by that "fear of life" of civilized peoples, which becomes translated into birth restriction and ultimately ends in the slow suicide of the race. In 1931 with a population of 65 millions new born children barely exceeded one million. In 1933 the number fell to 957,000. With 14.7 births for every thousand inhabitants, Germany had even fallen below France with its 16.3. Because of the progress in medicine and hygiene, the population did not decrease and the fall in births was compensated for by the decrease in mortality and especially infant mortality. This resulted in the prolongation of life but it brought about an older age average in the nation. The proportion between the number of young men capable of earning their living and that of old people who became charges either of their children or of the community, was being increasingly modified by the growing number of old people. People married less, married late and divorced more often. The voluntary restriction of births was an undisputed fact and practices of contraception developed to a disturbing degree. In the large cities the situation was much more serious. The cities were often spoken of as the "graves of the nation." In cities from 50,000 to 100,000 there was in 1913, for every 10,000 inhabitants an excess of births of 128; in 1932 this fell to 31. In cities of more than 100,000 inhabitants the figures were respectively, 98 and 8. In Berlin in 1933 there was an excess of deaths over births of more than 14,000.

The demographic prospects were thus truly alarming. At the time Hitler wrote his *Mein Kampf*, in 1924, the situation was such that one could have predicted that a century later there would be 250 million Germans in the world. In 1934 statisticians estimated that if developments proceeded at the current tempo, Germany at the end of the 20th century would have 45 million inhabitants, of whom 8 million would be youngsters below the age of 15 and 11 million persons over 60.

National Socialism reacted against this state of affairs with extreme vigor. Hitler proclaimed the "health and security of the family" as the nucleus of society. He declared that the infant was "the most precious possession of the nation" and that it was a crime to "deprive the state of healthy children." The state was to be considered the representative of the millenarian future of the race and was to act vigorously against the egotistic desires of the individual. Hitler plainly wished to communicate to the German people the impression that they constituted a fertile group which could multiply without end and which, by reason of its fecundity, its vital spirit, and its dynamism, is destined to seek expansion outside. He endeavored to inculcate in them the consciousness that the German claims found some sort of biological justification in the never ceasing multiplication of the Germanic race.

This resulted in indefatigable propaganda by book, by word, by pamphlet, and by education. It also resulted in a series of legislative measures which aimed to encourage marriage and raise the birth rate. Among these measures were loans to aid married people in setting up housekeeping (*Ehestandsdarlehen*),* prizes for large families, gifts and baby carriages on the occasion of new born infants, financial privileges granted to large families and additional taxes imposed upon bachelors or couples without children. The thesis emphasized by the Nazis is that he who does not confine himself merely to working for his own livelihood but also raises a family and children does more for the community than he

* The latest figures of the Reich Statistical Office indicate that between August, 1933 and the end of 1936 the government financed 694,367 marriages, of which 485,285 children have been born thus far. In 1936 there were 171,391 marriages thus financed or 14,603 more than the preceding year. According to a dispatch to the *New York Times* of February 19, 1937, the Nazi press "is beginning to denounce it as a shameful insult to German motherhood, the intimation appearing . . . that government-financed marriages are more fertile than others because every child repays one quarter of the loan."—*Ed.*

who restricts himself to making his own way in the world and leaving for others the care of propagating the race. It is not a question of giving alms to large families and punishing bachelors and childless people. It is simply a question of measures of equity. It is necessary to provide for a just distribution of taxes so that no one shall have a privileged position,—neither the celibate nor the childless couple nor the large family,—but rather that the standard of living of all categories shall gradually become equalized as a result of the sacrifices imposed on the one and privileges accorded to the other.

The results obtained were remarkable. The jokes of clever foreigners regarding the consequences of the "directed marriage" in Germany are hardly in order. The number of marriages, which in 1932 had fallen to 510,000, rose in 1934 to 731,000, showing an increase of 221,000 or 43.5 per cent. The number of new births in 1934 again passed the million mark (1,181,000), exceeding the number in 1933 by 23 per cent. Even in Berlin the deficiency of 14,000 gave way to an excess of 5,474 in 1934. These results, of course, are not a final proof of success. Burgdörfer, the specialist in demographic statistics, has called attention to the fact that the increase in the number of marriages was in direct relation to the number of loans granted (225,000 *Ehestandsdarlehen*; 221,000 additional marriages!) and that the increase in the birth rate is the result of the increased number of young households established. Under such conditions no one can tell if this progress will be maintained during the course of the following years. Moreover, the results obtained remain insufficient. Burgdörfer calculates that in order to maintain the German population at its actual level, it would be necessary that the annual number of births rise not to 1,181,000 but to 1,400,000. No decisive gain has thus as yet been obtained and no one knows whether the German people wish or do not wish to propagate themselves.

157

It should be said, however, that the first results have been encouraging.*

The eugenic measures taken by National Socialism were, like the measures with respect to births, also based on statements made by German hygienists regarding the German youth, which were not very reassuring. According to these statements a third of the young Germans were not *"vol-leistungsfahig,"* i.e. they were able to accomplish the normal tasks entrusted to them in an indifferent manner, but they were incapable of furnishing work of a superior quality. Moreover, they did not have the necessary energy to utilize occasions for improving themselves. Their strength thus would be used up so quickly that their congenital weakness would not be slow in showing itself. It would seem, there-fore, that despite efforts made in Germany to better public health by fighting against contagious diseases, notably tuber-culosis and syphilis, or even against unhealthy workers' hovels and barracks that public health still left very much more to be desired.

National Socialism undertook the struggle in another way. They tried to prevent procreation by individuals afflicted with certain defects which are hereditary or dangerous for public safety. Hitler maintained in principle: "He who is not healthy in body and in spirit ought not to perpetuate his malady in the body of his children. In this regard the racialist state has to assume an immense educational task. Through education it must teach the individual that it is not a pitiable

* The results for 1935, the latest figures available, were not as satisfactory. According to the *Deutsche medizinische Wochenschrift* (1937, no. 4), "the German population movement in 1935 began once again to return to its normal course. This follows a year which was especially remarkable through the extraordinary increase in marriages and births. In 1935 there was a total number of 650,851 marriages in the Reich (against 739,449 in 1934), thus 12% less than in the previous year." On the other hand the mortality for 1935 was much greater than for 1934. According to the same periodical, there were 791,912 deaths in the German Reich during 1935 as against 724,668 in 1934. Between 1932 and 1935 the mortality rate has increased by 10%.—*Ed.*

but a deplorable misfortune to be weak and sickly. But on the other hand it is a crime and consequently a disgrace to dishonor one's malady by transmitting its defects to an innocent being." This resulted in the famous law of July 14, 1933 which instituted discretionary or even obligatory sterilization for certain categories of individuals afflicted with hereditary diseases. This also resulted in the establishment of a certificate of hereditary health which is required for the performance of any marriage and also the establishment of bureaus of health charged with giving the public useful hygienic information.

Interminable controversies were aroused by this law. It was attacked as contrary to moral principles of the Catholic religion and we shall have occasion to speak of this in a later chapter. For the present we shall confine ourselves to saying that on the National Socialist side there was also another reason for favoring the sterilization law. For in addition to its hygienic advantages, it involved a sure economic advantage. The sterilization of 400,000 individuals included in the categories covered by the law, would cost about 14 million marks. On the other hand the savings realized by the disappearance of these categories of diseased persons would, according to Lenz, in a single year amount to at least 350 million marks and according to Burgdörfer perhaps even to a billion marks. In any case at the end of a short period there would be a decrease of expenditures of several hundred million marks.

The sterilization law began to be enforced on January 1, 1934 and has already been applied to 200,000 cases. It is still difficult to predict what its general effects will be on public health. Hitler, in any case, has expressed the most decided optimism. He feels that six centuries of eugenic policy rigorously pursued will be sufficient to free the human race from all its hereditary maladies.

159

BOOK V

Spartanism

v. *Spartanism*

1. The Spirit of Sparta

A SOCIETY which is characterized by the predominance of what Sombart calls "economism," i.e. an attitude of mind which is directed primarily toward the acquisition of riches and comforts, invariably develops certain characteristic types of individuals. There is the *urban* dweller who is removed from the soil and from nature; the *bourgeois*, haunted by the anxiety of tomorrow, imbued with his prejudices of caste, and curdled in his narrow egotism; the *intellectual*, disdainful of manual labor and full of illusions regarding the powers of reason; and the *esthete* wrapt in a sterile dream of beauty and culture. Hitler wished to break violently with these follies which, he maintained, threatened to bring about a crisis in Western culture. He urged the organization of a new society founded on strong national solidarity, on the rude, coarse virtues of the peasant, the artisan, and the soldier, and on the practice of strict discipline and voluntary sacrifice by the individual for the community,—in a word a society founded on the civic, robust and virile qualities which, in antiquity, made for the glory of Sparta.

Hitler began to believe in the necessity for a Spartan training of the new generations very early in his life and in his *Mein Kampf* he presented a detailed program of the kind of education which he considered necessary.

The first duty of the state, he taught, is to take care of the bodily development of the child. The fundamental task of the National Socialist state is to form fine bodies, robust,

163

hardy and capable of enduring privation, rather than to develop minds crammed with a mass of scientific knowledge. Genius can never spring from a people of degenerates. What made for the grandeur of the Greeks was the harmonious union of healthy body, luminous spirit and noble soul. The physical development of the infant is not a task which should belong first of all to the parents and only eventually to the state. It is primarily the affair of the state and the state understands that the physical education of its future citizen is a vital question for the group as a whole. The state decreed compulsory education for all without consulting the individual desires of the parents. It ought to do the same for physical education. The schools should not be allowed to produce generations of pedants and milksops.

Nothing, however, had been done along these lines. In the secondary schools two hours a week were given to gymnastics,—and this was not compulsory. Hitler wants at least two hours a day for physical exercise and he is not satisfied with gymnastics alone. He calls for training in all sports, particularly boxing. It is necessary that the child should become strong, supple, capable of endurance and that he should have confidence in the defensive power of his own hands. Physical education obviously cannot make a hero out of a coward but it does give the ordinary individual confidence in himself. The state should thus direct the physical education of a young German from infancy up to military service, which is the last term in the education of a citizen. In the army the adolescent becomes a man. He learns the use of arms. He becomes accustomed to strict discipline and learns, as well, to command. At the end of his service the young German receives the diploma of citizenship and also the certificate of health which qualifies him for marriage.

Character formation comes after physical formation. Here too Hitler is well aware of the limits of the powers of education and of the impossibility of making a criminal into an honest man. It is, nevertheless, possible to improve the ordinary individual. The chief virtues which Hitler wishes to inculcate into the citizen are fidelity, the will to sacrifice, reserve and self-mastery. It is interesting to see that he condemns denunciation as an act of cowardice and he censures teachers who encourage it in their classes and who use it to increase their authority. He urges in particular the development in young people of will, determination and desire to assume responsibility, and courage of conviction.

Finally, Hitler demands that strictly scientific education should be considerably simplified. It is necessary to eliminate from the programs a lot of useless subjects which only burden the memory. He recommends in particular that the teaching of history be passed over lightly. It will be sufficient if a child knows the main lines of world development and understands the major role which the fact of race plays in human destinies. Even scientific and technical education should be simplified. The foundation of all instruction ought to be "humanism" and in particular the initiation into Greek civilization. According to Hitler, a scientific and technical education cannot flourish except on foundations of an idealistic outlook diffused widely through the nation. The final goal of all education is to fashion citizens conscious of the glory of their country and their race, proud to belong to it and full of fanatical devotion to the national cause. Out of all the citizens an élite should be formed,—an élite not only of riches and birth, but of culture and talent. Access to this élite shall be open not only to children of the older governing classes but also to the lower classes.

2. Spartan Regimentation

In order to realize this theoretical conception of Spartanism, Hitler has organized a series of associations in which the citizen finds his place from the time of his youth up to middle and even old age. At no time should the individual have the impression that he is alone, left to himself. During his entire lifetime he ought to be filled with the sentiment that he is part of a vast collectivity which provides him with support and guidance, which has its claims on him and to which he owes love and devotion.

First there are the youth organizations; the *Deutsches Jung-volk* which includes children from ten to thirteen years and the *Hitler-Jugend*, in which are enrolled adolescents from fourteen years up.* After the age of eighteen, the young Nazi goes from these youth organizations into the National Social-ist Party and eventually into the S.A., i.e. the *Sturm Abteilung*, which consists of those who voluntarily engage as militants in the "protective sections" of the party. After their nineteenth year the young Nazis are called for six months into the labor camps, or *Arbeitsdienst*, where they are subjected to manual labor and to camp discipline. Having gone through this com-pulsory stage, they go to the Reichswehr, where they serve their two years of military service, which is now compulsory for all. After this they return to the party and continue to serve either under the brown shirt of the S.A. or the black uniform of the S.S. i.e., *Schutz Staffel*. The Nazi thus finds himself regimented during his whole life. At every age of his life he marches before his *Führer* in one uniform or another, at the party congress, in the various drives which are con-stantly being organized or in the incessant parades which the leaders use for the purpose of making perceptible to all party members the collective life of which they form an integral part.

Let us now look at these various stages of the hierarchy in more detail. The youth associations play a very important role in the National Socialist state. Hitler himself took pains to define this role in the speech which he delivered before

* The newspapers have recently announced the establishment of the *Deutsche Kindschaft*, which will include children from four to nine years.

54,000 representatives of the *Hitler-Jugend*, who filed by
him at the Nuremberg Congress of September, 1935. What
we desire of youth, he said, is quite unlike what the former
generations desired. The ideal young German until lately
was the intrepid beer drinker, the *Bierspiesser*, the dull Philis-
tine of yesterday. Today he is the lank athlete, inured against
intemperance, "swift as the greyhound, tough as leather and
hard as Krupp steel." This is the new man that National
Socialism wishes to form in place of the degenerate of yesterday and it wishes to educate him in strict discipline and
perfect self respect.

In 1933 National Socialism took into the *Hitler-Jugend*
all the youth organizations already existing at that time and
as much of the hitherto unorganized youth as possible. After
that the leaders decided upon a pause in which to solidify the
organization, to take the leadership well in hand and achieve
strict discipline. Then a new effort was made to extend the
movement. An active propaganda was carried on in the world
of industry and crafts in order to enlist apprentices in the
Nazi youth organizations. In the schools, likewise, the teachers
were urged to induce their pupils to join. Parents were
reassured by the organization of medical supervision, which
provided full guarantees to the family. The Nazi leaders also
attempted to quiet the fears of the representatives of religion
by assuring them that the young people would not be im-
peded in the performance of their religious duties. Some real
success was achieved. Resistance on the part of parents and
schools was gradually overcome, although it still continued
on the part of religious organizations, as we shall see later. In
1935 the Hitler Youth formed an immense organization comprising almost 60 per cent of the German youth and placed
under the direction of *Reichsjugendführer* Baldur von
Schirach.* It has its special celebrations (the youth sport

* On December 1, 1936 a new law was promulgated which placed the
entire youth of Germany within the *Hitler-Jugend* and made the organization an integral part of the state machinery (see Appendix).—*Ed.*

festival celebrated throughout Germany on June 22 and 23), its medical corps, its schools for leaders, its Academy for leaders which was established at Brunswick, and a special law for the youth is in process of elaboration.

An important modification in the organization of the youth is being prepared according to the latest speeches of Baldur von Schirach. The *Jungvolk* will continue to include as much as possible of the entire youth of Germany beginning at the age of ten. At the end of four years, however, there will be a selection. The most capable will form the *Hitler-Jugend* where they will remain for four years. This will be the nursery from which the party will be recruited. The others will be organized into an association which will bear the name *Reichsjugend* and there they will be trained in the spirit of National Socialism. This does not mean that they will be considered subjects of second rank. All careers will be open to them. But for them there will be no prospect of being included amongst the political leaders of the nation.

From what has been said above, it is apparent that the principal problem before the Nazi youth is their relation with their parents and with the school. The thesis of the Nazi authorities is that the education of the youth ought to result from the harmonious co-operation of three factors of equal standing: the paternal home, the school, and the youth associations.

As for the school the question has been regulated easily. The first youth associations at the time of the *Jugendbewegung*, had often been looked upon with disfavor by the school authorities. They considered this attempt at emancipation of the youth as an irritating break with tradition and as a symptom of insubordination on the part of the new generation. They, therefore, often went so far as to ban these associations. Resistance on the part of school authorities has been eliminated now without difficulty by the institution of a time schedule. A definite time was set during which the youth associations were able to make use of their members. It was also agreed that pupils receive some credit in their rating for the exercises of these associations. A lad who had distinguished himself in the *Hitler-Jugend*, for example, would thus be able to count upon certain consideration in his final examinations. This done, the members of the teaching body have voluntarily become recruiting agents for the associations and have given their word of honor that they will, if possible, make all their classes join these groups.

The relations with the family have been more difficult to regulate. Resistance occurs daily. On the one hand there is opposition due to reasons of health, certain parents entertaining fears for the health of their delicate children. More significant are complications of family discipline. Many parents are afraid that their children have become too absorbed in the associations. From the moment the young Nazi begins to go to school, his time is almost completely taken up by classes, obligations, religious duties, physical exercises and scout life. The leaders of National Socialism have been careful to underscore the fact that affiliation with these Hitler youth associations is voluntary and that no one is forced to join them. In fact, however, this free choice is very dubious in character. Failure to join looks bad from the point of view of civic loyalty. The Nazi leaders loudly declare that the parents are severely to blame for setting obstacles in the way of their children who wish to join these associations. The children are tempted by what appears to them to be an act of emancipation. Above all they have a horrible fear of being treated by their comrades as cowards or milksops.

Thus all the time of the youth is monopolized. They have scarcely a free moment left for either family or personal life. The young German is fashioned in this collective kind of existence into a conformity of tastes and sentiments. He has the feeling that he is accomplishing a civic duty and that he has to react against the effeminancy of "bourgeois" culture.

He thus lives more with his comrades and is gradually weaned away from his family. The leaders do indeed say that in case of discord with their parents, youth ought always to remember that respect is due to those who brought them into the world. In practice, however, this respect is reduced to very little and the gulf between the generations, far from being bridged, is only becoming greater under the Spartan regime installed by Hitlerism.

Among the interesting tasks undertaken by the Hitler Youth in 1933 was the organization of the *Jugendherbergen*, or rest camps, in which young people hiking on foot might find a place for the night in return for only a small payment. The idea was an old one and had already begun to be realized in the course of the past twenty-five years. But National Socialism took it up and developed it with astonishing vigor. In 1933, 4,600,000 travelers took advantage of these camps and in 1934, 5,800,000. The Nazi leaders look toward the time when Germany will have a network of these camps spaced at one to every twenty or thirty kilometers.

The educational aim of this institution is obvious. On the one hand it is to develop among the youth the taste for healthy sport, which includes hiking. On the other hand it places them in contact with different aspects of the German land and initiates them into a living knowledge of rural life. There are about 2,000 of these shelters today. There the Nazis organize meetings and courses, which often last several weeks and which are directed by leaders who are specialists in the organization of hikes.

3. The Labor Camps

The law of June 26, 1935 made it obligatory for every citizen to serve in the *Arbeitsdienst*. Every German must normally enter a labor camp after he reaches the age of nineteen and before he gets to be twenty-five. The annual contingent which numbers about 200,000 men, is organized into two gangs, each functioning for six months. The National Socialists believe that this compulsory labor service, directed by Colonel Hierl (who began to plan this work in 1929), is an event almost as important as the introduction of compulsory education by Frederick II or of compulsory military service before the War of Liberation of 1813.

The idea of labor camps was inspired, in the first place, by economic considerations. As a result of the need for Germany to supply its wants without recourse to foreign imports, the Germans studied with the greatest attention all the possibilities there were of extracting more agricultural products from the German soil, now reduced in extent by the Versailles Treaty. Colonel Hierl stated that by properly managed works the value of German agricultural production could be raised by almost two billion marks. These works would provide employment to 250,000 workers for forty years. This resulted, during the formidable crisis of unemployment which affected Germany during the 1930's, in the idea of organizing, through voluntary enlistment, labor camps where the unemployed might find work and where the unoccupied youth might serve its first apprenticeship and acquire a sense of discipline instead of becoming habituated to vagabond life and idleness.

National Socialists often complain that this institution has not been well understood by foreigners. Some have looked upon these labor camps as an organization aiming secretly to organize the German youth into military formations. Others have looked upon it as a workhouse where the unemployed are tied down to forced work. The aim actually pursued is to carry out certain public works which have a definite value but which are too costly to be achieved by paid labor. They thus utilize the unemployed who have been put out of work by the economic crisis. These unemployed would in any case have to be supported. It is better, therefore, in every way, to provide them with a useful job which will at the same time assure them of lodging, food and a hygienic occupation.

Apart from its economic aspect the *Arbeitsdienst* has also a pedagogic and moral aspect which is even more important in the eyes of the Nazis. For them it is an indispensable complement to military service. The army takes young men from all social classes and molds them into the uniform type of the soldier. But in the eyes of the Nazis the type of manual worker who wields the shovel and the spade is as respectable as the soldier. It is desirable and useful, moreover, that young men of all types go through the training of a manual worker before they receive the soldier's training; that they be given a shovel before a gun and that they be made to feel the equality of all citizens not only with respect to national defense by the gun but also with respect to national work by the shovel of peasant and ditch digger. This the Nazis consider to be an essential aspect of civic education.

Civic service is therefore considered by them as a powerful means of bringing about the fusion of classes through common life and work. The labor service is distinguished from military service in that it is founded on camaraderie. The army is a school of strict discipline, of severe subordination, ruled by a complex hierarchy, and order is assured by strict penalties. In the labor service also, the maintenance of discipline is guaranteed by a strict code. But the leader is supposed to assure himself of authority and secure order by persuasion and not by punishment. If he does not achieve this he is quickly replaced. In the army there are superiors and subordinates. In the labor camps camaraderie reigns not only among workers of all classes—intellectuals, workers, artisans, peasants—but also between the workers and their leaders. The latter lead the same kind of life as their subordinates and they owe their leadership to their example and their persuasive powers. The leaders are gratified with the results obtained and they feel sure that their men have become impervious to any communist propaganda.

4. The Army

The civic service is followed by the military service in which the young men are trained to defend their country by force of arms. Hitler has always had unlimited admiration for the army. When the World War broke out he volunteered to serve in the German army and he was profoundly happy to have his request granted. He served with enthusiasm and with fanaticism. He was convinced of the unique value of the German army. In his eyes it was invincible and it remained unvanquished. He believed tenaciously in the legend of "the dagger thrust in the back." At the time he wrote his *Mein Kampf* he declared that the period of military service should be the crowning point of a citizen's education.

Under these circumstances Hitler never thought, when he created his party, of organizing an armed force capable of rivaling the Reichswehr. He always insisted that his brown militia was only for the protection of party meetings and nothing more. For a while he yielded in 1923 to the pressure of his collaborators and admitted that the S.A. was preparing for insurrection. But he soon recognized that this was a mistake. After the failure of the putsch of 1923 he was definitely set against allowing his brown shirts to become a secret army and he carried out his wishes despite the opposition of a number of his followers.

During this whole period there was probably a sort of tension between the Nazis and the army. It was the Reichswehr which by its firm attitude had caused the collapse of the 1923 putsch. From then on the Nazis and the army had very little to do with each other. The leaders of the Reichswehr showed no sympathy for a party "which aims to overthrow by violence the constitutional regime of the German Reich." The professional soldiers showed an instinctive disdain for the rowdy and undisciplined irregulars. On their side the Nazis detested the Reichswehr as the strongest support of the Weimar republic. In 1929 Gregor Strasser supported a motion of lack of confidence against General Groener which had been introduced by the Communists. Before the whole Reichstag he declared: "We are fighting for the ultimate setting up of a high court which shall condemn to hanging all these traitors to the German nation who have undermined its military power and weakened its military will."

Hitler nevertheless maintained his line of conduct. He concluded that he could never gain power unless the Reichswehr was with him and he attempted to win them to his cause. While Strasser was sending Groener, Schleicher and their associates to the gallows, Hitler was endeavoring, on the other hand, to show the military leaders the mistake they were making in allowing Marxism to gain the upper hand. "If the left wins," he said, "then you will don the Phrygian cap for all time and you will become police guards, instead of officers."

Up to 1933, nevertheless, the Reichswehr maintained a wavering attitude towards Hitler. In 1932, Groener dissolved the brown militia but soon thereafter he was overthrown by Schleicher. Schleicher in turn is said to have had the idea, when he was set aside by Hindenburg, of a military coup with the aid of the army against the President and von Papen.

By that time, however, it was already doubtful if the army would have followed General von Schleicher. If we are to believe the statements made by Major Foertsch* the Reichswehr knew that it could not halt the events by any military action and it did not wish to attempt any step of this sort. Under the Weimar republic the army had shown very little sympathy for the parliamentary state and consequently had always proclaimed its desire to remain *above the parties* and

* *Die Wehrmacht im national-sozialistischen Staat* (Hamburg 1935).

174

maintain its own autonomy as much as possible. But once National Socialism had assumed power the attitude of the army changed. Hitler had told the higher officers that he considered the army one of the fundamental pillars of the new state. And the army on its side felt that Hitler was a soldier in thought and will, and the kind of state which he conceived was exactly adapted to the views of the army.

The crisis of June 30, 1934 brought the *Führer* and the Reichswehr still closer together. It seems, indeed, that the Röhm revolt had, in part at least, been directed against the privileged position of the Reichswehr as the single armed force in the Reich. In quelling this rebellion of his old comrades, Hitler made the position of the Reichswehr even more firm. When Hindenburg died at the beginning of August, 1934, and when by the law of August 1 the functions of the President of the Reich and Chancellor were combined in the person of Hitler, he became commander-in-chief of the army and by virtue of this title he immediately received the oath of allegiance of the Reichswehr. The Minister of the Reichswehr, General von Blomberg* frankly admitted that for the Reichswehr, National Socialism as the foundation of the new state, was above any attack and that it would find in the army "a source of National Socialist spirit." This does not mean that the army, until lately above parties and outside politics, had now become the instrument of a party and its policy. It means simply that the army which from 1918 to 1932 had developed *outside* the political framework of the nation, from now on placed itself voluntarily *within* this framework, which had taken on a new form as a result of the Nazi action. The state and the army now co-operate for the realization of the same national ideal. "The political function of the army in the National Socialist state," writes Foertsch, "is most happy and most honorable. It is, together with the party, the

* *Völkischer Beobachter*, March 23, 1935.

solid foundation of public power. It represents the nation and is its educator."

The proclamation on March 16, 1935 of the re-establishment of universal compulsory military service accorded completely with the wishes of the army, as General von Blomberg explained in the above cited article in the *Völkischer Beobachter*. In no country in the world, said he, did the idea of Scharnhorst that *all* the inhabitants of a country are its born defenders, so capture the hearts of the people as in Germany. The training which makes the citizen into a soldier is a national need for him. He considers it unbearable to see military service, which he holds to be the right and privilege of every free man, become the apanage of a tiny minority of specialists, no matter how well chosen these might be. Everyone looks upon military service as the great school of the nation and nothing else can replace it. It is a school of discipline, camaraderie and solidarity, where the character of young generations is formed. The youth of former years, which had lacked this training, has shown by its discord and its restlessness how indispensable this sturdy school is for moral soundness. The new generation will know how to show itself worthy of this "right of arms" which has been restored to it. It will find in the army a source of National Socialist spirit and of national solidarity. An army cannot develop except upon the ethnic base from which it has sprung and which supports it. It is inconceivable without a direct connection with the forces and ideas which manifest themselves among the people. The re-establishment of compulsory military service is, therefore, not a return to the past. The army serves the Germany of today and prepares the Germany of tomorrow. This had been proclaimed in the soldier's catechism of Marshal von Hindenburg: "The service in the army is a service of honor to the German people." The army will show itself faithful to the oath which binds it unto life and death to Adolf Hitler, the creator and the *Führer* of the New Germany.

How far is this complete community of spirit between army and government a reality? It is certainly difficult to say. It has often been alleged that the army has retained its autonomy and its particular spirit. It has been maintained that in disarming his brown shirts Hitler destroyed the force which had led him to power and that he now has only a guard of several thousand men at his personal disposal. He is, therefore, at the mercy of the army, which could at any moment bring about his fall and in his place install one of its own men. The most varied kind of rumors circulate in the press regarding the personal attitude of particular generals toward the *Führer*. Thus, for example, the change of General von Reichenau gave rise to all sorts of comments. What weight do these rumors carry? At present there does not seem to be any serious reason to suspect the accuracy of official pronouncements. The re-establishment of the national army certainly aroused an immense wave of enthusiasm in Germany and the entire nation is thankful to Hitler for having dared, and successfully accomplished, the liberating move which broke the chains of Versailles. It is difficult, moreover, to understand why the army should not adhere to its loyalty to him who has restored new force to it and who has made rearmament one of his major tasks. Hitler needs the army—that is obvious—but the army in its turn needs the popularity of Hitler. It has become more and more impregnated with the principles of National Socialism. The privileges of class and caste have disappeared. Volunteering for a year has been discarded. The probabilities are, therefore, that in the very near future the army will be completely refashioned in accordance with the new spirit.

5. The Role of the Brown Militia

As the second pillar of the National Socialist state alongside the army there is the party. In the party the brown militia, or the S.A., is the volunteer organization of party militants. There were no doubt disagreements within this body. It was possible to look upon the S.A. as an armed band, after the fashion of the Italian fascist militia, and constituting, parallel to the Reichswehr, an homogeneous force, militarized and completely subordinated to National Socialism. This was the conception of certain lieutenants of the *Führer*, among whom probably was Röhm, the chief of staff of the S.A. This point of view, however, had always been rejected by Hitler. Finally on June 30, 1934 Hitler crushed the rebels in most brutal fashion.

On the other hand Hitler felt very keenly the necessity of maintaining the party organization and assigning to it, alongside the administration and the bureaucracy, the important role in the state which we have described above. Consequently it was also necessary to maintain the S.A. organizations as a force—unarmed, but sturdy and active, and capable at any time of making sure that the will of the party was carried out.

The S.A. rank and file have no doubt passed through a crisis. They are conscious of having been the makers of Hitler's victory. Now that they have triumphed they feel that they have not been repaid in proportion to their merits. Hence there was a feeling among them of having been deceived which gave rise to a spirit of bitterness. There were also many difficulties of a passing character. It was necessary to purge the S.A., to decrease their number and to replace a great many of the leaders. We do not have all the details of this work of reorganization, which was indicated in passing allusions in speeches by Hitler, Goebbels and chief of staff, Lutze. We simply know that the S.A. remains as a group of volunteers, freely consenting to devote a part of their time to the service of the party. This militia is not kept in barracks. It is allowed to accept former army soldiers who have completed their period of service. On October 19, 1935 Goebbels defined the task of the S.A. as follows: "The S.A. is an historic fact and no one can imagine its disappearance. There are some organizations which act simply by their presence. An army is not obliged to demonstrate its *raison d'être* by making war. By its mere presence it very often prevents war." In the same way the enemies of National Socialism have not yet disappeared. If they do not show themselves it is because they know that the S.A. is ready to suppress any act of sabotage. The S.A. is the vigorous arm of the party to which Hitler will always make his appeal for the maintenance of *internal* order while the army and its bayonets is charged *exclusively* with the defense of the frontiers.

The S.A. comprises active service (18 to 35 years), a reserve (35 to 45) and a *landsturm* (over 45). Its supreme chief is Hitler and the chief of staff is Major Lutze. It is divided into 21 groups which in turn are subdivided into 97 brigades with 627 *Standarten*, each one comprising between 1,000 and 3,000 men.

Beside the brown militia there is also the black militia (S.S. i.e. *Schutzstaffel*) which comprises about 200,000 men under the command of Heinrich Himmler and is divided into 85 *Standarten*. It is the personal guard of Hitler, and fulfills the function of political police and the duty of surveillance of the concentration camps. "From this center of information," we read in the *Völkischer Beobachter* of January 30, 1935, "all political life in all its details and all its manifestations is watched and judged according to the principles of National Socialism. The S.S. has erected this organization against all those who are hostile toward the *Führer* and the nation. In the same way it furnishes a great number of men for service in the secret police."

The National Socialist state thus presents a Spartan appearance. This Spartanism shows itself in the propaganda for marriage and children, which is to insure the infinite development of national strength, and in the policy practiced with regard to women, who are placed in the position of dedicating themselves completely to the triple function of mother, educator and guardian of the hearth (*Kinder, Küche, Kirche*) and who are therefore freed from outside obligations and are even prevented from competing with men in many fields. It is also evidenced in the eugenic work of preventing the spread of social diseases (through sterilization), in the effort to bring back into being a class of hereditary peasants who are sturdy and strongly rooted in the soil, in the organization of a hierarchy of associations which from the *Hitler-Jugend* up to the army and the S.A., train the child, the adolescent, the young man and the mature man in the practice of national solidarity, in the reform of education which gives the primary place to the training of the body and to the formation of character, and in the effort toward a simplification of the material existence, toward social and moral discipline and toward a reform of habits. Even the institution of the *Eintopfgericht*, the single dish to which every citizen has to restrict himself on certain days, brings to mind the "black broth" of ancient Sparta.

The question may certainly be raised if this Spartanism is a psychic reality betraying a real will towards heroism, or if it may not in certain respects be merely a façade which conceals a more prosaic reality. It is difficult to give a precise answer to this question. The simplification of German life is a fact. But this may be due more to an inevitable lowering in the standard of living rather than to a desire for asceticism. There has also been some question as to whether there actually has been any progress in public morality. Corruption, perhaps, has not merely been obliged to seek cover more than formerly, but even more, it has been passed over in silence by a regimented press. There is also the question whether Hitlerism has in fact restored the German family or whether the regimentation of children and men into these various associations has not really further aggravated the disintegration of the family. I do not pretend to have an answer to these doubts. I can only confine myself to saying that the stranger who returns from Germany, after seeing the meetings of the youth, visiting the labor camps or attending the grand public demonstrations such as the party congresses at Nuremberg, carries away the strong impression that German life has been vitalized. It presents new aspects, of little attraction perhaps for those who do not share the Nazi conception of life, but nevertheless clearly indicating the considerable influence which the National Socialist ideology of heroism has exercised over the nation.

Finally I should like to stress the point that Spartanism is not in any way synonymous with dullness of mind. It is hard for me to believe that Germany has suddenly become a land of barbarians. I feel, as do a great many of those who have had the occasion to observe the situation at close range, that the "eternal" Germany still lives under the brown shirt of Hitlerism as it did under the tinsel of the era of Wilhelm. Cultural preoccupations are quite evident among the representatives of Hitlerism. They all agree that the Third Reich, far from disdaining culture, ought to bend all its efforts to promote culture and to demonstrate that Germany, "purified" of Judaism, will necessarily develop a culture and science superior to that of the past.

Hitler expressed this sentiment in a forceful way in his Reichstag speech of March 23, 1933. "Parallel with the cleansing of political life," he said, "the government will also proceed to purify completely our social organism. The entire system of our educational institutions—the theater, cinema, literature, the press and the radio—will all be considered as means for attaining this end—and appreciated as such. All are obliged to work for the preservation of the eternal values immanent in our ethnic personality. Art will always be the expression and the mirror of the aspirations and realities of an epoch. The world of bourgeois passive contemplation is rapidly disappearing. Heroism raises itself as the coming creator and leader of political destiny. It is the mission of art to give expression to this *Zeitgeist*. Blood and race will again become the sources of artistic intuition. It shall be the task of the government of national awakening to see to it that it is precisely in a time of restrained political influence that the living values and the national will to live shall find most energetic expression in the cultural field. This decision imposes upon us a grateful admiration for our glorious past. In all fields of historical and cultural life the knowledge of our tradition ought to be the glory of our present and should constitute a transition to the future."

On the other hand there are many reservations which, I believe, can be made with respect to the cultural tendencies in the Third Reich. Undeniable are the losses which have been inflicted on science and the arts by the policy of systematic "purification." It is certainly no small matter that Germany has rejected men like Einstein, Thomas Mann or Richard Strauss. One may also entertain doubts as to the efficacy of the Nazi manner of regimenting art. The question may be raised as to whether the practical tendency, so distinctive of Hitlerism, is very favorable to the progress of art and science and whether truth and beauty do not, in the National Socialist ideology, cease to be ends in themselves, disinterested and freely pursued, but become instead instruments of propaganda for the purpose of developing as complete an intellectual conformism as possible. One may likewise remain skeptical of the Nazi notion of a "political" university and there is room for fear that the German spirit developing along these lines will still further accentuate the divergences which separate it from the spirit of other nations.

Nevertheless, as numerous trustworthy observers have maintained, German publications still continue to maintain a high level of scientific value. The Germany of today contains sources of culture which are of primary importance and there is nothing to indicate that they are destined to disappear in the near future. The German spirit remains alive and active under Hitler as it did under William II. It may temporarily assume certain aspects which displease or shock us and we are not bound to admire these unreservedly. But we must also concede that its development is not incompatible with the new Spartanism, either in theory or in fact. Spartan ideology might not seem attractive or palatable to us, with its vexatious exclusivism. But it remains an ideology and it would be intransigeance and foolish dogmatism on our part to view it as barbarism and not to recognize many of the spiritual values which it possesses, no matter what our reservations regarding it might be.*

* During the more recent period, however, the deleterious effects of Nazi rule on German culture have become more evident. These are revealed in many ways. Learned journals and learned societies have been forced to cease their activities. The distinguished *Verein für Sozialpolitik*, in existence since 1872, voted on April 25, 1936 to dissolve because it could not accept the demands imposed upon it by the Minister of Education and maintain, at the same time, the intellectual independence and freedom of action which the organization owed to its members. The most celebrated German historian, Friedrich Meinecke, was forced out from the editorship of the *Historische Zeitschrift* and such famous and completely Aryan scholars as Spranger and Jaeger found the intellectual climate of Nazi Germany so oppressive that they voluntarily expatriated themselves.

The nationalization of science has proceeded at an accelerated pace. At the anniversary celebration of the University of Heidelberg in the summer of 1936 the statue of Pallas Athene on the façade of one of the buildings as a classic head of the Republic of Letters was replaced by the German eagle and the inscription "To the eternal spirit" was changed to the nationalist "To the German spirit." The preface to the first issue of the *Deutsche Mathematik* (January, 1936) shows how far this has progressed even in the realm of natural science. "We serve the German way in mathematics and wish to cultivate it. We are not alone in this world: other peoples have the same claim to express their way in mathematics. Various points of contact exist between the mathematical work of the different peoples. Our review has an open mind for the suggestions and information which may derive therefrom for us, also. But we see everything from the standpoint of the mathematical accomplishments of our people. For it, our labor is meant, conscious of the fact that creative mathematics also develops the stronger and achieves the greater importance for the world the deeper it is rooted in the national spirit." (Quoted in Kohn, Hans, *Force or Reason*, Cambridge, Massachusetts, 1937, pp. 133-34).

The tragic situation of the genuinely creative spirits in Germany is perhaps best indicated in a speech which the poet Ernst Wiechert delivered before the students of the University of Munich in the early part of 1936. The speech was to be published but it was banned by the censor and is now passed secretly from hand to hand in typewritten form. Wiechert belonged to the conservative group of German writers who looked hopefully to the revolution of 1933. His words, couched in figurative and somewhat symbolic language betray his keen disillusionment in the cultural state of Nazi Germany. (See Appendix.)

For the problem of culture and education under the Nazis see Thompson, Dorothy, "Culture under the Nazis," and Beard, Charles, "Education under the Nazis," in *Foreign Affairs*, vol. xiv (1936), pp. 407-23 and 437-52. See also the author's concluding remarks on pp. 288-90.—*Ed.*

BOOK VI

The Religious Problem

VI. The Religious Problem

1. The Crisis in Protestantism

AMONG the issues in present-day Germany there is scarcely a problem more pathetic than the religious problem.* Let us first look at the situation of Protestantism.

In order to understand the evolution of German Protestantism in the nineteenth century it is necessary to distinguish between the Protestant spirit and the Protestant church. The history of the spirit of Protestantism, in so far as it is a principle of spiritual and moral life, is of significant interest. Protestantism, in the course of its evolution, has tended to strip religion of its objective, historical, and absolute character. Christianity did not appear to the Protestant spirit as a set of revealed truths which are external to the faithful and which must be *believed*. It conceived of Christianity as a state of consciousness which each individual was obliged to *live*. Protestantism did not force the individual to believe in the reality of certain historical facts. Protestant exegesis ended by demonstrating that the Gospels were the mythical expression of the religious experiences of a primitive community and the personality and doctrine of the historic Christ was not to be seen except through an increasingly impenetrable mist.

Protestantism also tended to strip Christianity of its quality as a revealed religion, one and eternal. Christianity is only one of the innumerable forms of the religious conscience of humanity,—an admirable form no doubt, superior perhaps, but

* For the religious problem in Germany consult, Gurian, Waldemar, *Hitler and the Christians* (London 1936).

187

never unique, probably not even eternal, and in any case variable in form. In a word, Protestantism tended to fashion a Christianity which was without dogmas and which "becomes" a subjective religion engaged in a continuous process of evolution.

By its very nature Protestantism aimed to create as perfect a synthesis as possible of the two great opposing conceptions in the modern world, Christianity and scientific rationalism. German Idealism, from Kant, Fichte and Goethe up to Hegel and Eucken, despite its independent appearances and despite its frequent semblances of irreligiousness, always remained profoundly conscious of its ties with Christianity. Philosophers and artists were at one in regarding the modern "religion" as being identical with the religion of Christ. German Idealism thus appeared as a new combination of the two great elements of Western culture, the classical element and the Christian element, and as an ingenious and profound attempt to unite into one original synthesis the spiritualized religion of Christ with the religion of science and beauty.

Less glorious, no doubt, has been the history of the Protestant church. The official church, having become conservative and merely an appendage to the state, barely maintained itself amidst the almost general dissatisfaction of the people. The large cities became "spiritual cemeteries" in which there were hardly any believers apart from the official world which still professed a strict evangelical faith. The enlightened bourgeoisie, by force of tradition and convenience, continued to associate religion with the important acts of life but in general it lost all living faith. The working masses, influenced by socialism as well as of their own accord, were suspicious of the pastor as an accessory to the gendarme and of the church as working for the safety of the throne and the security of the moneyed interests. Even in the country the sermons of the preacher did not seem to have much influence on the peasants or on public morality. In general it seemed that the

Protestant spirit always felt itself imprisoned within the rigid framework of the state church,—the creation of a past epoch which no longer provided satisfaction to the modern spirit. To many the church appeared as a body without a soul, as an institution of pomp with an imposing façade which concealed rather poorly its actual internal decay.

What was the attitude of the new racialist and Germanic "religion," which had developed so strongly since the end of the 19th century, towards Evangelical Christianity and the Protestant church? *A priori* there is no reason why the "religion of race" should not, like the "religion of science," attempt to harmonize itself with Christianity. This tendency was revealed in one of the most important personalities produced by the racialist movement. Houston Stewart Chamberlain, whom National Socialism views as one of its most eminent prophets, was a deeply religious person. For him the Christ who is revealed in the Gospels was a teacher of life to whom one gives oneself not by reason of theological speculations but under the stimulus of spontaneous and living intuition. For him Christianity does not belong only, nor even principally, to the past; it also holds the future. One may say even more perhaps, namely that the Christianization of the Western world has scarcely begun. On the other hand Chamberlain was deeply steeped in the highest scientific, philosophic and esthetic culture of the modern age. Besides being a botanist he was one of those who best entered into the spirit of Kant, Goethe and Richard Wagner. Conforming to the tradition of German Idealism he saw no difficulty in harmonizing Christianity with the cult of science and art. At the same time, in his *Foundations of the Nineteenth Century*, Chamberlain attempted to incorporate the racialist theory into a general world view which would satisfy both his religious needs and the demands of his scientific spirit and his esthetic soul. Chamberlain's religious sympathies, it should be noted, were always for Protestant Christianity. We find in him that very marked hostility, distinctive of racialism, towards Roman Catholic universalism. He considered this universalism as a deviation from true Christianity. He detested in particular the Counter Reformation and the Jesuit spirit as it appeared in Ignatius Loyola. In the person of the latter he saw the typical representative of the non-Aryan Basque, fundamentally incomprehensible to any of the Aryan race.

During the World War the great experience of the *union sacrée* had given birth in the hearts of many to the hope that the dream of an interconfessional and *national church*, so often entertained in the past by generous and tolerant souls, would now become a realized fact. Catholic and Protestant had fought side by side in the trenches. They felt that the spiritual element which united them, their common love of the German fatherland, for which they had offered their lives in sacrifice, was deeper than the confessional differences which separated them. These from now on appeared to them to be negligible or at least secondary. The common national experience of Christians of all creeds and rites being faced with death aroused among them a genuine religious fervor and made them desire the coming of a new church where all Germans,—Catholics, Lutherans or Calvinists,—would be able to kneel, without distinction, before the "German God."

I am inclined to believe that this intuition is at the bottom of Hitler's attempt to harmonize racialism and Christianity. The founder of National Socialism presented his doctrine as neither a religion nor as a successor to any religion. He considered National Socialism to be a *Weltanschauung* compatible with any positive religion. His attitude towards religion is very clear. Whatever may be his personal feelings towards religion, either Catholic or Protestant, he declares in his *Mein Kampf*: "For a political leader the religious teachings and institutions of his people should remain above attack. Otherwise he ceases to be a politician and he should become a reformer if he possesses the necessary ability."

The Religious Problem

Hitler understands the primary importance of faith and religious institutions in human society. He has not only never refrained from heaping scorn upon the atheists who oppose science to religion and see in religion only a superstition destined to disappear rapidly, but he has expressly condemned every anti-clerical policy, which, according to him, can only result in failure. Bismarck had failed in his *Kulturkampf*. The pan-German policy of the Austrian, Schönerer, had come to naught because he had taken as his slogan *"Los von Rom."* Schönerer had launched abuse against ultramontanism and in this way he had alienated the petty bourgeois and populist elements who could have brought about the triumph of his cause.

Later Hitler revealed himself to be even more severe against the incoercible antagonism toward Christianity of his racialist allies, Ludendorf, Graefe and Reventlow. After he left prison in 1925 Hitler separated himself distinctly from his old friends. He declared categorically that he never had and never would combat Rome. He broke definitely with Ludendorf, whom he held void of all political sense. Hitler's point of view, therefore, is very clear. It is not at all that of a *homo religiosus* who confesses his faith. We shall not pretend to decide the question whether Hitler is, as has been stated, a sincere if not a fervent Catholic, or whether, as he appears to Archbishop Söderblom of Upsala, he is "fantastically free of all traces of Christianity." In his writings he always declares himself a politician who compromises with the "force" which religion represents among a people, who regards irreligion as characteristic of individuals ignorant of realities, and anticlericalism as false tactics, particularly in a country as divided in religion as Germany is. Article 24 of the official Nazi program specifically proclaims the adherence of National Socialism to positive religion. "We demand liberty for all religious confessions in the state, in so far as they do not in any way endanger its existence or do not offend the moral sentiment and the customs of the Germanic race. The party, as such, represents the standpoint of positive Christianity without binding itself confessionally to a particular faith. It opposes the Jewish materialistic spirit within and without and is convinced that permanent recovery of our people is possible only from within and on the basis of the principle of general welfare before individual welfare." Hitler's attitude after he came to power conformed to this program. He has repeatedly come out against atheist materialism, and against the skeptical relativism of the "scientific" epoch and of Marxism. He has expressly declared "that he considers both Christian confessions as the most important factors in the ethnic personality of the Germans."

Within the party, however, the attitude towards Christianity has plainly been more critical. Rosenberg, in his *Mythus des XX. Jahrhunderts*, goes much farther than his leader. He takes up the theses of Chamberlain on Catholic universalism and develops them and accentuates them with more vigor. But, without going so far as to reject Christianity completely, he strongly emphasizes the "oriental" elements, unassimilable for Aryans, and he states that there are fundamental differences between the Christian mentality and the German mentality. These ideas gained considerable ground in racialist circles.

Fanatics like Ludendorf are rare. Ludendorf has gone so far as to end up with a German neo-paganism. Recently he published a message in which he took pride in the growing number of Germans who were leaving the Christian church. He invited all his compatriots to refrain from sending their children to church and to religious schools and he concluded as follows: "Your most important duty is to protect your children from Christian influences. They destroyed our people, and only priests and Jews have profited thereby."

More numerous is a group of thinkers among whom religious interest is allied with a decided cult of race and often also with more or less hazardous speculations regarding pre-history and the origins of Germanism. Wilhelm Hauer repre-sents an individual of this type.* Manual laborer, then pastor, theologian, missionary to the Indies and professor at a uni-versity, Hauer is an original and strong personality. He is a captivating speaker and he exercises a certain suggestive power. He began as a fervent Protestant and he showed a growing exasperation with the absurd divisions within the Evangelical Church. These he attributed to the personal in-sufficiency of the official representatives of Christianity. He pointed to the growing dissatisfaction of the faithful and he explained this by the fact that the church had always been too far removed from the people. He sketched a plan for over-coming this decadence but he met with a rebuff. He then turned his back on Christianity and left the church. But de-spite it all, he had need of a god and he went to seek it in the revelation brought by National Socialism.

God, said Hauer, reveals himself to us directly in the blood which flows in our veins, in the smell of the earth, in the beauty of rivers and mountains, in the daily life, and in the revelation of the community in the family, commune or state. For him heaven is on earth and God is within us. He, there-fore, deliberately rejects Christianity and considers it to be fundamentally opposed to Germanism. These two have been battling each other from the time of the conversion of the Germans up to the present. Even the person of Christ, for whom he has profound respect, contains, according to Hauer, too many strange elements to serve as the object of German piety. German youth ought to be formed by the study of its own history and not by the study of a strange world. "Why should any history whatsoever be more sacred to us than our own German history?" He provides his disciples with such

* Hauer resigned as president of the German Faith Movement in 1936 because of the severity of the attacks which many of his adherents directed against Christianity.

slogans as "Our Holy Land is Germany" or "By German faith to religious unity!" It is probable, perhaps, that these neo-pagans are only a small sect without any profound influence on the religious life of the people. They have also renounced spontaneously all public propaganda. According to a recent statement this movement does not actually number more than fifty-three thousand registered members. Hitler has never made common cause with them and has only accorded them disdainful tolerance. He might even be ready, if necessary, to combat neo-paganism, as he has combatted free thinkers and atheists, in order to give proof of the sincerity of his Christianity.

More important is the movement of the German Christians. They do not seek to oppose Christianity but attempt to capture the Evangelical Church from within. It seems that even the origin of this group is political and not religious. In a circular issued in February 1932 by a Nazi functionary in Silesia are found for the first time the guiding principles given by the central direction of the party for the formation of an association of *Evangelische Nationalsozialisten*. These should base themselves on positive Christianity, breathing the very spirit of Luther, but they should retain full consciousness of the essential principles of National Socialism. They should attempt to capture within the Evangelical Church the influence to which their numerical importance gives them the right. In the course of the year 1932 the group was organized, had its first successes in the ecclesiastical elections, constituted itself on June 6, 1932 under the leadership of the Nazi leader in Prussia, Kube, and took the name of *Deutsche Christen*. They presented a program, attracted such people as the pastor Hossenfelder and the future Reichsbishop Ludwig Müller, and at the beginning of 1933 became the most influential party within the Evangelical Church.

Such briefly is the spiritual "climate" which the intrusion of racialism into German religious life has created. Let us now see how Hitler's religious policy developed within this milieu and what the reactions of the Christian world were towards this policy.

Hitler's leanings in the religious problem were revealed very distinctly from the very moment he assumed power. Hitler is not, or in any case does not wish to be considered, an anti-Christian. He glories in the belief that he saved the world from the assault of Marxist materialism and that he reduced to naught the free thinkers and the atheists. He has no sympathies for neo-paganism. He senses the artificial character of this movement and if necessary he would attack it if any advantage for his policies would result therefrom. He insists on the fact that he has defended Christianity against the perils of bolshevism in a more effective way than did the churches and their pastors.

On the other hand the *Führer* is fundamentally indifferent to divergencies in dogma or cult between the various confessions. It matters little to him if one is Catholic or Protestant, Lutheran or Calvinist, orthodox or liberal. In this respect he professes complete tolerance. He wishes to see the realization of a "Third Church," of the "superconfessional" church which the soldiers in the trenches dreamed of during the World War. Everything smacking of theological controversy and disputes of ministers is totally alien to him. He aims for a synthesis of national and religious faith and for the advent of a German church which shall be as free as possible of Roman influences and which shall include the many Protestant sects whose members will pray in common in the patriotic faith compulsory for every citizen of the Third Reich. This very indifference places him in profound opposition to those Christians who cling to the traditional and historical elements of their religion and for whom the discussions of dogma or rites which led to the breaking up of the primitive Christian unity into rival confessions are something more than empty prattling. They perceive that this attitude of supreme disdain for problems whose tragic seriousness they feel implies an indifference towards the religious truth to which they are attached.

There are some flagrant contradictions between the Nazi *Weltanschauung* and the Christian *religion*. Racialism, which is based on the fact of blood, posits the fundamental inequality of the human races and has for its goal the flowering of *one* chosen race, the Nordic, Germanic, Aryan race. The Christian believes in the equality of men in so far as they are free personalities, and he teaches that Christ died for all humanity. Racialism hurls anathema against the Jews while Christianity accepts among its sacred books the Old Testament, which is the history of the Jewish people. Christianity also admits that Christ, even if he were not a Jew by blood, in any case was subjected in the most profound way to the influence of Jewish religious thought. It need not be held *a priori* that it is impossible to harmonize these two beliefs. In fact they were harmonized in the case of a thinker like H. S. Chamberlain. But this accord has been more difficult to establish than the Nazis believed and the confrontation of these two doctrines may well culminate in a violent conflict.

The contrast between the two conceptions is no less striking from the moral point of view. Racialism places at the head of its scale of values heroism and honor. It glorifies struggle and combat. Christianity is a religion of peace and love. It reproves the arrogant and promises salvation to the humble and the disinherited. Racialists are well able to point to the famous verse in *Matthew* 10:34, "Think not that I am come to send peace on earth: I came not to send peace, but a sword." But they cannot without paradox make Christianity into a doctrine of war and in practice they often reproach it as a religion of slaves, incapable of satisfying such heroic souls as those of the Germans.

Finally, Hitler is inclined to confine Christianity strictly within the domain of religious intuition and the inner world of the soul, and to contest its right to exercise any influence on practical life. There too he has met with firm resistance. Christianity cannot indeed allow itself to be relegated to a place outside the sphere of secular life. It tends irresistibly to make its influence felt in the world of reality and considers itself unfaithful to its essential principles if it renounces any reforming action in temporal life.

We cannot enter into a detailed history of the conflict between National Socialism and Protestantism. We shall confine ourselves to sketching briefly the main direction and moments. It was necessary at some time for the Christian conscience to measure the gravity of the situation which the triumph of Hitler had brought about. Immediately following the advent of Hitler, officials as well as church goers of both the Catholic and Protestant sides, rallied to National Socialism with a docility which could only disappoint and sadden independent spirits. One might have believed at a given moment that complete agreement had been reached between National Socialism and the various Christian churches and that a certain religious conformism was going to become almost a compulsory article of Nazi faith.

Soon after he came into power, meanwhile, Hitler announced his desire to unify the organization of the Evangelical Church. He held it absurd to allow the continued existence of some thirty rival churches which do nothing but tear each other to pieces. All were agreed, German Christians as well as Confessional Protestants, in admitting the need for unification and a central administration which would, however, respect the internal life of the churches. The representatives of the evangelical churches approved the general lines of policy laid down for the reform of the constitution of the churches and on May 27, 1933 designated Pastor von Bodelschwingh as Reichsbishop. He was one of the most universally respected personalities in German Protestantism. This choice immediately aroused the protests of the German Christians who wanted as bishop a man who had taken an active part in the national movement. They demanded that the head of the church be elected by the faithful. A certain uneasiness developed in the evangelical churches and in order to put an end to it the Prussian Minister of Ecclesiastical Affairs designated Dr. Jäger on June 24, 1933 as Commissar of the Evangelical Church in Prussia.

This appointment immediately brought about the resignation of Bishop von Bodelschwingh. The latter thought that the appointment of a government commissar made impossible the task of church reorganization which he had assumed. Reform was soon made by direct governmental stimulus. On July 14, 1933 the Reich cabinet issued the law on the constitution of the evangelical churches. On July 23, there were church elections which resulted in a great victory for the German Christians. Almost everywhere they received majorities ranging from 51 to 100 per cent. On September 27, the Bishop of Prussia, Ludwig Müller, confidant of Hitler, was appointed Reichsbishop. On October 5 a number of German Christians were named bishops. Soon the rumor spread that Müller was going to put through a wide movement of recalls and changes to the detriment of those who were not members of the German Christian party. From then on the Confessional Protestants were under no illusions. Protestantism was threatened from within by the development of the German Christian party in the very body of the Evangelical Church. From the outside it was threatened by the fact that Hitler had appointed to the highest post in the ecclesiastical hierarchy an adherent of the German Christians, who was his devoted follower, and who worked with all his energy to make the principles of National Socialism prevail within the church and to fill the ecclesiastical hierarchy with his people. The autonomy of the churches was thus threatened by an administration imposed by the government, which acted in arbitrary fashion without considering the interests of the faith and the will of the church members.

In the meantime, however, the German Christians compromised themselves gravely in the eyes of evangelical opinion by the meeting which they organized in the Berlin Sportpalast on November 7, 1933. Here, before an immense audience, among whom were a number of high church dignitaries, Dr. Kraus boldly formulated the essential aims of the movement. They may be summarized as follows: (1) The totalitarian dogma of National Socialism ought to be extended to the religious domain. The recognition that there is a sort of privileged exemption for matters of faith would constitute capitulation. In religious matters as in all other matters there is only one sovereign law, that of Hitler. (2) The Lutheran reformation should be crowned by the racialist principle. Luther's work will not be complete unless the Nordic soul triumphs over "oriental materialism." (3) The Judaism of the Old Testament, which represents the rapacious and greedy soul of Israel, should be eliminated from the educational program of Germans. It is also necessary to eliminate the "Jewish" elements which had seeped into the New Testament. Above all it is necessary to expunge all "the theology of sin and inferiority of Rabbi Paul." The prayer "deliver us from evil" is antipathetic to the German Christian, for it is, according to the expression of Pastor Gebhard "synonymous with renunciation of the vital struggle" and "unworthy of an heroic heart." (4) Christianity ought, finally, to be systematically purged of everything which has made of it a doctrine of suffering and humility, good at most for slaves. "We reject the crucifix," concluded Kraus, "we wish an heroic Christ."

The meeting at the Sportpalast caused a scandal. In the unrestrained language of Dr. Kraus the German Christians revealed themselves as real kinsmen of the neo-paganism of Hauer and Reventlow. A serious crisis developed among them. At one stroke they became suspect to the mass of faithful, who soon left them as rapidly as they had at first ranged themselves under their banners. The "Confessional" church, or to be more exact the church "of those who adhered to the evangelical faith" (*Bekenntnisskirche*),* rose to defend itself.

The conflict developed gradually. There were now two rival authorities in Protestantism. There was on the one hand the Reichsbishop and the ecclesiastical hierarchy, together with the assemblies which he had convoked and where he had assured himself of a majority. On the other hand there was the Confessional front which included all the opposition elements and which rested on the confessional evangelical synods and the Brotherhood Council.† The latter held that it was the sole legitimate authority in the church. The Reichsbishop acted through decrees which he issued by virtue of the plenary powers with which he was invested. His method was simple. Meeting with opposition in the national evangelical synod he assumed the right, by a decree of July 7, 1934, of purging the synod of all members who did not appear to him to show the desired guarantees of docility and he replaced them with "proved men of the church." He thus purged the synod of about twenty of its members and acquired a majority for his plans. These included unlimited power for the central authority, suppression of church emblems and flags and their replacement by the swastika, an oath of fidelity to the race doctrine to be demanded from all pastors, and the suppression of voting by the national synods, although discussion was permitted. The Reichsbishop was protected by Hitler even against the judgments of tribunals and complaints of bishops.

---

* In the spring of 1933 the orthodox and liberals in Prussia, who ordinarily fought each other in the church elections, published a common manifesto. At the same time, in May 1933, a reform movement was organized under the name of *Evangelium und Kirche*, which set up opposing lists to the German Christians in the church elections. It is in an appeal of this party that we find for the first time the formula "*Wir kämpfen für eine bekennende Kirche.*"

† The *Bruderrat* was designated as the directing council by the Confessional Synod of Berlin-Dahlem on October 24, 1934.

The Religious Problem

The resistance of the Confessional Protestants first took a legal form. They protested against the arbitrary acts of an authority whom they held to be illegal and whose measures they reported to the tribunals. But their resistance revealed itself in a particularly striking fashion along theological lines. This was the position taken by the celebrated Heidelberg professor, Karl Barth. Barth carefully refrained from making an attack on the National Socialist regime but he criticized in the most incisive manner the theology of his adversaries.* The opposition clergy, however, based their stand not only on the ground of law and theology: it was in the name of the Gospels that they rose against the violence committed by Hitlerism to the religious sentiment. In March, 1935, the Confessional Synod of the Evangelical Church held at Dahlem solemnly accused National Socialism "of setting up the myth of race and people, of making idols out of blood, race, nation, honor and liberty, in place of God, and of demanding, as a new religion, faith in eternal Germany and of wishing to supplant by this new faith the faith in the eternal realm of our Lord and Saviour Jesus Christ."

This conflict aroused immense confusion in the Protestant world. The administration proceeded against the recalcitrants with disciplinary measures, enforced retirements, dismissals, changes, etc. But they could scarcely succeed. The dismissed pastor, and with him his entire parish, held null and void any dismissal issued by an authority which they did not recognize. The pastor continued to minister to his parishioners, supported by the faithful who assured him his subsistence if his salary had been cut off and who found a meeting place for

* Karl Barth, Swiss-German theologian, is one of the leading figures in world Protestantism to-day. As a result of his refusal to take the oath to Hitler he was removed from his post in 1935. "I was a professor of theology in 1921 in Göttingen," says Barth, "and in Westphalia in 1925; then for ten years I was at Bonn University on the Rhine, until I refused to open my lectures on God each day by raising my arm and saying, 'Heil, Hitler!' I could not do that; it would have been blasphemy. And so I was compelled to come to Basle University." (*Manchester Guardian*, April 23, 1937).—*Ed.*

worship if he was driven from his church. The parish, more-over, refused to recognize the new pastor named by the central authority. There were countless trials before the tribunals to regulate these conflicts and in many parishes they no longer knew who was the real pastor.

The increase in the opposition movement was very great. At the end of 1934 it was estimated that out of 16,000 pastors there were scarcely 3,000 who had ranged themselves freely behind the banner of Bishop Müller while 13,000 others or more were won over to the ranks of the Confessional front or else observed an attitude of prudent expectancy. The situation thus became increasingly difficult for the Reichsbishop. He could not conceal the fact that he had been disavowed by the majority of Protestants and that he risked seeing the "Confessionals" constituting themselves as a dissenting church without ties to the government and in direct opposition to the central authority.

How could these disagreements, which the Evangelical Church was incapable of solving by its own means, be ironed out? Hitler thought that only the intervention of the state could bring about a solution. In June, 1935 he created an arbitration tribunal of the last resort for regulating any ordinary ecclesiastical litigations. He also designated Minister Kerrl as arbiter between the parties and gave him full powers to direct the affairs of the church. After having been allowed several months for reflection Kerrl appointed a Reich committee (*Reichskirchen-Ausschuss*) to deal with the necessary task of arbitration within the Reich and a series of regional committees (*Landeskirchen-Ausschüsse*) to which he entrusted the same mission in the various states, Prussia, Hesse, Saxony, etc. By the decree of December 2, 1935, moreover, he withdrew from "associations or church groups," i.e., the Brotherhood Councils of the Confessional churches, the right to name their pastors, to ordain and examine candidates for pastoral functions, to inspect parishes, to convoke synods, etc.

The Religious Problem

The decree no doubt allowed the Confessional church and its Brotherhood Councils to continue but it deprived them of all administrative power. The intention of National Socialism was to institute one "free" official church where all tendencies would have the chance and the right to defend freely their dogmatic point of view but where the pastors of all shades of opinion would recognize one single administrative authority emanating from the Reich committee and the regional committees.

It was quite doubtful whether this compromise would be acceptable to the representatives of the Confessional church. Minister Kerrl and his committees presented themselves as "arbiters" between conflicting parties in the Evangelical Church. But did these arbiters reveal the desired guarantees of impartiality? Nothing was less certain. Immediate protests accumulated against the appointment of the church commissars for the Reich, and it was not at all certain that the regional commissars would enjoy any great authority. Under these conditions this newly created "arbitral" authority encountered the same opposition which Bishop Müller had encountered. The adherents of the Confessional church had serious reasons to fear that in the church administration the Confessional tendency would be at a distinct disadvantage in comparison with the German Christians and the neutrals. They suspected that they might be progressively eliminated, if they would allow themselves to be deprived, without guarantees, of the prerogatives exercised provisionally by the Brotherhood Councils, which are direct offshoots of the community of the faithful. Certain moderate elements of the Confessional church such as the Bishop of Hanover, Marahrens, inclined, it is true, towards conciliation and offered their collaboration to the Reich committee, but they were disavowed by the majority of their co-religionists. Conflict has been proclaimed as inevitable by eminent personalities in confessional Protestantism, such as the pastor Dibelius, who calls upon his brethren to brave "martyrdom."*

Will this conflict result in a separation of church from state? It is said that Minister Kerrl held this threat over the opposition clergy in the hope of breaking down their resistance. This separation would, indeed, imply the immediate confiscation of all Protestant church property, the value of which is considerable. It is understood that the interested parties hesitate to allow a step fraught with such consequences to be taken. We may add that the Evangelical Church would find itself in serious financial difficulties, and separation would be contrary to the very spirit of Luther, who always desired an intimate alliance between temporal and spiritual authority. Above all, the separation would perpetuate a schism in the Evangelical Church. From then on there would be a state church and a dissenting church and this would create a most dangerous situation for the very idea of Protestantism.

One sees the gravity of the conflict. National Socialism declares that it is a *Weltanschaung* and not a religion, and it demands that every citizen loyally accept that concept. On

---

* Dr. Dibelius was formerly General Superintendent of the Lutheran Church in Prussia. In an open letter to Minister Kerrl, circulated in March, 1937, Dr. Dibelius said: "Let me ask you one question, Herr Reichsminister. If, in the morning's religious instruction, the children are told that the Bible is God's word that speaks to us in the Old and New Testaments and when, in the afternoon, young people have to memorize: 'Which is our Bible? our Bible is Hitler's *Mein Kampf*,' who is to change his doctrine here? This is the decisive point. When you demand that the Evangelical Church shall not be a state within a state, every Evangelical Christian will agree. The Church must be a church and not a state within the state. But the doctrine which you proclaim would have the effect of making the state into the Church in so far as the state, supported by its coercive powers, comes to decisions with regard to the sermons that are preached and the faith that is confessed. Here lies the root of the whole struggle between the state and the Evangelical Church. The struggle will never come to an end as long as the state does not recognise its own frontiers . . . Hitler's state can count on the service of Evangelical Christians . . . but as soon as the state endeavors to become Church and assume power over the souls of men . . . then are we bound by Luther's word to offer resistance in God's name. And that is what we shall do." (Reported in the *Manchester Guardian*, March 12, 1937).—*Ed.*

the other hand it claims that this concept is in no way opposed to the Christian idea and it intends to remain within the Evangelical Church. Above all, it has put its hand upon the government of the church and rules it with the aid of bishops and committees as it sees fit. The Confessional Protestants defend themselves as best they can against this seizure. They reject as unholy the "corrections" which the Nazis have made in traditional Christianity. They insist that *Wotanized* Christianity is no longer Christianity and that German Christians in rallying without reservation to the racialist doctrine have banished themselves from the community of the faithful. Finally, they refuse obedience to ecclesiastical superiors who do not, in their eyes, represent the community of the faithful but who were imposed from without the church by the political authorities.

Between these two points of view conciliation is difficult and no compromise has as yet been found which should satisfy one or the other. The disadvantageous position of the Confessionals is apparent. Their opponents occupy the dominant position in the church and it seems at present difficult to dislodge them from this position. But the threat of persecution has given renewed vigor to the impulse of the opposition clergy to resist the attacks of the Nazis, who display their customary fanaticism even in the domain of religion. Future events alone can settle the matter. The Nazis are confident of success. They have the youth with them, they contend, who will follow them with enthusiasm. If the Confessionals remain obstinate in their resistance, say the Nazis, they will find their churches deserted and they will see the youth disappear over the horizon following the banner of Hitler. The real question lies in the power which traditional faith exercises today over the new generations. Summoned to choose, will the youth go towards Christ, towards Wotan or towards a Wotanized Christ? That is all. The importance of the decision which the responsible leaders of Protestantism are going to make is keenly appreciated by everyone.*

2. The Crisis in the Catholic World

The situation in the Catholic Church was less critical at first than that in the Evangelical Church. Hitler, in fact, hastened to conclude a Reich Concordat with the Roman Curia on July 20, 1933 (ratified on September 10), which confirmed the Concordats previously made by Bavaria in 1924, by Prussia in 1929 and by Baden in 1932. The Catholic episcopate immediately abandoned the wary attitude which it had adopted toward National Socialism in the beginning. A declaration of the Bishops at Fulda expressly proclaimed: "We shall no longer consider it necessary to continue those admonitions and defensive measures which we took at a time when there was just anxiety regarding the maintenance of the integrity of the Catholic faith and the safeguarding of the indefeasible rights of the Church." The bishops endeavoured to live on good terms with the new regime. They loyally attempted the experiment of conciliation in the hope of sparing their followers embarrassment and persecution. They were undeniably in a better position than the Protestants. The Catholic clergy was not subjected to the same oath of allegiance which was exacted from the Protestants, the formula of which placed loyalty to Christ and loyalty to the *Führer* on the same plane. No bishops were suspended. The Church was not subjected to the interference of arrogant commissars nor to the authority of a Reichsbishop. It was never threatened from within by the development of a Germanic Chris-

* Since this section was written the Reich Church Commission for the administration of the Protestant Church, under the chairmanship of Superintendent Wilhelm Zoellner, resigned in protest against the high-handed manner of Minister Kerrl. All the efforts of the latter toward solving the conflicts in the Protestant Church failed and Chancellor Hitler ordered new church elections and stripped Kerrl of most of his powers. These elections were postponed several times.—*Ed.*

tianity. It always remained intact and autonomous in its organization. It had the immense advantage of obedience to a head situated outside the sphere of the National Socialist government and having as its charter a concordat which guaranteed to it by treaty its essential rights.

Hitler had no reason for raising an issue against the Roman church: this he had always condemned as grave political imprudence. The Catholics have often suspected him of entertaining the idea of unifying the Catholic and Protestant faiths or of favoring the development of a Germanic Catholicism free of all attachments to Rome. I see no reason why Hitler should feel impelled to make such a move. All such attempts up to the present have failed. It was in his interest, on the contrary, to compromise with Catholicism,—in any case up to the time the Saar question was regulated,—for the attitude of the clergy could have had a very great influence on the results of the plebiscite.

It is none the less true that despite the external truce there was a latent hostility between Catholicism and National Socialism. There had always been a very clear antagonism between Hitler and the Catholic Centre Party, which he considered responsible for the mistakes of the Weimar regime and which he accused of having made common cause with the Socialists and of having co-operated with the bolshevists against nationalist Germany. The Catholic Centre Party, however, was not to be identified with Catholicism. The Centre Party, at the peak of its success, never gathered round its standard more than 5 million voters while the Catholic population numbered 21 million in 1935. Despite this, however, there is a strong bond between the Catholic Centre Party and the faith, so much so that National Socialism has carried over a good part of the hate which it has for the party to the Catholic religion. These suspicions were stirred up by the fact that in the plebiscite of August 19, 1934 it was the "black" Rhineland which delivered the greatest number of opponents to the regime. Whereas, for example, at Koenigsberg, the proportion of negative votes to affirmative votes was about 1 to 25, in Cologne it was 1 to 4 and in Aix La Chapelle it was almost 1 to 2. Under these circumstances the Catholics soon felt themselves the object of a growing mistrust. They were watched and spied on. Every priest was a suspect traitor. Any militant layman who was a member of the Catholic Action risked his position and the upkeep for his family. Positive Catholics were systematically eliminated from the administration and particularly from the educational system.

Let us survey the principle points concerning which there were conflicts between the Catholics and the Nazis. One of the difficulties which recurred most often was in respect to the laws of sterilization. The National Socialists deemed it intolerable that ecclesiastics who, in accordance with the Concordat, had promised to respect the laws of the Reich, allowed themselves to condemn a measure which the government considered so essential for the protection of the race. On their side the Catholics, basing their stand on article 32 of the Concordat which granted the priests the right to teach publicly "the doctrines and the precepts of the Church not only as relating to dogmas but also to morals," declared that it was inadmissible for the National Socialists to prevent Catholics from holding as untenable a law contrary to the teachings of the Church and condemned by divine law. From that they inferred that the German state cannot prevent either the clergy or the lay Catholics from showing their convictions regarding the law of sterilization and acting according to their conscience.

The conflict was even more serious on the question of education. It is well known with what energy National Socialism claims the right to mold the spirit of the children by education and instruction. "The youth belongs to us," said Goebbels at Essen on August 4, 1935, "and we will yield them up to no one." But on this point he comes into conflict with the equally absolute claim of the clergy to maintain its hold on the spirit and the soul of the youth. The Catholic Church is able to find support for this point in the Concordat which guarantees the maintenance of confessional schools and which in article 31 declares that Catholic organizations "should be protected in their institutions and their activity." National Socialism is at bottom hostile to this privilege. We have seen above the fierceness with which the representatives of Germanism demand a single school for all. Since the terms of the Concordat render impossible the suppression of confessional schools, they insist at least that every one devoting himself to education be strictly obliged to observe not only a negative neutrality with respect to state institutions but to support the regime positively in all respects. They rage pitilessly against any one who disregards this injunction. They do not conceal their satisfaction each time they are able, on one point or another, to register a check to confessional education. Still more aggressive is the campaign waged to enroll the Catholic youth into the *Hitler-Jugend*. The Concordat forbids the suppression of Catholic associations, but the Nazis do everything in the world to make the young enroll in the Hitler Youth. Catholic organizations have been forbidden to wear uniforms or insignia, they are not allowed to have standards or music, to carry on sport activities or to make group excursions. For them that whole external and corporate life which has so much attraction for the young German has been forbidden. The young Catholic, faithful to his association, is condemned to lead the solitary life of a semi-pariah, happy when he is not treated by his Nazi comrades as a renegade and traitor to Germanism and is not insulted or beaten. The Catholics have made every effort to maintain their associations, for they realize the danger for their flocks of contamination by the "pagan" surroundings of the Nazi associations. The Catholic associations have suffered considerable loss in strength, more in certain regions than in others, although in the associations of young girls they have held their ground nearly everywhere.

Catholic propaganda, either from the pulpit or through the press, has also met with more and more serious obstacles. Have Catholics, under the pretext of defending their religion and moral principles, carried on polemics against the acts of the government and laws of the state, and asserted their opposition to the totalitarian idea of National Socialism? This in any case is the thesis of the Nazi leaders. They accuse them of organizing "by means of hitherto unknown propaganda grand processions and church festivals which really are political demonstrations." Göring, in his famous circular of July 15, 1935, wrote: "It has come to the point where Catholic believers carry away but one impression from attendance at divine services and that is that the Catholic Church rejects the institutions of the National Socialist state. How could it be otherwise when they are continuously engaging in polemics on political questions or events in their sermons! In certain regions hardly a Sunday passes but that they abuse the so-called religious atmosphere of the divine service in order to read pastoral letters on purely political subjects." In reply to what they consider to be "provocations," the National Socialists have multiplied the trials for abuse of the pulpit, they have muzzled the Catholic press, censored or stopped bishops' letters, even suspending the little weekly or diocesan religious bulletins. In the Catholic world information has come to depend on typewritten sheets which circulate under cover or on oral communication by trusted emissaries.

Catholicism, moreover, has been hit in its material interests. It is easy to understand why some Catholic individuals might have thought that under the present circumstances it might be wise for certain religious organizations or establishments to take a part of their possessions out of Germany. How many capitalists have not at one time or another practiced the "flight of capital?" It is not glorious, it is not patriotic. All that can be said is that this is an offense which has been frequently committed by people of standing as well as by innumerable speculators. In Germany it is dealt with under the very rigorous provisions of the exchange laws. The government had to act forcefully against the religious groups who attempted to export capital illegally. Prosecution was carried out with exceptional severity against the most diverse kinds of people, beginning with church members, nuns and convent superiors up to university professors. Even the Bishop of Meissen was arrested on October 10, 1935 and confined in the Moabit prison. The sentences which were pronounced were undoubtedly legal, but from a human point of view it was startling to see severe prison sentences inflicted on religious individuals who probably never had a clear idea of the crime they were committing and who, very certainly, did not act because of any personal interest. The huge fines inflicted have also led many to wonder if the state in this way did not really aim to despoil the property of the religious corporations in Germany.

The reaction of the Catholics was rather slow in coming. It was only towards the end of 1933 that attention was attracted to the preachings of Cardinal Faulhaber at Munich, which were stigmatized by the Nazis as defiance of the regime. In 1934 there appeared the pastoral letters of the Cardinal of Cologne, of the bishops of Berlin, Münster and Ermeland, and of the Archbishop of Freiburg, which denounced the persecutions in which Catholics were the principal victims. In 1935, after the Saar settlement, the conflict became more heated. With increasing bitterness the National Socialists complained of the attitude of the clergy, who under cover of religion were attempting to make anti-Nazi propaganda and were in this way reviving Centrist tendencies. They declared that they would crush this resistance and smite without mercy all those whom Goebbels called "priest politicians" and whom they openly accused of collusion with Marxists and Jews. On July 15, 1935, Prussian Prime Minister Göring addressed a circular letter to the administrative and police authorities ordering them to prosecute with all the rigor of the law any political activity of the clergy or of the Catholic organizations. The tone adopted by the minister was one of extraordinary violence. After indicating that he had no intention of unloosing another *Kulturkampf*, he plainly stated that National Socialism will never tolerate the revival of Centrist aspirations and that he would fight the aspirants even if they hid themselves under the cloak of religious activity. Protected by the state which guarantees it the integrity of its institutions, the Catholic Church "does not have the right to invoke God against the state, a monstrosity which we witness every Sunday, nor to organize political formations under the pretext that it is defending itself against a danger which it pretends to find in the state." After a diatribe against the subversive activities of priests, Göring concluded with the threat to suppress all youth organizations which meddle in politics and called for the active co-operation of administrative and judicial authorities of state and party to put an end to this intolerable situation.

This time the reply came directly from Rome. Following another aggressive speech of Minister Frick, the *Osservatore romano* complained in measured but clear terms of the unfortunate situation of the German Catholics, which was incompatible with the assurances given by the Chancellor. On August 3, the *Osservatore* heightened its tone and wrote: "It is intolerable that in a country under a Concordat a high state functionary should publicly insult the supreme head of the Catholic Church and abuse his power in order to carry on an anti-Christian campaign. It is intolerable that after promising in the Concordat friendship and protection for the Catholic Church they should permit this same Church to be attacked by the supreme dictator of German culture and education. It is intolerable that they should make an appeal to the Concordat at the same time that they preserve an attitude contrary to the Concordat. It is intolerable that they should remind the Church of the engagements into which it had entered and which it had loyally observed and at the same time take unilateral action such as the law of sterilization or the exclusion of Catholic organizations from all activity." The article then concluded: "The *Kulturkampf* in Germany is no longer, unfortunately, a danger for the future. Thanks to Rosenberg and his allies, it is a tragic reality of the present."

Thus we see that the situation in the religious domain has tended toward extreme tension and it may at one moment or another lead to serious complications. It is scarcely probable that Hitler himself desires a violent conflict. In his speech to the National Socialist Congress at Nuremberg on September 11, 1935 he spoke with great vigor against what he called "political confessionalism," i.e., the intrusion of the clergy into the domain of politics. Recalling that he had crushed the Centre party and chased from power the "political clergy" at a time when he had not yet possessed governmental power, now that he had that power, he added, he would not tolerate the resurrection of a clergy which attempted to meddle in affairs of politics. He would resolutely oust those priests who failed in their vocation and in place of being pastors of souls, had become politicians. He concluded by emphasizing that the real danger for the church as well as for society was bolshevism. If bolshevism triumphed it would soon sweep away the thirty evangelical churches as well as Catholic Centrism. Hitler again insisted on the fact that he had never entertained any idea of a conflict with Christianity and that he continued to hold the Christian religion and the ancient idea of the state as the two fundamental elements of German spiritual evolution.

Many of the party leaders surrounding Hitler, however, are firmly convinced that serious conflict between the churches and National Socialism is inevitable. One might judge the violence of their tone by the following quotation from a book by Arthur Dinter: "The Judeo-Roman Church cannot, without denying itself, abandon the struggle against National Socialism. It tends completely towards the dream of a divine state established on an international basis, within which, under the authority of the so-called representative of God on earth, i.e., the Roman Pope, there would be imposed upon the entire humanity those unhealthy Judaic-Pauline myths. In place of this National Socialism proposes to realize practically in the German National state of Adolf Hitler the positive Christianity, i.e., the pure doctrine of Jesus. From this follows the hatred of the Judeo-Roman church which ardently desires to tear down an intolerable rival."

Might the collision perhaps be avoided or adjourned? There appear to be some moderates among the Nazis and even among the smaller group of leaders who have not abandoned this hope. Among the ministers, men like Schacht, Blomberg and Neurath, for diverse reasons, counsel against pushing things to the breaking point. There are also conciliating elements both among Catholics and Protestants who do not aspire to martyrdom and who would not reject a compromise. At Nuremberg, however, Hitler made concessions to the radical elements of his party, particularly on the Jewish question. He has given free rein to the extremists who rave against the priest politicians, who proclaim that the enemies of Germany are "Judea and Rome," who accuse the clerics of being in league with the bolshevists and who "threaten to reopen the old case" and divulge the separatist activities of the Centre Party after 1918. The possibility of a new *Kulturkampf* is not at all excluded and it occupies the attention of the more far-sighted leaders of the German Catholics. What reaction will the Germans exhibit in such an eventuality? It is difficult to foresee. All that may be said is that the religious domain represents an

214

undeniable source of fermentation which might cause serious embarrassment to the Nazi regime.*

* On March 21, 1937 the Pope issued an encyclical on Germany, which was read from Catholic pulpits in Germany. It represented the first direct papal intervention in the Nazi-Catholic Controversy. The Pope accused the Nazis of violating the terms of the Concordat and declared: "With pressure veiled and open, with intimidation, with promises of economic, professional, civil and other advantages, the attachment of Catholics, especially of certain classes of Catholic government employees, to faith is exposed to violence as illegal as it is inhuman.

"With paternal emotion, we feel and suffer profoundly with those who have paid such a great price for their attachment to Christ and to the Church; but the point has now been reached where there is a question of the final and highest end, of salvation or of perdition, and therefore the only way to salvation for the believer is that of generous heroism."—*Ed.*

BOOK VII

Agricultural and Industrial Organization

VII. *Agricultural and Industrial Organization*

1. Nazi Economics

NATIONAL Socialism has undertaken as its goal the total refashioning of bourgeois society. We shall not attempt to treat here of the place of Nazi doctrines in the general history of social thought. We shall simply indicate in summary fashion some of the fundamental tendencies of the social measures undertaken by the Nazis and then see how these tendencies are manifested in the two great domains of human activity, agriculture and industry.

National Socialism adheres to the system of capitalism in that it admits of private property, recognizes the utility of competition and attempts to achieve a maximum of individual achievement (*Leistung*). It retains at the head of every business and industry entrepreneurs who assume the risks, manage their enterprises as best they can and collect the profits or make good the losses according to the good or bad fortune which they had in the management of their affairs. The Nazis consider it essential to maintain competition among these entrepreneurs in order that the weak may be eliminated and only the most fit survive. Likewise among the workers, artisans and peasants, National Socialism allows for the play of emulation. This assures material advantages to the individual who makes the best use of his particular talents, carries them to the highest development and makes them yield a maximum of useful results.

Although Hitler allows for competition he does not, however, want unlimited competition. He sets up the principle of "general welfare before individual welfare." Competition is useful only in so far as it shows itself favorable to the general interest. As soon as it becomes a principle of destruction Hitler condemns it and fights it. Not for a moment would Hitler consider the idea of allowing the peasant class to disappear because the German farmer is unable to withstand the competition of the new countries across the sea. He admits neither the master's right to exploit the worker nor conversely the worker's right to ruin the master by excessive demands. In the same way he attempts to draw a clear line of demarcation between fair and unfair competition, the latter being a condition where one attempts to ruin his competitor by unfair or malicious practices.

For the principle of the struggle of classes, organized in an anarchic multiplicity of unions arrayed against one another, Hitler wishes to substitute one single corporate and professional organization. This organization is to suppress useless friction and injurious conflicts between the various social groups and is to teach the workers and the employers the difficult art of harmonious co-operation in the enterprise for the general welfare of the community.

The ideal goal towards which National Socialism aims is the autonomous administration (*Selbstverwaltung*) of business in all fields. This autonomy is to be organized, however, not on a democratic but on an authoritarian plan. This means that power shall never be exercised by a majority group; it should be delegated at all stages of the social hierarchy to individuals, who are not named by an electoral college, but who impose themselves upon the choice of the masses by the superiority of their abilities and are responsible not to their subordinates but to their immediate superior. Under such conditions, and particularly during the transition period necessary to effect the education which will teach the various social groups the art of free collaboration, the authority of the leaders at the top is very considerable. In fact Germany lives today under a dictatorial regime where the *Führer*, through the intervention of his direct representatives, the Ministers of Agriculture, Economics and Finance, and of his trusted advisers, exerts an almost unlimited power as *organizer* of the new society, as *animator* in the "battle of production" and the "battle of employment" which are to heal the crisis in which the country found itself at the advent of National Socialism, and as *arbiter* between the various social groups.

2. Agricultural Organization

From the first day National Socialism came to power it affirmed its interest in the protection of agriculture. In the program of February 1, 1933, we find the express stipulation that "in the period of four years the German peasant would be freed from the misery in which he is steeped." Eight months later in his speech of October 1, 1933, Hitler declared that "the ruination of the German peasant would be the ruination of the German people." A ruined artisan class might conceivably regenerate itself; a middle class reduced to misery might one day recover its affluence; industry reduced to nothing might rehabilitate itself through its own efforts; a town pauperized and depopulated might conceivably raise itself to new prosperity. But the peasant driven from his land disappears forever as a peasant and it is impossible to bring about the rebirth of a peasant class after it has been allowed to disappear. The peasant not only assures the nation of its daily bread; he is the guarantor of its future and provides a people with force, health, equilibrium and endurance.

The German peasant was particularly hard hit by the world crisis through no fault of his own. For a long time unable to maintain competition with the new countries where land is cheaper and where agriculture has been mechanized, he was on the road to ruin because of the tremendous decline in prices of agricultural products. Despite all the repeated protective measures undertaken in his behalf by the former governments the peasant sank more and more into debt and was unable to sell his products at a profit. It was necessary to come to his aid if he was to continue to supply the country with the quantity of grain, vegetables, milk and meat which were needed for nourishment. The previous aid given to agriculture was based upon the maintenance of large estates, especially in the east, and there had been notorious scandals in connection with these which had contributed much to the increasing confusion of the previous years. The measures undertaken by National Socialism were inspired by quite different considerations.

The Nazis first attempted to group the entire peasant class into one vast and centralized corporate organization at the head of which was placed the leader of the peasantry (*Reichsbauernführer*), and of which Hitler himself became the patron. This vast work of reorganization was begun on April 4, 1933 by a commission which brought together the principal previously existing agricultural groups. It pursued its work with redoubled vigor after the resignation of Hugenberg and the appointment of Darré as Minister of Agriculture for both the Reich and Prussia. The corporate organization of agriculture into the *Reichsnährstand* and the *Stand der deutschen Landwirtschaft* was a tremendous task. It was necessary first of all to set up with care the limitations of the agricultural "sector." This comprised not only production of grain, fruits, vegetables, cattle, milk, etc., but extended also to trade in skins, hides and fish, the mineral water industry and the manufacture of mayonnaise, and to organized industries like those of margarine, sugar, chocolate, biscuits, canned foods, beer, sparkling wines, frigorifics, etc. In order to fuse these different divisions of the sector into the framework of a single organization, it was necessary to do away with hundreds of existing groups and undertake an immense job of adaptation. In most essentials this task has already been achieved.

With this accomplished, Hitler then attempted, by the law regarding hereditary domains, or *Erbhöfe*, (May 15 and September 29, 1933), to consolidate the position of the peasant class by establishing a category of stable middle-sized peasant proprietors, bound to the soil and possessing farms as large as 125 hectares,—i.e. enough for the maintenance of one family, and not big enough to constitute an estate of capitalist exploitation. An *Erbhof* of this type becomes the material center of a family tradition. It cannot be divided and it passes on to only one heir. The latter attaches to his name the name of the domain and thus becomes in a certain way the manager of an estate which is the inalienable apanage of his family, and which the individual cannot dispose of at his own will. He cannot sell or divide up the land except with the authorization of a special tribunal, the *Erbhofsgericht*. There are in Germany about 845,000 holdings which belong to this category and they comprise about 44 per cent of the arable land. About 700,000 of these holdings can become hereditary holdings. These family holdings may be held only by Germans of pure race, Jews and colored people being excluded. The National Socialists think that in this way they can bind the peasant more firmly to the soil while building up in him an attachment to the aristocratic family tradition as well as the sentiment of national and historical solidarity.

Another set of measures aimed to protect the peasant from the operation of the law of supply and demand. These measures fixed a minimum price for agricultural products, and above all for grain, and thus assured the producer the sale of his products at an equitable price. This price is determined by the agricultural organizations and the government. Freed from the bonds which enslaved him to the capitalist system, the worker in the fields is no longer to be an agricultural *entrepreneur* like the American farmer but a genuine *peasant* invested with a social function, which implies not only rights but also duties. It is necessary that the peasant manage his land in an honest and economical fashion; it is necessary that he learn to adapt his production to the needs of national consumption; it is necessary that he feel conscious of the solidarity between the city and the country. Supported by the sacrifices made in his favor by the community, he, in turn, is to work for the benefit of the community and not alone for his own egotistical advantage.

This also represented a considerable task of organization. The Nazis began by regulating the sale of grain—first of wheat and rye, then also of oats and barley. Then they decided not only upon minimum prices but upon fixed prices, with variations for region and season. From then on every producer has not only the right but also the duty of bringing into the market a fixed quantity of products at fixed times. All the intermediaries between the producer and the consumer, the grain merchants, the millers, the flour dealers, the bakers, etc., are likewise forced to observe the fixed prices and to sell fixed quantities of products for consumption. The producers and middle men are organized into one syndicate, the *Hauptvereinigung der deutschen Getreidewirtschaft*. If there is an excess or a deficit the grain office or *Reichs-getreidestelle* intervenes; it assigns the stocks and places in circulation the existing supply and it alone has the power to import or export the quantities of cereal necessary in order to assure the balance between production and consumption. Little by little almost all the branches of the agricultural sector have been organized in the same way as grain. Milk, butter, cattle, margarine, sugar and fish have been organized along the same lines.

The measures taken by the Nazis aim to realize as far as possible the autarchy of the Reich in food supplies. Germany, however, has never been able to produce the entire volume of products necessary to feed her population. It is estimated that in 1934, for example, she lacked about 20 per cent of the total number of calories necessary. The shortage was mainly in fats, albuminous foods and fodder. Before the war this deficit had been made up by considerable annual imports. Then the deficit decreased. For while the economic crisis made it necessary for Germany to restrict imports, by protective measures she made a considerable increase in the volume of her production. It is estimated that for the period between 1924 and 1934 this increase amounted to 30 per cent. In a speech in October, 1935, Goebbels stated that imports which until lately had amounted to two and a half billion marks had dropped to about a billion.

The need to make up this shortage still remained, however. It did not amount to very much in an exceptional year like 1933, but the shortage became considerable in 1934 when the crop yield was bad and in 1935 when it was merely average. The shortage appeared acute, moreover, because between 1933 and 1935 the unemployment crisis had been mitigated and the purchasing power of the workers and their expenses for food had somewhat increased. There were also the labor camps and the larger army, which increased the demand for food.

The increased shortage came at a most inopportune time for, as a result of the financial crisis and the scarcity of foreign exchange, it was necessary to reduce imports to a minimum. This was all the more serious because it was necessary at all costs to import the most essential materials to keep the factories going and insure rearmament. For this reason food imports had to be reduced to a minimum. The Nazis thus had to choose between two alternatives: either to reduce imports of raw materials and thus risk aggravating unemployment and retarding the re-equipment of the army—or to reduce imports of necessities, which would involve difficulties of subsistence. The choice of the Nazi government was never in doubt.

Without hesitation it pronounced itself in favor of the second alternative. In 1935, therefore, there were many difficulties in satisfying the demand for foodstuffs. There was a scarcity of fruits and vegetables and prices rose considerably. In the spring certain regions had difficulty in the apportionment of beef; toward the middle of the summer the supply of eggs was insufficient; in the fall and in the early winter there was a shortage in fats and pork. The members of the government multiplied their exhortations for discipline, patience and resignation. Germany, the propagandists repeated everywhere, will submit with good will to a few privations in order to be able to continue the "employment battle" and complete the re-equipment of the army. She will not capitulate before the ordeal of food restrictions.

The Nazis also ran afoul of a new phase in the "battle of production." In the beginning the Nazis had been concerned with protecting the living of the peasant by assuring him, through price regulation, a sufficient return for his work. Now it became the principal concern of the leaders to realize the greatest possible yield from the soil. This was necessary in order to reduce imports to a minimum.

This ultimate reduction of imports is not altogether impossible. There are "reserves" in Germany that can be utilized. Out of the three million small or middle-sized agricultural holdings there are comparatively few that are managed in the latest technical manner. The great majority of the peasants work with obsolete, unimproved methods. Since they are not stimulated by the incentive of competition, they readily allow themselves to drop into routine farming. When the yield is bad they prefer to stint themselves rather than make an effort to better their production. They lack the necessary technical information. They are, moreover, conservative, slow to accept new ways and mistrustful of trained agriculturists. Progress in agricultural technique is, in most cases, fairly slow. But time pressed on and if the Nazi rulers desired to mobilize rapidly all the latent reserves they could overlook nothing to further the maximum development.

On the other hand the Nazi leaders refused on principle to institute a general plan for agricultural production. They wanted to leave to the peasant the responsibility of freely exploiting his land. The collective agriculture as practiced in Russia is repugnant to them. All they can do is to exercise a certain pressure on the peasant in order to shake off his apathy and provide him with the necessary improvements to insure a better yield.

The solution of the problem involved the following considerations. The grain crop in normal times is almost sufficient. But there is a great shortage of fodder (Germany produces only 50 per cent of her consumption needs), in albuminous foods (a shortage of 20 per cent) and in textiles (hemp, linen, wool). It was therefore a question of seeing how this shortage could be made up or reduced. They had to determine what areas could be utilized for various types of cultivation, by what methods they could be exploited, what were the indispensable expenditures for new installations (e.g. for the construction of silos for fodder) and what modifications would have to be made in the organization of work in the various regions of Germany in order to obtain the desired results.

Various plans were suggested to accomplish this. They attempted, first, to set up in each region a general staff of model peasants, or *Fachbauern*, who would direct the "battle of production" and would be charged with giving advice to their colleagues. While the peasant generally mistrusted the advice of a graduate engineer he would willingly consent to hear what a neighbor would tell him about his experiments.

Then they attempted to make an appeal to the pride of the peasants. They instituted inspections of the holdings, fields and stables, following which the peasants received certificates according to the progress realized. Eventually there were also awards of prizes and distinctions. They thus established competition between the peasants of the same village and between groups of peasants of various regions.

Finally, they adopted certain forceful measures to increase the yield. They contemplate imposing a small number of types of seed for sowing, which have been developed in the experimental laboratories. At the same time they do not allow any but the best known types of animals to be used in breeding. They plan also to organize obligatory control of milch cows. This has yielded some excellent results among certain groups of dairymen, and if applied to all the cattle it would lead, they believe, to an appreciable increase in the yield.

The situation did not undergo any essential modifications during the course of the year 1936. There was fear for a time that there would be a serious crop shortage for that year. According to the most recent estimates, however, there will have been some improvement, as compared with 1935, in grain and fodder accompanied by a considerable decrease in live-stock, which declined from 3430 million tons to 1730 million. The pressing exhortations addressed to the peasants at the end of the year to assure the stipulated deliveries of grain leave room for suspicion that there was reason to fear failure. In other respects the crop appears to have been good. The crop of potatoes, especially, increased from 41 to 45.72 million tons. Revenue from agriculture increased and in 1936 there were close to two billion marks more in receipts than the figures showed for 1932-33. This situation allowed the agricultural groups to make various technical improvements to intensify production. The development of agricultural machinery has been particularly marked and expenditures for such purposes rose from 84 million marks in 1934 to 240 million in 1936.

In what measure has the German peasant shown recognition for the solicitude of the Nazis for him? It is difficult to say with certainty. Skeptical observers maintain that the German peasant at bottom has a horror of all that smacks of regimentation and blunt meddling in his affairs. They aver that for some time he has been applying himself systematically to evading the official regulations. Rather than yield to the injunctions of Nazi officials he is said to have reduced the land sowed, to have given false information on the condition of his crops, to have slaughtered more of his cattle than necessary, and to have practiced "retrenchment" in secret in order to sell his products at a higher price to clandestine buyers rather than to bring them on the legal market at the official price. In what measure is this little war between peasant and the authorities a reality or in what measure has it been invented or exaggerated by the enemies of the present regime? A foreigner is not able to venture a reasonable opinion on this question. All that can be stated is that for a number of essential products the crops of 1935 were less than the average for the six years before. There have been renewed food difficulties in the cities and the clandestine buyer, who buys up food necessities in the country, has again made his appearance in Germany just as during the war. Can one infer from these facts that the harmony between peasants and Nazis is not as perfect as the party organs pretend? We shall confine ourselves merely to posing the question without definitely answering it.

In general Germany does not and never will cover all her consumption needs. The importation of foodstuffs, however, which in 1936 remained at almost the same figure as for the preceding year, did not exceed 1370 millions for the first eleven months of 1936. Can one say that under these conditions Germany is suffering privation? One must guard against exaggerations on both sides. It certainly is absurd to say that the German population is lacking in everything and that people are dying of starvation as during the World War. It is no less absurd to pretend that the Germans are living in plenty and lack nothing. I am also very skeptical of the thesis of certain very ingenious critics who aver that the government

itself has manipulated the privation in Germany by storing up
supplies for the army and by secret sales abroad. This, they
say, the government has done in order to provoke resentment
among the masses against foreign powers, who by their policy
of encirclement are held responsible for having brought into
effect an economic blockade.

On the whole, if one can believe the testimony of unbiased
observers, the food situation for the German people is, except
for certain trifles, almost identical with that of France. The
bread is poor because it is necessary to mix a certain quantity
of rye flour with the wheat flour. But Switzerland also has a
regime of "federal bread" despite which she is not very badly
off. There is a sufficient quantity of bread in Germany and
it has not been necessary to introduce bread cards. There is,
however, a definite scarcity of fats. As of January, 1936, no
one can obtain fats unless he is on a customers list (*Kunden-
liste*) and beginning in February, cards for fats were distributed among a certain number of families. The government
officially announced its intention to reduce consumption of
fats by 25 per cent. There are also certain difficulties in assuring sufficient supplies of meat and meat consumption has
declined considerably. Eggs are also scarce. In general these
represent only small discomforts which cannot lead to serious
disturbances of the national life.

3. Industrial Organization

Let us now pass from agriculture to industry. We will first
see how National Socialism distinguishes itself from the economic "liberalism" to which it is opposed. The old order, say
the Nazis, rests on the idea of the struggle of classes and on
unlimited competition. The head of an enterprise and the
worker always stand opposed to each other like two antag-
onistic forces constantly in a state of war. The entrepreneur
is free to make arrangements with his workers as he pleases.

Working conditions are discussed privately and depend on the scarcity or abundance of labor on the one hand and the business orders on the other. If the workers are dissatisfied they can go on strike and conversely the owner has recourse to a lockout or he may close his plant. On both sides there are powerful organizations which zealously defend the respective interests of the worker who wishes to better his lot, and the employer who wishes to reduce wages as much as possible in order to lower his net costs.

These organizations are agencies of conflict and their role is to organize the class struggle. The government, in theory, has nothing to say even if it is persuaded that the employer is exploiting his workers or that the workers by their unreasonable demands are threatening to ruin the business. In practice, however, the state has been led to intervene wherever there was conflict. It passed laws for the protection of the worker, which forbade the grosser kinds of exploitation; it regulated the working conditions of women and children; it fixed a maximum working day of eight hours. It also instituted arbitration between the two opposing parties. In case there was a dispute between employer and workers, the conflict was brought before the arbitration board and this board attempted to bring about a compromise. These various measures mitigated the divergencies but did not suppress the battle which flared up at every turn. There was no end of charges and counter charges. The workers defended with all their energy "the conquests of the revolution" against their employers. On the side of the employers some maintained that as a result of the action of the arbitration boards and by indulging in blackmail and calling strikes the organized trade union workers had really become a privileged group who made use of the fear which they inspire to exact more pay for their work than they merited, thus exploiting the community.

The fundamental principle of National Socialism is that the class struggle is absurd and criminal. An industrial enterprise

231

forms an indissoluble whole to which both employer and workers ought to give their entire devotion. Far from being rivals, they are all soldiers of the selfsame army of labor, merely occupying different positions in the hierarchy. In a military regiment there is no antagonism between officer and soldier. Each knows very well that he cannot do without the other. The fact that one commands and the other obeys is not sufficient to impair the effectiveness of their relations. The German in particular voluntarily accepts commands if he feels that he is being *well* commanded. He obeys a leader who knows his business and who works for the common good. The great cause of disagreement in the field of industry in most cases, say the Nazis, is the capitalist profiteer who comes between the leader and the "soldier." This profiteer, moreover, is often of an alien race.

The necessity for maintaining private property and individual initiative is one of the fundamental axioms of the Nazi movement. It was proclaimed by Feder in the early period of the party. It was confirmed by repeated declarations by the *Führer* and his ministers. It was particularly emphasized by the Minister of Economics, Kurt Schmitt, in his speech of March 13, 1934. In that speech Schmitt asserted that it was not his intention to destroy the variety and multiplicity of German economic life. National Socialism too has need of the independent producer whose existence is inextricably bound up with that of his establishment. He who directs a business should have the responsibility for it. If he manages it well it is legitimate for him to derive personal profit from it. If he does not manage it well, it is no more than right that he suffer for it and not be able to shift on to others the consequences of his mistakes or make the workers or society bear his losses. The competition between rival businesses is necessary and fruitful. It is an indispensable condition for the attainment of a "maximum of production" through healthy emulation. In his speech of May 17, 1934, Hitler also declared that it is impossible to abolish the egotism of the individual who endeavors to raise himself to a better condition of living by increasing his "output." The only thing necessary is to ennoble this egotism by proper education, to inculcate the spirit that this egotism is not an end in itself but only a means, that private welfare should always give way before the general welfare and that superiority of output also implies an obligation towards the community.

This kind of harmonious co-operation between employer and worker cannot be realized in one day. In his *Mein Kampf* Hitler insists on the need for educating both sides. It is necessary for the employer to get rid of his arrogance and learn to respect manual labor. The worker, on the other hand, must free himself from the feeling of envy and become more conscious of his own value. In an age of unceasing progress, where the tempo of production is being constantly speeded up, where greater skill is always necessary in order to remain "at the top," it is important that the worker, through systematic professional training, acquire that pleasure in the accomplishment of his task which will give him a feeling of ownership and a consciousness of his own worth. It is necessary, finally, that workers and owners in every factory learn to collaborate in joint committees in which the entrepreneur co-operates with men who possess the confidence of the workers. On the day when the consciousness of the solidarity between employer and worker will have been sufficiently developed, the enterprise itself will regulate the conditions of work, each according to its capacities. The owner will have no more idea of exploiting his workers than the workers will attempt to ruin the enterprise by excessive demands.

Since this educational task requires time and the formation of this new type of worker and owner cannot be achieved in one day, National Socialism advocates as a transitional measure the establishment of "just" price agreements, i.e., those which take into account the needs of the workers and the conditions of the various establishments. If no agreement can be made between the interested parties, the state then intervenes to maintain social harmony. Strikes and lockouts are not permitted.

4. The Labor Front

The Nazi program demanded the elimination of trade unions since Hitler looked upon these unions as the incarnation of the Marxist principle of the class struggle. The task of disposing of them was relatively easy after the great political defeat suffered by socialism. It was realized without much difficulty soon after the installation of the new regime. At the huge workers festival celebrated on May 1, 1933 Minister Goebbels indicated that National Socialism would soon tackle the difficult and complex task of re-establishing social peace in the world of labor and of integrating the worker into the national community as an element enjoying fully deserved rights. At ten o'clock in the morning on May 2, Dr. Robert Ley, at the head of a "committee of action for the protection of German labor" occupied by force the offices of all the trade unions and imprisoned several of their most important leaders. He met with no resistance. In the course of several days all the socialist as well as Christian associations, together with 169 trade union organizations, were placed under the control of the Nazis. On May 10 the Nazis held the first meeting of the organization which was designed to replace the trade unions, namely the German Labor Front (*Deutsche Arbeitsfront*).

Hitler prided himself on having won the workers from Marxism which had never done anything positive for them. He declared himself ready to assume the role of protector over the vast organization which was set up on a dual foundation; the German workers front and the German employers front. Dr. Ley was placed at the head of the entire organization. The reorganization and unification of this vast system of unions required almost a year and a half. It was completed in October, 1934. From then on unity in administrative functions was completely realized.

The *Arbeitsfront* comprises almost the entire labor world of Germany. It includes more than 20 million members. Its receipts for 1935 were about 311 million marks, it owns property worth about 250 millions and its budget showed a monthly reserve of four to five million marks. Its bank, at the end of 1934, had a balance of 303 million marks. In his speech at Nuremberg on September 13, 1935 and in statements made to the foreign press, Dr. Ley summarized the achievements of the Labor Front as follows: The management of the *Arbeitsfront* has been more economical than that of the trade unions. With an average assessment which was reduced from 3.60 marks a month to 1.52, the *Arbeitsfront* was able to accomplish considerable work. It distributed financial assistance amounting in 1935 to about 100 million marks. During the same year it spent 30 million marks for workers' education and 18 million for the construction of buildings, particularly schools; it provided legal advice to more than two and a half million workers. It also procured for the worker paid vacations, guarantees in case of breach of contract, improvement in professional education, stabilization of wages, improvement of family wage, above all for work at home, and it put at the disposal of the worker a professional press the circulation of which reached between 12 and 15 million copies.*

* In his speech at the Nuremberg Party Congress on September 13, 1936 Dr. Ley gave the following figures for the year 1936: the average monthly receipts of the *Arbeitsfront* rose to about 30 million marks with a monthly surplus of 7½ million marks; the property owned amounts to 300 million marks; financial assistance totaled 87,469,029 marks; legal consultation was supplied to 3½ million people and the circulation of the labor press increased to 20 million.

According to the *Deutsche Arbeits-Korrespondenz* of December 18, 1936, the cash assistance given by the *Arbeitsfront* for the years 1933-36 was as follows: 1933, 18 million marks; 1934, 64 million; 1935, 80 million, and 1936, 78 million.—*Ed.*

Special mention should be made of the Strength Through Joy (*Kraft durch Freude*) organization, one of the most interesting creations of the *Arbeitsfront*. It is used for organizing the leisure of the workers. The Nazis hold that it serves the interests of the worker, who, thanks to the vacations given to him, now maintains himself in better physical condition, and at the same time also serves the interests of the employer, who can expect a better output from a happier and less tired worker. The association organizes hikes and tours which range from the simple weekend excursion up to vacations of ten days aboard a steamer, or trips abroad at extraordinarily reduced rates. An elaborate project, approved by the *Führer* and requiring ten years for completion, calls for the construction of enormous hotels, rest houses, ships, etc., which will permit 14 million workers, laborers, artisans and peasants to make trips every two years at astonishingly low rates. Beside this touring organization, which already has a following of more than 5 million members for its hikes and excursions, the association also favors the development of sports (there are 38,200 play fields with more than 2 million participants), the spread of education through 150 people's colleges, the esthetic education of the worker by providing him with practically gratuitous access to all kinds of artistic, musical or theatrical performances and finally the adornment of the factories and workshops for which it has already spent about 200 million marks.*

With the establishment of the Labor Front the Nazis assumed control over the entire world of labor and they organized it into one firmly knit organization. The accomplishments of the Labor Front in the field of rational organization of production and the professions were, however, not so marked. It was confronted with a situation where there were

* For a critical estimate of the *Arbeitsfront* and the position of labor see Thomas, Norman, "Labor under the Nazis," in Foreign Affairs, vol. xiv (1936), pp. 424-36, and Franz, Leopold, *Die Gewerkschaften in der Demokratie und in der Diktatur* (Carlsbad 1935).—Ed.

numerous groups, many of them duplicating each other, but all of them maintaining that they were indispensable for the functioning of the economic machine. The Nazis wanted to introduce order in this field also, to create a single corporate organization and make their own social conceptions prevail. But it soon became evident that in this field there were more serious difficulties than in the field of labor. The socialist and other trade unions had not offered any resistance to the will of Hitler. It was not the same with the employers. The Nazis preserved private property and individual initiative. Hitler rejected the socialization of production. For him joint ownership and joint decisions by the workers smacked of Marxism and would necessarily bring about disorder. The employer, therefore, remained master of his establishment, free to manage his business in his own way with his administrative councils, cartels and employers' organizations.

Whenever Hitler found himself in the presence of an organized force and a definite and well known authority such as the army or the diplomatic staff, he always inclined to compromise with them. The captains of German industry also represented for him an imposing force, an organization of technical capacity which he could scarcely do without. His instinct immediately led him to seek some arrangement with them rather than to engage in a violent struggle. He did not, therefore, give free rein on this point to the "socializing" wing of his party which would have willingly "brought into line" the industrial magnates and invested a corporate organization with authority over them.

Dr. Ley, it is true, announced in May, 1933: "The major lines of the corporate structure of the German people have been completed. Today I shall submit to the *Führer* the completed plan. It will be one of the most important works accomplished by the revolution. It is nothing less than the establishment of an organic bond between the employees on the one hand and the employers on the other, and the integration of both into one economic organization." Actually matters were by no means that far advanced. Hitler soon foresaw the danger to economic life which the "individual actions" of his too zealous followers would involve. He did not hesitate to reprove forcefully this "sabotage" of the National Socialist idea. Under such circumstances he also decided not to proceed with complete reorganization but rather to delay and to allow the projected corporate organization to be realized of itself through gradual stages. In a speech delivered on July 13, 1933, in the presence of Hitler himself, the Minister of Economics, Dr. Kurt Schmitt, declared in very clear terms: "The corporate organization which ought some day be established in our Reich, . . . is for the moment adjourned and postponed, not because it ought not to be made, but because there is the danger of seeing certain undesirable elements devoting themselves in this domain to experiments of a kind which will disturb the economic order, creating for themselves spheres of influence, strengthening their positions and realizing the most diverse plans. It is the *Führer's* will that we begin by drawing a clear line and following the long and slow path of healthy evolution."

What then are the main changes brought about by the Nazis in German economic life?

(1) The law of May 19, 1933 instituted the office of *Treuhänder der Arbeit*. The function of these officials is defined as follows: "Until the reorganization of the social constitution, the *Treuhänder* replace the workers' trade unions and the employers and their organizations in the task of concluding agreements regarding contracts for work which shall be agreeable to all the interested parties." The *Treuhänder*, numbering thirteen to correspond to the thirteen economic regions which were established in Germany, are named by the central government. They are responsible to it and receive their instructions from it. The decree of March 10, 1934 provided that they receive the assistance of committees of experts

composed of representatives of the workers and employers. The institution of *Treuhänder* is to be temporary. As soon as the education of employers and workers shall have been completed and all shall have become conscious of the solidarity which unites them, then the contracts will be concluded by the industrial groups themselves. For the present it is impossible to entrust this work to men who have been brought up in the idea of class antagonism and whose whole mentality has thus been corrupted. It is indispensable that there be for these people a state organ which can carry into effect the National Socialist principle of "general welfare before individual welfare." In practice this means that the delicate function of exercising the posts of arbiters of last resort between employers and workers has been entrusted to a group of Hitler's trusted followers.

(2) The Nazis instituted honor courts which are invested with very important powers. These courts consider complaints against employers accused of being guilty of anti-social acts, and they have the power to declare such individuals ineligible to conduct their business. These courts are also empowered to control the relations between employers, to see to it that competition is "fair" and to determine where unfair competition begins.

(3) In a series of laws and decrees (February 27, 1934; May 1, 1934; December 2, 1934) the Minister of Economics drew the framework of a vast organization comprising, on the one hand, professional groups—industry, crafts, commerce, banking, insurance, power and transportation—and on the other hand, regional or geographic organizations corresponding to the thirteen *Treuhänder*. This immense aggregate is eventually to become an autonomous and self-governing corporation. A series of committees were established at the various stages. These range from the shop committee which is the primary cell of the organization, through local works committees and regional economic chambers and labor chambers

up to the Reich Economic Chamber and the Chamber of Labor. One after another of these various parts of the system were instituted during the course of the years 1934 and 1935. The whole system is still too recent, however, to make possible any appraisal of its functioning and its efficiency.

(4) On March 26, 1935 at the Congress of the *Arbeitsfront*, Dr. Schacht announced that after long negotiations he had come to an agreement with Dr. Ley regarding a very important point. The establishment of the double organization of the *Arbeitsfront* on the one hand and the professional and regional groups on the other hand, declared Dr. Schacht, had made possible a reform of economic life along the lines of National Socialism and had paved the way for the advent of a system founded no longer on the class struggle but on the free co-operation of employer and worker in one unified enterprise. A dualism nevertheless still existed between the *Arbeitsfront*, which is concerned with the *social* aspect of the problems, and the professional industrial groups which look at these problems principally from the *economic* aspect. A closer collaboration between the two organizations, however, is necessary since their ties threaten to remain precarious as long as they develop independently. The March congress of the *Arbeitsfront* attempted to realize this co-ordination by instituting experiments in practical co-operation between workers and employers calculated to train them in the habit of working together. Schacht emphasized the major significance of this experiment. It was heralded as the continuation of the emancipating work of Baron vom Stein, the great organizer of administrative autonomy in Germany.

As a result of this agreement the group of industrial associations now entered the *Arbeitsfront* and collaboration was instituted between the *Arbeitsfront* and the agencies of the industrial groups at all stages of the organization. This was done through committees established on the principle of parity of representation of workers and employers and all problems were to be studied both from their social and economic aspects.

In this way the Nazis hope to solve certain difficulties for which up to the present they have had recourse only to the good offices of the state. It was quite evident that the arbitration tasks of the *Treuhänder* had become more and more overwhelming and that they were called upon for mediation in a host of cases which were hardly important enough to bother the state. Dr. Schacht and Dr. Ley, therefore, never stopped insisting to the representatives of the economic groups that they ought to become accustomed to regulating their own affairs among themselves. The state, said Ley, in a speech delivered at Kaiserlautern on September 4, 1935, is not a nurse to whom the child appeals for aid at all times. The members of a family arrange matters among themselves and they regard it as dishonorable to have to appeal to a court to settle a dispute. The same should also hold true for an industrial enterprise for it also constitutes a unity just like the family. It is absurd to call upon *Treuhänder*, party, *Arbeitsfront* or state at every instant. Business enterprise ought to direct its own affairs, assume responsibilities and move along through its own means. The true leader is one who can convince his subordinates that he is acting for the common welfare and does not need to hide behind the decision of some superior official. In the future the state will say to the complainants: "Lock yourselves up in a room, discuss, argue if necessary, but find a compromise and do not lazily hand over to another the task of solving the difficulties which arise."

The significance and value of the corporate reform attempted by the Nazis has been appraised in very different ways. There is no lack of skeptics who insist that the "socializing" plebeians have been vanquished by the crafty industrial magnates and that Minister Schacht gave to Dr. Ley nothing but purely verbal satisfaction. The co-operation between employers and workers, they say, is an illusion which is limited only to the field of *social* policy. In matters of wages and working conditions, on the contrary, control is maintained by the capitalists, who continue to manage their affairs sheltered from control and supervision. They claim that the chief goal of these permanent consultative agencies which have been established is to create a rational bond between big business and the state. The co-operation between the state and big business in the economic field is, as we shall presently see, becoming more and more intimate. Consequently the so-called "corporatism" is really only a dictatorial regime in which the real power belongs to the captains of industry who are allied with the Nazi functionaries.

It goes without saying that within Germany great hopes have been placed upon this new organization. The Nazis undoubtedly feel that for the moment it is hardly more than a framework depending for its character upon what those who become members of the various recently organized committees make of it. They expect these committees to be something more than mere discussion clubs and that not only social problems but also economic questions will come up for adjustment. They will not be miniature parliaments, where rival groups struggle for power and attempt to get majority control, but veritable schools of co-operation where employers and workers will learn the difficult art of amiably coming to terms for the proper management of affairs.

It is difficult at present to pronounce definite judgment on this question. The inner character of German economic life is little known to us. Relations between employers and the labor world do not seem to have been easy to regulate. On the Nazi side we have witnessed the successive fall of several men who had been entrusted with this task: Dr. Otto Wagener, head of the economic section of the National Socialist Party who first began the struggle with the powerful Reichsverband der Industrie; then successively Philipp Kessler and Count Ruediger von der Goltz, who had been appointed as leaders of the economic organization. On the side of the employers it seems that for different motives, individuals like Krupp von Bohlen und Halbach and Thyssen have left the party. It is obvious that labor conflicts have been numerous and the tasks of the *Treuhänder* very heavy. We also learn from the press of numerous cases in which the honor courts pronounced condemnations against employers. Finally, the antisemitic campaign together with the litigations which this has brought about and the greatly increased liquidation of Jewish concerns during the last years, have contributed to the disturbance of the economic world. A study of the reports of the *Treuhänder* would undoubtedly permit a better appraisal of these struggles. At present, however, these conflicts appear only as a vague and muffled echo. The significance of the work accomplished by the Nazi revolution in the social sphere can therefore hardly be measured in objective terms.

BOOK VIII

The German Economic System

VIII. *The German Economic System*

1. The Economic Situation at the Beginning of 1933

IN ORDER to understand the economic achievements of the Third Reich let us first attempt to outline the situation which prevailed in Germany when Hitler came to power in the beginning of 1933.*

The year 1932 marked the culminating point of the economic crisis which hit Germany and the entire world from 1929 on. In Germany the year 1931 had already been distinguished by violent disturbances. Between the summer of 1931 and the summer of 1932 the situation became still worse. A number of definite symptoms testified to the growing seriousness of the economic crisis through which the country was passing. There was increased unemployment, reduction in the volume of trade, decrease in export surplus, decrease in public savings, considerable slackening of production, constant decline in the index of prices, a catastrophic crash on the exchange, decrease in the gold reserve and foreign exchange held by the Reichsbank, an alarming budget deficit, financial difficulties of municipalities and general tightening of credit.

Even after the Lausanne agreement of July 8, 1932, which freed Germany entirely of reparation payments, it was doubtful whether Germany could pay the interest on her foreign

* For detailed analysis of Nazi economic measures and their effects see the London *Banker* (February 1937) which contains a critical analysis of four years of Nazi economic policy. Valuable also are M. Florinsky's *Fascism and National Socialism* (New York 1936); John C. de Wilde's *The German Economic Dilemma* (Foreign Policy Reports, March 15, 1937) and two articles by Horace Endemic in the *Annalist* (August 7 and 21, 1936), pp. 180-81 and 284-85, 310.—*Ed.*

debts. There was speculation as to how the Reich, the states and the towns, with their ever-increasing deficit, would be able to meet their most important obligations. Above all, the enormous army of unemployed workers and intellectual proletariat demanded work and bread and they showed increasing exasperation with the absolute impotence of the government to find any effective way to better their situation.

In August, 1932, however, several signs of improvement and of a business upturn began to show themselves both in America and in Germany. From then on there was increased hope that the lowest point of the depression had been passed, that the business cycle was on the upswing again and that business would improve. At the same time the idea developed that the state could perhaps, by a bold plan of grants for public works, crank up the industrial machine and thus shorten the period of stagnancy and trial of the national economy.

Chancellor von Papen boldly set forth this plan in his famous speech at Münster on August 28, 1932, in which he developed his economic program. This program was inaugurated with his decrees of September 4 and 5 and in later ordinances. The business world was afraid of any hazardous experiments at the time. There was talk of forced loans, of a levy on capital, of inflation, of a compulsory reduction in the interest rate and of recourse to a regimented economy. The September decrees, however, did not attempt any revolutionary innovations. By the establishment of advance tax certificates, by instituting an important program of public works and by bonuses accorded to employers of new workers, the Chancellor created an increase in credit of 2 to 3 billion marks. This was accomplished by means equivalent to an internal loan, which the Reich promised to pay back in 5 years beginning with 1934. It thus attempted to revive economic activity and galvanize private initiative by giving it opportunities to make use of its powerful energy. In practice this meant that his program was a draft on the future and the Chancellor admitted it without hesitation. He discounted in advance the surplus of revenue which might result from a general business upturn and he sought to hasten this upturn by boldly pledging the future. He acted *as if* prosperity would necessarily return beginning with 1934, without considering too much the financial difficulties which might devolve upon the country if this eventuality did not materialize or if it came at too slow a pace.

The von Papen program was at first very well received by the business groups but it soon raised increasing opposition in the country. Labor revolted against the measures which permitted employers to reduce wages and to break collective agreements. Discontent showed itself in movements like the transportation strike in Berlin in November 1932, in which Communists and National Socialists combined to prevent the application of measures condemned as anti-social. The Chancellor saw rising opposition also among agrarians and industrialists in his own party. Papen had sought to win the agrarians by quota regulations which aimed to protect national agriculture. These measures, however, soon showed themselves ruinous for export commerce, since the countries which suffered as a result of the quotas, notably Holland, the Scandinavian and Baltic countries, Italy and France, retaliated immediately by announcing restrictions on imports of products manufactured in Germany. The quota plan was dropped as a result of the opposition which these dangers raised in the camp of the industrialists. The agrarians in their turn raised indignant complaints and made insistent demands for more efficient protection. There was, therefore, almost unanimous protest against the economic measures of the Chancellor.

2. *Economic Dictatorship*

When the Nazis came to power the economic crisis had reached its most acute point. On February 15, 1933 the number of unemployed totaled 6,047,000 while the number of employed workers scarcely amounted to 11½ million. It was clear that such a situation could not continue without soon leading to catastrophe. The new leaders could scarcely do anything more than revive the plan of their predecessors. This they did, however, under better conditions and with redoubled and persevering energy. The only chance of saving the country was through the vigorous intervention of the state. There could be no question of increasing taxes since the taxpayers were at their last gasp and already weighed down by the burden of charges. It was equally impossible to have recourse to a loan under such critical conditions. The only possible expedient was to proceed as von Papen had already done, with credit expansion to encourage public works. As a result in January 1933 there came the Gereke program of 600 million marks and in June and September the two Reinhardt programs of 1,000 and 500 million marks. The state resolutely took the initiative with measures which aimed to extricate the economic system from the marasmus into which it had fallen.

It was not that Hitler underestimated the importance of private initiative. He did not think of suppressing competition and he never ceased repeating that he needed enterprising industrial leaders who would dare to take the lead and assume risks. He also did not ignore the dangers of bureaucracy and excessive organization. But he thought that temporarily at least the state should assume the major role in order to set recovery in motion. He installed a regime of economic dictatorship. It was exercised by a small number of leaders in whose hands more and more extended powers came to be concentrated. The best known of these was Dr. Schacht, president of the Reichsbank since March 15, 1933 and since July 30, 1934, Minister of Economics. Beside him may be cited Count Schwerin-Krosigk, Minister of Finance and his aide, Fritz Reinhardt. Their authority was practically unlimited.*

* By a decree of April 17, 1936 General Göring was charged with the control of all measures relating to foreign exchange and imports of raw materials and also with the task of co-ordinating the work of the various ministers hitherto charged with the regulation of these matters. This meas-

The German Economic System

Under their impulse governmental action has up to the present been preponderant. Not only has the state not given way to private initiative but it closely supervises private enterprise and often suppresses it. In certain industries like potash and textiles, for example, it has gone so far as to forbid new installations. Since it reserves for itself the right to put capital in circulation, it also decides in what manner the available capital shall be used. The Statistical Office calculated that out of 8¼ billion marks devoted in 1934 to expenditures for equipment, 70 per cent went into public installations and only 30 per cent into private industry. This proportion is an altogether unusual one and it was increased still further in 1935 when the total for equipment rose to 11 or 11½ billions.

The "employment battle" begun by the new leaders of German economic affairs soon showed some remarkable results. At the end of 1933 there was a decrease of a million and a half in the number of unemployed. On July 1, 1935 the total of unemployed fell to 1,754,000 showing a decline of nearly 4,300,000 from the number in February, 1933. At the same time the number of workers employed increased to 17 million by the summer of 1935. All the unemployed thus put to work did not find normal and permanent positions in industry. Many were employed in temporary works made possible by state subsidies. In such cases it might be said that the state, in place of giving them unemployment relief for doing nothing, was using them for works of general usefulness. This is the case for example, with the men who serve in the *Arbeitsdienst*, with those employed in emergency works (*Notstandsarbeiter*) and those used to help in agricultural work (*Landhelfer*).

On the other hand the Nazis endeavored to provide employment for a greater number of workers through better

ure, which made Göring economic dictator of Germany, was interpreted at the time by some as a direct attack on the authority of Minister Schacht which would lead to a crisis in German economic life.

distribution of work. This they did by the suppression of multiple jobs, by the elimination of women in certain categories of work and by shortening the hours of labor. Here too it was not a question of creating new work. The same amount of work was distributed among a greater number of people without the state being obliged to make any sacrifices. The results obtained by the struggle against unemployment were no less considerable. By the end of November 1935, the number of unemployed fell to 1,980,000 and thus below the number in 1929 (2,040,000). Of this number it was estimated that there were about half a million persons who were unemployable. Another half million constituted the fluctuating mass of the labor army necessary in every epoch. There thus remained only about one million unemployed for whom work had to be found. This number becomes larger in the winter when an increase in unemployment is always due. The crisis had, therefore, not ended. But it had been reduced to proportions which no longer constituted an imminent danger for the national life.

3. Juggling Accounts

Toward the middle of 1934 another grave problem presented itself, the problem of balancing accounts.

In order to understand the significance and gravity of this problem it is necessary to begin with the fact that Germany was a debtor nation. She had, it is true, been freed from her war debt properly speaking by the Lausanne agreement of 1932. But there remained important commercial debts contracted abroad, particularly in America, during the years which followed the restoration of the mark in 1923. It is well known too that beginning with 1930 the question of the payment of short term credits and service charges for the long term credits had caused the most serious embarrassment to Germany and even imperiled in various ways her entire financial structure.

By reason of the enormous economic development during the 19th century Germany had become a country of large industry, incapable of deriving from her own soil the necessary products to feed her ever increasing population. In order to exist Germany had to pay with exports of manufactured articles for the necessary imports of foodstuffs and raw materials required for her industry. If this kind of payment was not made, German economy found itself in danger. If Germany did not export enough to pay for these imports, it was necessary either to pay for the imports with the aid of the gold reserve and foreign exchange owned by the Reichsbank, which in such an eventuality was in danger of being drained, or else to restrict imports. In the latter case, however, there was the danger both of undernourishment and of bringing about a stoppage of industry, which would be unable to carry on without certain foreign raw materials.

One therefore sees the capital importance for Germany of an equilibrium in her trade balance. It is essential that by her exports of manufactured goods Germany procure the resources which will permit her to regulate (1) the interest on her foreign debt; (2) the imports of foodstuffs; (3) the imports of raw materials. If these payments are not made, then Germany exposes herself to bankruptcy, poverty and the cessation of her industries.

In 1932 and 1933 such regulation presented no difficulties. The trade balance was in fact favorable to Germany. Exports exceeded imports and left a credit balance which in 1932 amounted to almost 265 million marks per quarter and which even in 1933 was still 165 millions per quarter. Out of this balance Germany was able to pay the interest on her foreign debt.

The situation changed in 1934. On the one hand the need for imports increased. Due to the very improvement of the

253

internal situation following the credit extended by the Reich for public works, German industry showed an increasing demand for imports of raw materials. On the other hand the export trade was confronted with mounting difficulties. There was the world wide increase of customs barriers, there were the measures of quota restrictions undertaken in many countries, there was the devaluation of currency like that of the pound sterling, the dollar, the belga, etc., which placed at a disadvantage the countries whose money had not been devalued, and there was, finally, the political boycott of which Germany was often the victim. Under these conditions not only did the trade balance no longer show a surplus but in 1934 there was a debit of 34 millions for the first quarter, 161 millions for the second quarter and 52 millions for the third.

There was no other way, therefore, of paying the foreign debts except by recourse to the Reichsbank. The gold reserve and the supply of foreign exchange visibly diminished. At the beginning of 1934 the Reichsbank still had in its vaults about 400 million marks in gold.* Four-fifths of this sum disappeared in the course of the first half of the year. Payment of interest on foreign debts soon became almost impossible. On June 15, Dr. Schacht saw himself obliged to decree a moratorium on foreign payments first for six months and then for a year. This measure never worked completely for he was obliged to enter into agreements with certain European creditors whose imports from Germany exceeded their exports to Germany. In general, however, the saving realized amounted to about half of the foreign payments.

This measure, nevertheless, did not solve the financial problem posed by the trade deficit. How was the balance between exports and imports going to be re-established? The first step, for a long time practiced by the Reichsbank, was that of

* When the Nazis came to power in January, 1933, the Reichsbank had 821,900,000 marks worth of gold and 100,600,000 of foreign exchange. In the beginning of 1937 these holdings had shrunk to 67,200,000 and 5,600,000 respectively.—*Ed.*

quotas for foreign exchange. The bank provided the importers with a definite quota of foreign exchange wherewith to make their payments abroad. From May, 1932 to February, 1934 this quota remained fixed at 50 per cent of the figure for imports for 1930-31. Since during this period of time the volume of trade had diminished considerably, business men did not find it too difficult to adjust themselves. But from February to June, 1934, the quota was successively reduced to 45 per cent, then to 35, 25, 10 and finally to 5 per cent so that in the last week of June, the bank, in order to avoid the complete disappearance of its reserves, had to establish the rule of not giving to the importers any more foreign exchange than came into the treasury. The distribution of foreign exchange operated according to an emergency schedule among the various importers. The result of these measures was not long in revealing itself. Since the bank was very far from satisfying the demands for foreign exchange, the importers found themselves unable to pay their foreign tradesmen at average maturity, and little by little an ever increasing arrears of debts was accumulated.

Another manner of paying foreign debts was then devised. A certain number of foreign banks, particularly those of the Balkan countries and Sweden, had individual accounts in marks at the Reichsbank. Their credit balance permitted them to buy German merchandise. Thanks to these accounts (*Verrechnungskonten*) the foreign payments, in place of being made in foreign exchange, were made simply by means of transfer of bank balances. Importers used this method of payment to a large extent. The result was that the balance in marks of these accounts increased greatly and the foreign bankers found it increasingly difficult to find place for this balance, which could not be used except for acquiring German merchandise. The *Verrechnungsmark* was thus rapidly devalued and could no longer be negotiated except at a considerable loss.

255

Under these conditions there was an enormous increase in payment agreements (*Zahlungsabkommen* and *Verrechnungsverträge*), which succeeded each other with such dizzy rapidity that importers and exporters found it more and more difficult to find their way in this fast-moving chaos of regulations.

It was then that Dr. Schacht found himself forced to take a new step forward. He announced his plans in the speech which he delivered at the opening of the Leipzig Fair in August, 1934. His "new plan" which came into effect on September 21, was based on one leading idea. Up to then the government, in order to avoid the complete disappearance of the reserves of the Reichsbank, had controlled foreign payments either through foreign exchange restrictions or through the payment accounts. It was now necessary to go one step further and establish control not merely over the payments but also over the imports themselves.

In the early spring of 1934 the government had already realized that any consistent policy, whether it be to develop exports by devaluation of the mark or to renounce this and stimulate domestic trade by a program of public works, would have disastrous effects on the general economic system. One single way remained open in order to re-establish the equilibrium which threatened to be broken between the inflow and outflow of money. It was necessary to restrict imports. On March 24, 1934 a law regarding trading in industrial raw materials or semi-manufactured articles had been promulgated. This law instituted inspection offices first for the imports of wool and cotton, then also of metals other than iron, and then of a series of other products such as hides, rubber, fats, etc. The economic leaders believed that it was possible to restrict imports of raw materials since there was a relatively large accumulation of stocks from 1933, and there was no urgency to renew these immediately. The result however did not correspond with the attempt. In place of importing raw materials they brought in semi-manufactured or even finished goods, which, in the final analysis, did not improve the situation.

It was amid such conditions that Schacht saw himself forced in his "new plan" to extend control over all imports. The number of supervisory boards was increased to twenty-five and they exercised their control on the importing of all kinds of merchandise.* From now on no one could import anything without their authorization. This draconic measure made it possible for imports to be exactly proportioned to the available foreign exchange. Only the importer who had received from the supervisory board a certificate placing at his disposal a certain amount of foreign exchange was to be assured of the power to pay his creditor within a given time. In practice it became evident that a foreign merchant would hardly decide to trade with an importer who had not obtained the certificate in question for then he would have no chance at all of being paid.

In short, the state, through these supervisory boards, exercises a very considerable influence on German economic life and, as in Russia, it has a monopoly on imports. It depends on the state whether a factory does or does not obtain the raw materials necessary for its functioning. Its influence extends over the choice of raw materials to be used, over the organization of the work and even over the methods of production. The state has in fact assumed enormous responsibilities. The supervisory boards determine and classify in order of their importance the quantities of raw materials to be imported which are to be used for the manufacturing of particular indispensable articles; they regulate the distribution of the imported quantities among the various factories; they take into account the necessity of maintaining as many factories in operation as possible; they favor factories which export more than they import; they manage the clientele of

* The number of boards was later increased to twenty-seven.—*Ed.*

buyers of German products and foreign suppliers; and they must consider the interests both of the important firms and those of the entire country. This work has become even more complicated by the fact that trade has come to be carried on more and more by barter, each country buying from the other only the equivalent of what it sold to it. This shows how enormously complicated are the steps necessary to procure for Germany the raw materials which she needs and at the same time balance exports and imports with each country.*

In order to maintain German exports in the face of competition by countries with devalued currency, it was necessary to keep the price of export merchandise from rising any higher. The price of the export goods, however, stood in a necessary relation to domestic prices. It was, therefore, essential to keep the domestic prices as stable as possible. But in the case of agricultural products, we should remember, it was necessary to allow an increase in prices in order to maintain the peasant class. The watchword from then on became the prevention as far as possible of any increase in prices for other products, despite the fact that the general tendency of the price index was upward.

The only possible way to accomplish this was to force the producers and traders to renounce all avoidable increases in their selling prices and reduce to a minimum their margin of profit. Thus, after having established control over imports, the government also found itself led to control prices. On November 5, 1934 Gördeler was named Reich Commissar for the control of prices. His task was an infinitely delicate one. The economic policy of the government aimed to revitalize the industrial life and combat unemployment by a program of public works. But every improvement in business tended to bring on an increase in prices. It was the task of the controller, therefore, to establish a distinction between justified

* The London *Banker* reports that in a deal involving the purchase of 10,000 lbs. of wool against which German toys were exported, about 680 official forms had to be filled in.—*Ed.*

and unjustified increases, to prohibit the latter vigorously and to combat as far as possible the causes of the former. It was also often necessary for him to oppose the action of cartels which had been made compulsory in many cases by the Nazis and which tended normally towards increasing prices.*

Germany thus lives under a regime of directed economy, and the action of the state assumes an ever increasing importance. It is the state which by its works of general utility has revived the industrial life of the country and provided work for millions of unemployed. It is the state which has decreed the corporate organization of peasants and industrial workers. It is the state which has been led to control, successively, distribution of foreign exchange, then the volume of imports and finally price fluctuations. On all these points state action and action by the bureaucracy which it has instituted have been substituted for the action of the individual entrepreneur. This represents a disadvantage of which the Nazi leaders are fully conscious. Dr. Schacht himself has said: "The new plan is a terrible thing because it necessarily presupposes an increase in bureaucracy and organization." And he added: "We are all agreed on one thing, namely that the standard of life of our people cannot be maintained by means of the bureaucratization of our entire economic life." The disadvantages of bureaucratic action are well known. They are schematicism and lack of elasticity. When individual initiative finds itself replaced everywhere by the decision of an omnipotent authority, the dangers of serious mistakes which might affect the entire economic structure of the nation will be

---

* Gördeler resigned as Price Commissar in the summer of 1935. He became convinced that his post served only as a smoke screen for Schacht's policies and that prices could not be kept down under such conditions. Gördeler thereupon sought to influence Hitler to stop rearmament for a half-year and inaugurate a foreign policy which could make this possible. Hitler, influenced by Schacht, rejected this plea and Gördeler left his post. He was succeeded by Joseph Wagner, a district leader from Breslau. I have this explanation of Gördeler's resignation from a reliable authority who received it directly from Herr Gördeler.—*Ed.*

found to have considerably increased. In principle the Nazis, therefore, maintain private initiative and free competition between business enterprises. In practice, however, they greatly reduce this initiative, and they entrust the task of enormous and perhaps overwhelming direction to a small number of leaders and a huge bureaucracy. It is a dangerous experiment and of great interest, but it is still impossible to make any prediction as to its success.*

4. Financing Rearmament

In the fall of 1934 the economic situation became more complicated by a new problem which emerged for the leaders of the Reich. Beginning with October 1, 1934 preparatory measures were undertaken for the re-establishment of compulsory military service for one year and it was officially proclaimed on March 16, 1935. It was a question, therefore, of preparing for German rearmament in an industrial as well as financial way.

This was a formidable task. Just at the time when the expenditures for cranking up industry were beginning to be diminished and the "new plan" of Dr. Schacht was just beginning to be put into operation, German economic leaders were faced with the serious problem of how to meet the enormous expenditures required by the re-equipment of the German military forces. This included costs of armaments, equipment, reorganizing the artillery, tanks, airplanes, and stocks and provisions of all kinds for an army which had been greatly enlarged. "This creative work which they demand of us," said Dr. Schacht, "far surpasses all the sacrifices which had been asked of citizens of any nation at any epoch." Hitler did not hesitate to demand these sacrifices. For him politics comes before economics. Not that he underestimates the capi-

* It has been estimated that between 700 and 1,000 special ordinances dealing with economic control come into force every week.—*Ed.*

tal importance of economics and finance in the life of a people.
But he never loses sight of the fact that there is a hierarchy
of problems and that the interests of national defense come
before every other kind of consideration. It is indispensable,
of course, to economize, and the preaching of a very rigorous
economy is one of the constant themes of the Nazi propagandists. But in no case should it be necessary to be niggardly
regarding expenditures for rearmament. For the reflection of
German *force* is the *sine qua non* of any real revival of German *prosperity*. The raising of the standard of living is one of
the constant cares of the *Führer*, but he does not hesitate to
declare in the most categorical fashion that the people must
willingly resign themselves for a time to rationing of fats,
butter and pork so that rearmament may proceed at the
desired pace.

The magnitude of the sums expended for German rearmament remain entirely unknown. After the works programs of
1933 and 1934, which granted credits amounting to about
5 billion marks, the government, by a law of February, 1935,
authorized the Minister of Finance "to raise, by means of
credit, resources the figure for which is to be fixed by the
Chancellor and *Führer* on the advice of the Minister of
Finance." From that time on, therefore, we have no information concerning the credits extended by the Reich. Beginning
with 1935 the Reich, moreover, has entirely ceased making
its budget public. We have no information concerning the
Reich budget except in so far as rare indications are provided
by the ministers in their speeches. All figures found here and
there in the press rest on suppositions or combinations which
are of doubtful objective value. Thus the deputy Edward
Grigg, in a speech of February 24, 1936, estimated that for
the preceding three years Germany had spent 800 million
pounds sterling annually for rearmament. The *Financial News*
estimated these expenditures at 15 billion marks and Mr.
Winston Churchill at 11½ billion pounds sterling. Another

English publication, basing itself on the statistics of public investments published by the Institut für Konjunkturforschung, proposes the figure of 1 billion pounds sterling while the correspondent of an important French newspaper holds it reasonable to suppose that the annual expenditures made by Germany for rearmament are more than the entire French budget.*

There are of course some very definite indications that the costs of rearmament have been enormously increased. There is first of all the fact that rearmament has more than absorbed all the increased revenues from which the Reich budget benefited in the last few years and which reached a considerable sum. The total revenues from taxes according to the budget of 1932-33 had fallen to 6,647,000,000 marks. Following the business improvement, the receipts for 1933-34 topped this figure by almost 200 million, those for 1934-35 by nearly 2 billion and the receipts for 1935-36 amounted to 9.650 billion, thus showing an increase of 3 billion in comparison with those of 1932-33. The revival of industry, on the other hand, brought about a saving of almost 1½ billion marks on unemployment expenditures, which had fallen from 2,8 billion marks in 1933 to 1,4 billion in 1935. Finally the general conversion, in January, 1935, of all investments to the uniform interest rate of 4½ per cent resulted in a corresponding decrease in the service charges on the debts (540 millions). The resources of the German budget were therefore increased by more than 4 billion marks between the years 1933 and 1935. The Nazi leaders, however, have not only expressly

* The authoritative London magazine, *The Banker*, in its issue of February, 1937, gives the following estimate of expenditures for rearmament in Germany:

1933-34	Rm. 3,000,000,000
1934-35	Rm. 5,500,000,000
1935-36	Rm. 10,000,000,000
1936-37	Rm. 12,600,000,000

Total for four years, Rm. 31,100,000,000 *Ed.*

warned the taxpayers not to count on any cut in taxes and that the government needs receipts at least equal to the present amounts, but they have also intimated that it might become necessary to increase the taxes. The Finance Minister added, in effect, that despite the considerable increase of receipts, his budget *always showed a deficit.*

The economic leaders have never made any secret, however, of the means whereby they have financed the "employment battle" and Reich rearmament. In order to pay for the expenditures of the Reich, they have drawn drafts on the future by discounting in advance the increased revenue which might result from an upswing in business. They repaid as much as possible of the extraordinary credits involved in these operations to the extent that the increased revenue was realized. They thus attempted gradually to incorporate into the budget the expenditures for rearmament. But the Minister did not hide the fact that the military expenditures had been covered *only in part* by the amounts listed in the budget. The rest was to appear in the form of an increase in the Reich's debt. The Institut für Konjunkturforschung provided an estimate of the German debt as of June 30, 1935. According to its figures the recorded debt of the Reich amounts to 13,161 billion marks and that of the states, Hanseatic towns and municipalities about 12,04 billion.* To this figure it is necessary to add a total of about 5 billion marks in the form of advance-tax certificates, employment-creation bills, interest-subsidy certificates and other Reich bills.† This debt totaling about 30 billion marks is not exorbitant. It is less than the

* According to the statement submitted by the German government to the United States Securities and Exchange Commission the Reich funded debt was 11,620,028,787 reichsmark and the floating debt 2,918,302,089 reichsmark, as of March 31, 1936.—*Ed.*

† Most foreign experts put the figure for these bills at a much higher sum. The *London Economist* (August 1, 1936) set the figure at between 13 and 15 billion marks while the London *Banker* (February, 1937) set it at almost 16 billion marks. Others have estimated this so-called secret or unofficial debt at between 20 and 25 billion marks.—*Ed.*

German pre-war debt of 32½ billion, and also less than the British debt of nearly 9 billion pounds sterling, of the French debt of 340 billion francs and of the debt of the United States of almost 30 billion dollars. It is also not fair to reproach the Nazis with having too greatly accelerated the tempo of indebtedness, since between 1928 and 1931, under the Weimar republic, the debt had been increased by 10 billion marks. It is, however, a matter of serious concern that a large share of this amount is in short term loans, payable to the creditors, at least theoretically, at one moment or another.

The financial leaders, under such conditions, insisted on the danger involved in resorting indefinitely to credit inflation. Dr. Schacht as well as Herr von Schwerin-Krosigk are in agreement that the time has come to return to a more normal situation. This is to be done by consolidating, by means of loans, the sums invested by the government for the stimulation of German industry and for rearmament, by practicing a policy of rigorous economy in the smaller things in order to be able to make certain very large and indispensable expenditures and even by supplying, through fiscal reform, certain additional resources to the regular budget. They therefore never miss an occasion to address the most pressing warnings to the public. The German people, they say, should be prepared for a period of great sacrifice. At the present time there can be no question of any one increasing his profits. He must be satisfied with maintaining his *status quo*. They emphasize the point that it is the strict duty of all those who have realized any benefits from increased employment to place these benefits at the disposal of the state by subscribing to the loans which are floated. They do not hide the fact that it is idle under such conditions to hope for a decrease in taxes or an increase in wages. It is rather to be expected that prices will mount and the cost of living increase. "Nothing will be given to us gratis," said the Minister of Finance in a speech on November 8, 1935. "We cannot count on any miracle. We

264

must conquer everything by the force of work and, for that reason, by consenting to make sacrifices." The state floated some very large loans in 1935. In January it borrowed 500 million marks from the savings funds and 300 million from the insurance companies. In September it borrowed 500 million from the savings funds and 500 million were distributed among the public.

5. A General Appraisal

How ought one to appraise the economic situation of Germany? When reading the German newspapers and official publications one finds that the dominant note throughout is one of keen satisfaction with the results attained by Nazi Germany after four years of effort. They point to a number of favorable symptoms which show that on the whole the country, after a period of atrophy and depression, has returned to relative prosperity. They point to increased activity of the railroads and navigation companies and to an improvement in sales of shares, the market price of which increased from 54.5 per cent of the market price of the period between 1924 and 1926 in 1932, to more than 89 per cent at the end of 1935. The market price of bonds for the same period increased from 76.32 per cent to 95 per cent. They also stress a marked increase in the profits of many businesses, a decrease in losses and an increase in social insurance funds as well as savings funds. The latter rose from 10 billion marks in 1931-32 to more than 13 billion at the end of 1935. This represented an increase in disposable funds which not only made possible the loans which were mentioned above but also the redemption of almost 2 billion marks of foreign debts which were liquidated between March, 1933 and September, 1935, including 1.287 million marks for the Reich, 194 million for the states, 131 million for the Hanseatic towns and 325 million for the municipalities. As a whole, therefore, the tendency is toward

optimism. Hitler, in his New Year's speech of 1936 emphasized the advances accomplished in the struggle against unemployment and he prided himself upon the "consolidation"
of the economic situation.

Upon looking more closely at what constitutes this new
economic activity, we immediately see that it was stimulated
chiefly by state orders, that it reveals itself very much more
in industries of producers' goods rather than in consumers'
goods industries, and that, everything taken into account, it is
expressed in an increase in stocks of tools and armaments
rather than in an improvement in the standard of living of
the people themselves.

The revival of German industry in 1933 no doubt had an
effect also on the income of the workers. Between 1932 and
1933 the national income of Germany increased from 45,3
billion marks to 56 billion and during the same period the total
of workers' wages and salaries increased from 26 billion to
31,7 billion. However, since the number of workers employed
during this period had increased by 4 to 5 million, a simple
calculation shows that the amount of fixed revenue during
the three years was increased by 20 per cent but the number
of workers who shared in this amount increased by 25 per
cent. This indicates that the average wage and salary had *decreased*. Moreover we have seen that the policy of the economic leaders tends less to improve the condition of the
workers than to maintain it at a constant level. Beginning with
1934 the curve of the number of workers employed and that of
workers' incomes progressed in strictly parallel fashion and
the hourly wage both for skilled and unskilled workers remained the same since 1933, namely, 78.3 pfennig and 62.2
pfennig respectively. This represented a decline of 22 per
cent from the average wage in 1929.

This does not mean that individual wages remained the
same during the entire period. The wages of certain groups
of favored workers certainly increased. In a large section of

German industry, it must also be noted, the average length of the working day increased from 6.94 hours in 1932 to 7.60 hours in 1935, indicating an increase of 10 per cent. In general, nevertheless, it is obvious that the principal aim of Nazi economic policy has not been to increase the purchasing power of the masses by increasing wages and decreasing taxes, nor to satisfy their growing needs by developing consumers' goods industries, as normally occurs during periods of prosperity. These consumers' goods industries have shown only a slight revival,—about 10 per cent as compared to 1932, but very much below the level of 1928. Under these conditions the standard of living of the masses has scarcely changed. It did improve for the agricultural workers because Hitler, as soon as he came to power, took forceful measures to protect the peasant class whose existence was threatened by economic developments. The workers employed in those industries which have benefited from the favorable economic situation have also improved their position. For the great bulk of the workers the standard of living remained the same or was even lowered. It is perhaps necessary to give this much credit to Hitler and his aids, that they did not lure the workers with deceitful promises and did not conceal from them the fact that they had to postpone temporarily the realization of their personal desires, accept without murmur the restrictions imposed upon them and willingly yield to the necessary privations.

The economic revival which German publications emphasize, therefore, was not produced except in the relatively narrow section of capital goods industries and particularly those of the war industries, i.e. construction industries, steel, metals, machinery, transportation, etc. There production has on the average doubled since 1932. In certain favored industries like the automobile and cement industries production has even tripled and quadrupled. Almost everywhere it went beyond the level of 1928. Factories are working in full force, often to absolute capacity. In some branches of industry, especially in the construction industries, it is claimed there is even a scarcity of skilled specialists in some regions. Statistics cited by the *Frankfurter Zeitung* indicate that the volume of business in the capital goods industries increased from 4 billion in 1932 to 8¼ billion in 1934 and 11 or 11½ billion in 1935. But the Statistical Office has estimated that of the figures for 1934, 70 per cent went to state agencies and only 30 per cent to private industry. During 1935 the proportion of public business increased.* This is a very unhealthy proportion and shows to what extent the revival of German industry has been government-financed.

The economic leaders of the Reich are well aware of the difficulties which such a situation presents. They have on various occasions in the last years indicated that the period in which the state takes the initiative in economic affairs would have to end. They now appeal to individual initiative and urge the business men to stop counting on the gifts of state orders and to dare to take risks once again. The business men should inscribe on the first page of their ledger the old formula *"Mit Gott,"* a symbolic expression of the responsibility which they assume before their conscience and their people. The leaders emphasize the fact that alongside the public works of the state, which meet the needs of the general welfare, there should also be an increase of profitable industrial enterprises, which apart from the profits which their owners will legitimately derive, will also create the superior values necessary for the nation in order to cover its expenditures and make possible the servicing of the German debt. Up to the present, however, individual initiative has hardly responded to this appeal.

* It continued to increase also in 1936 as indicated by the annual report of the Reichsbank. The report states that "in 1936 German business continued its upswing, which was primarily determined by the Reich government's tremendous measures" and that in the money market "the available means were put more comprehensively than ever in the service of public tasks." (See *New York Times*, March 16, 1937).—*Ed.*

The German Economic System

What makes the economic situation of Germany particularly critical is the fact that the vital question of exports has never yet been regulated in any satisfactory fashion. The total volume of German trade has not stopped decreasing. In 1933 it amounted to more than 9 billion marks, in 1934 it barely reached 8,6 billion and in 1935 it was no more than 8,4 billion. As a result of the circumstances which make it absolutely necessary for Germany to reduce her imports she has not been able to participate in the improvement in world trade which has been evident during the last years. She has succeeded in balancing her exports and imports in the sense that the excess of imports of 284 million marks which was registered in 1934 gave way to an excess of exports of 111 millions in 1935;* but this favorable balance was absorbed by reimbursement of old commercial debts, by the servicing of foreign debts and also by the necessity of stretching the period of payment for exports. The situation whereby Germany found itself forced to proceed generally by barter, not buying in the various countries any more than the sum equivalent to the exports sent to that country, resulted in a complete confusion of trade statistics. Imports from European countries were increased while at the same time exports to overseas countries also increased. This often involved very unfavorable consequences. A typical example of this is furnished by the cotton trade. In 1934 Germany covered 80 per cent of her needs of cotton in America, where she found the best quality at the cheapest price. Today, as a result of the necessity to adjust as much as possible exports to imports, she was forced to reduce her imports from America by more than half while her purchases from Brazil, the Congo, Sudan and Egypt

* In order to develop its exports Germany created a revolving fund, which in 1935 was raised to one billion marks (of which 720 million were furnished by industry). This was to be renewed that year, industry furnishing 600 million, and agriculture, the banks and commerce 400 million. It may be questioned whether exports at the cost of such sacrifices do not risk becoming a substantial loss.

increased in formidable proportions. But they also became, by force of circumstances, infinitely more burdensome for her.

Another dark spot in the situation is the fact that the question of German commercial debts abroad has not yet been settled. Dr. Schacht was forced to suspend the servicing of these debts in June 1934 for one year and this moratorium was extended for another year up to 1936. But it is altogether impossible for Germany to further reduce its imports of food stuffs and raw materials. These have already been reduced to a minimum. It is difficult to anticipate an improvement in exports, especially since the prices of raw materials are tending to rise and the foreign nations seem little disposed to compensate for the increased costs to Germany resulting from that by a corresponding increase of their imports of German manufactured goods. Under such conditions, since the interest on the debt cannot be paid except through foreign exchange furnished by an excess of German exports over imports, one can scarcely see how the actual situation can be modified. Dr. Schacht, who is fully aware of the harm which this absence of assets has done to German credit, recognizes in principle Germany's obligation to honor the liabilities which she has assumed toward foreign private lenders. In fact, however, he does not see the possibility of resuming the servicing of the interest charges at the rates stipulated at the beginning. He brought about a general decrease of interest rates in order to suggest to Germany's creditors that they enter into an arrangement with Germany and consent to a decrease in the interest rates on their debts. Up to the present no agreement of this kind has been made and because of this fact there is a certain tension between Germany and her creditors, particularly those in the United States.

It is very difficult to appraise the German economic situation in its entirety. If one places the emphasis upon the exceptionally favorable situation revealed in the producers' goods and equipment industries, one can, as do the apologists for the regime, proclaim a healthy optimism and envisage the future with full confidence. If, on the other hand, one emphasizes more strongly the dangers which are inherent in the situation—deterioration of consumers' goods industries, privations imposed upon the masses of the population, difficulties encountered in increasing exports, the exorbitant extension of influence of the state over economic life and the diminution of private initiative—one arrives at very different conclusions. Even an industrialist like Klockner, who belongs to the group of actual beneficiaries of the regime, recently raised the question, not without some distress, as to what will happen when the state will slow up its orders and stop its credit expansion. And if, as the opponents of the Nazi regime and certain foreign observers maintain, there is a suspicion that German official statements are guilty of an excess of deliberate optimism, that there is a "secret debt" of the Reich, which does not appear in any of the statistics, that beside the number of unemployed admitted there is also an army of "invisible" unemployed, that the costs of rearmament rise to sky high figures, that the antagonism between the employers' aristocracy and the masses of poor workers is sharper than ever before and that a rumbling of discontent has begun to show itself below the surface among a disillusioned people, then the German situation obviously may be represented as being almost desperate and an imminent cataclysm might be expected. The Nazi press and officials continue to protest against these rumors and they denounce indignantly the campaign of "calumnies" waged against the Reich. "We shall not provide the evil minded people abroad," said the Minister of Finance recently, "with the pleasure of an economic and financial collapse."

I have neither the positive information nor the necessary technical competence to take definite sides in this controversy. I limit myself merely to pointing out the perplexities of opinion in the face of the German situation. The facts alone give reason for both the optimism of the one and the pessimism of the others. As far as I am concerned I shall confine myself to one remark of simple common sense. I do not think it would be wise to predict with certainty that this economic collapse which has been heralded for so long a time and which has not as yet been manifested, will be produced in a *very short time*. Germany is a country where governmental authority is very strong, where technicians are in a position to exercise an almost unlimited dictatorship over the economy and finances of the nation, where the masses are endowed with extraordinary patience to suffer the most extreme privations, as they showed in amazing fashion during the World War, and where moreover they are infused with the Spartan spirit which inclines them to accept without revolt the sacrifices which are demanded from them in the name of the general welfare. It may be that the optimism of the Nazi propagandists is exaggerated. It may be that if the general situation does not change, Germany will find it increasingly difficult to maintain herself. But I do not believe that any one can make any certain prediction as to the tempo of future evolution. For my part I merely raise the question whether Germany might not be capable of carrying on for a period of time, the duration of which it is impossible to determine, under a regime of a closed economy where exports will be strictly adjusted to imports. Theoretically this period might last for as long a time as the people will resign themselves to accepting a greatly reduced standard of living, which will be imposed upon them by the combination of economic fatalities which hangs over us all at the present time.

6. *Economic Developments in 1936*

Economic developments in 1936, as recorded in German official publications, followed the general lines of development of the first years of Nazi rule. The crisis of unemployment, they claim, has been overcome. In September 1936 the number of unemployed fell to 1,035,000 as against 17,900,000 employed workers. It may be said, therefore, that almost the entire healthy population has found employment. There may even be a considerable scarcity of skilled workers, particularly in those capital goods industries which have been especially developed. This situation is being remedied by the organization of apprenticeships and by restoring skilled workers, who in order to avoid unemployment had accepted work outside of their specialized fields, to their former trades. The average of the hours of work had increased to 7.80 hours in November 1936. Labor productivity has also increased. Taking 100 as the average labor productivity for one hour in 1928, the number estimated for 1935 would be 128.

Nothing in the general lines of economic policy was changed. The aim continues to be to maintain as stable a level of wages as possible and consequently also the standard of living of the workers. Excessive development of consumers' goods industries continues to be discouraged and capital goods industries, particularly those necessary for the restoration of German military power, are fostered, following the well-known formula of "cannons rather than butter."

The great innovation of 1936 was the new four year plan promulgated by Hitler in his proclamation to the German people at Nuremberg in September. "In four years," said the *Führer*, "Germany must be wholly independent of foreign countries in respect to all those materials which can in any way be produced through German capability, through German chemistry, or by our machine and mining industries. The creation of this great German raw material industry will employ productively those masses freed by the completion of rearmament." It is principally a question of reducing imports of four fundamental materials, fuel and oil, rubber, textiles and iron ore. As for iron, they have sought to do without foreign imports by exploiting the mines as much as possible even if the yield be indifferent. They also use a great deal of scrap iron, which is always found in great abundance in a country of rapid industrial development. On the other hand they have manufactured synthetic fuel by the distillation of lignite, which Germany has in great abundance. They have also produced artificial rubber by synthetic processes. Cotton, wool and silk have been replaced by the development of rayon and artificial wool (*Zellwolle*), 30 per cent and more of which must be incorporated into the fabrics used for manufacturing purposes.

Considerable results have already been achieved along these lines. Germany counts on being able to furnish 75 per cent of her fuel needs for 1938 out of her own artificial fuel. Altogether it is probable that technically Germany has a good chance if not to free herself entirely from foreign dependence, at least to diminish considerably her imports and thus realize important economies in foreign exchange. For the time being the successes which have been produced have been very costly. Synthetic rubber is four times as expensive as imported rubber and artificial fuel costs twice as much as natural oil. *Astrara*, a fabric which contains 50 per cent *Zellwolle*, costs 80 per cent more than wool fabric. They hope, however, that the net costs of these products will be reduced after new technical perfections will have been effected and after the installations have been paid off. The primary thing for the Nazis in the present state of the world, however, is not to provide the consumer with products at a cheap price but rather for Germany to support herself and to economize on foreign exchange. The Nazi program has therefore been accepted with enthusiasm and initiated with energy and spirit.

According to official publications the economic situation continues to improve regularly. The national income increased from 56 or 57 billion marks in 1935 to 61.5 billion in 1936 and from the point of view of the purchasing power of

money it is estimated that these 61.5 billion are the equivalent
of 74 billion in 1928. In the latter year, a year of special
prosperity, the national income was estimated at 75 billion.
This would therefore signify that the total income of Germany after having fallen to about half in 1932 was now
returning to a level almost equivalent to that of the prosperous
years.

In the field of consumption the differences between 1935
and 1936 were insignificant. Governmental authority made
itself felt more forcefully. Its aim was to "orient popular
consumption in the direction of articles which can be furnished to them by our own national production." Thus they
tried hard during the autumn to foster the consumption of
cabbage, pork and fish; they forbade the manufacturing of
whipped cream, fatty cheese and rye brandy. They also
forbade the use of copper for household goods and of rubber
for children's toys and bathroom supplies. The population
yielded without too much protest to this adaptation of consumption to production.

Public finances continued to thrive. The Reich revenues
increased by more than 2 billion marks in 1936 and for
1936-37 will reach a total of about 11,8 billion marks (15,5
billion for the total revenues of Reich states and municipalities). If one considers that during the same period the Reich
saved 1,850 million as a result of the decrease in unemployment it may be said that as compared to 1932-33 the Reich
has realized an increase in revenue of 7,140 million and for
the entire period of 1933-37 an increase of about 15 billion.
This large sum, however, has not been sufficient to meet the
needs of the treasury and the Reich is still increasing its debt.

The year 1936 witnessed the development anew of private
investment. This showed itself in the increase in savings
funds; in October 1936 the total volume of savings funds
increased to 14,300,000,000 marks, an increase of one billion
marks over the figure for 1935. It also showed itself in the

increase in insurance funds which rose to 22,8 billion marks in 1936. But more than in these it showed itself in the increase in bank credits, in the taking over by private economy of large parcels of shares belonging to the state and by the setting aside of reserves which permit business concerns to finance their own new installations. This improvement in the capital market not only permitted the state to float a new loan of 600 million marks on November 6 but also made possible a considerable increase in investments. These reached the total in 1936 of 13,5 billion marks, an increase of 2 billion over the figure for 1935. It is therefore not astonishing that under these conditions the movement of the stock market has on the whole been upward. While stocks with fixed profits remained practically stable between 95 and 96, the course of other shares advanced from an average of 54.5 in 1932 to 106 in October, 1936.

The dark aspect of German economy continues to be the difficulty for Germany of balancing her exports and imports. Figures, it is true, show an export surplus in 1936 of 550 million marks. But it cannot be concealed that the export business is becoming more difficult, in the sense that the price of raw materials which are imported is increasing and the price of manufactured articles for export is decreasing. Moreover, the effects of devaluation by France, Holland, Switzerland, Italy and Czechoslovakia threaten to aggravate these difficulties still more. These countries have absorbed practically 38 per cent of Germany's exports in Europe and 27 per cent of her total export. But it is necessary to count on a decrease in these exports as a result of these devaluations and perhaps also on an increased competition by France in Central Europe. In any case German exporters will find themselves obliged to make price concessions in order to maintain their position. Devaluation, it has been calculated, resulted also in a loss for Germany of between 80 and 100 million marks in foreign exchange. If we take into consideration the fact that despite the moratorium the servicing of foreign debts continues to absorb annually more than a half a billion marks and that the gold reserve of the Reichsbank fell in 1936 to 72 million marks, it is not difficult to understand why from this angle, the German situation still appears critical.

Under such conditions any attempt at a general evaluation must remain hesitant. Pessimists persist in estimating that Germany is at the end of her rope and that her development towards autarchy has led her to a more and more alarming state of asphyxia and that she can only choose between economic collapse and war. The intensification of the colonial demands, the peregrinations of Dr. Schacht through Europe in search of outlets for German exports, the draconic penalties promulgated on December 1, 1936 for evasions of exchange regulations are all interpreted as symptoms which herald an imminent crisis. The optimists, on the other hand, place their emphasis on the successes which have been obtained, on the improvement of the domestic situation from the standpoint of industrial production as well as from the financial standpoint. They affirm that the German situation today is healthy and that although Germany desires a resumption of European and world economic co-operation, she is none the less ready to hold out as long as the other powers persist in their state of economic irrationalism and extreme nationalism which has provoked the paradoxical confusion in which the civilized world finds itself today.

BOOK IX

A Frenchman
Looks at Nazi Germany

IX. A Frenchman Looks at Nazi Germany

Retrospect

EVERY day Germany becomes more and more difficult for the French to understand. We had sufficient difficulty, several years ago, in becoming familiar with the Germany of the "left." However, despite frequent misunderstandings and persistent mistrust, a *rapprochement* had finally been outlined. We inclined towards the feeling that by a slow evolution toward democracy in Germany reconciliation between the two countries would slowly be achieved. In the intellectual and spiritual world, in any case, we felt that fruitful intercourse might be established between the two countries.

Suddenly in one day, almost all the Germans of distinction whom we had known suffered persecution, were ferreted out, imprisoned, exiled and spurned. Suddenly their friends, i.e., the people of the left among us, already enemies of Italian fascism, have become the bitter opponents of Nazi Germany. Conversely, certain groups oriented to "the right" and until lately strongly mistrustful of the Germany of "the left" have been seized with tenderness for the dictatorship established across the Rhine by Hitler, while often still retaining many of their old prejudices against "militarist" and "imperialist" Germany. A complete confusion has thus been brought about. We float about amidst thousands of conflicting sentiments ranging from decided horror through mistrust and uneasiness up to curiosity mixed with sympathy and regret that we do not have a "strong man" like Hitler in France.

I should like to indicate here those aspects of National

Socialism which I consider most difficult for Frenchmen to accept today.

I have the feeling, first of all, that we are generally grieved by what I have called the deliberate intolerance proclaimed by the Nazis, by the appeal which they make to the fanaticism of the masses and by the determined brutality of the measures whereby they seek to impose their power. I do not believe that we have been shocked so much by the theories professed by the Nazis. The disdain which Hitler reveals for the intellectuals and the esthetes is nothing particularly offensive to us. There was a "smart" period when we too heard a great deal concerning the treason of the intellectuals, the impotence of science, the foolish pretensions of reason and the timidity of the fastidious. We swallowed, without so much as making a face, the *Reflexions on Violence* of Georges Sorel and we listened, without being scandalized, to the paradoxes of Nietzsche on the will to power and his apology for the "barbarian" and the "blond beast." I do not know if I need develop any further after so many others have done so, the thesis, strongly contested as a generalization, of the innate "moderation" of the French in contrast to the natural "immoderateness" or impetuosity of the German. I do believe however, that the French react instinctively against Nazi fanaticism and that they rise up in opposition before their *calculated* violence. The terrorism *en acte* which the Nazis perpetrate against their enemies repels us and we were tremendously shocked by the executions of June 30, 1934. The French instinctively retreat from a regime which employs such drastic measures. They feel unresponsive to a country which submits in silence, without protest, and without revolt, to the treatment which the Nazis inflict upon their vanquished enemies, and they gaze with astonishment and hardly with sympathy upon the blustering clamor with which the victors celebrate their triumph.

Another point on which there is a clear divergence between

A Frenchman Looks at Nazi Germany

French and German sentiment is that of the question of race and the practical consequences which National Socialism derives from this doctrine. The overwhelming majority of French opinion maintains an irreducible skepticism towards the race myth. It does not deny in any way the importance of the phenomenon of race nor the dangers of racial deterioration. But it thinks, rightly or wrongly,—and I shall not enter into the question here,—that science is very far from having given us a complete explanation of problems so prodigiously complex as those of race and heredity. Guidance, for the present, must be sought in the counsels of experience and common sense. These teach us that all the great nations of Europe,—the French, the Germans and the English,—are the products of an inextricable mixture of races. We are all of mixed blood and we are at present profoundly ignorant of the reasons which make a particular crossing desirable and another one dangerous. To us it appears that even a crossing between heterogeneous races is capable in very many cases of producing favorable results.

Under such conditions Nazi intransigeance in the Jewish question remains incomprehensible to us. We cannot believe that, under the pretext of difference of race, it should be permissible to oust from the national community a group of citizens who were guilty of no positive offense and who have so often asked nothing but to become merged with this community. The ways in which Nazis have sorted out Aryans from non-Aryans and the hunt for "Jewish ancestors" to which they have devoted themselves in order to find a pretext for ostracism, appear to us both debatable and ridiculous. The whole movement seems less an act of purification than a measure of arbitrary proscription. It appears to be dictated less by a pretended "race consciousness" than perhaps by a sentiment of envy of an intelligent, rich and often encroaching minority. The French, who until now have resisted the anti-Jewish and anti-Protestant campaign waged in certain

283

opposition circles, remain strongly incredulous of the idealization of race. They are insensitive to the arguments by aid of which the Nazi prophets attempt to motivate an attitude which is not understandable to us and which we find warranted neither by facts nor by justice.

The race theory involves another consequence no less important. It emphasizes in an exclusive fashion the *differences* which separate men from each other. It is one of the fundamental convictions of racialism that the unity of the human species is an absurd hypothesis and a simple abstraction. In reality, they say, there is an ultimate plurality of races, each with its own scale of values, its particular conception of the beautiful and the good, and its own religion. At a congress of jurists held recently under the presidency of Carl Schmitt, the proposal was put forward to suppress the juridical notion of *man*. "The juridic notion of 'man,' in the sense of article 1 of the Civil Code, obscures and falsifies the differences which are designated by such terms as 'compatriot,' 'citizen,' 'foreigner,' 'Jew,' etc." For these jurists it is important to suppress such scientific abstractions which, they feel, have nothing to do with real life. It is necessary to think in the concrete, to see like with like and unlike with unlike, and, therefore, to take into account the essential differences which separate from each other men of different races, different nations, and different professions. These differences are, according to National Socialist phraseology, "realities instituted by God."

A Frenchman finds it difficult to rally to such exclusivism. It seems to us that the *resemblances* between the various types of human beings rather than the *differences* are the "realities instituted by God," and we protest when only one of these two factors is recognized. We refuse to hold as an empty abstraction the category of the "universal human," so dear to Goethe. We recognize with Kant the absolute value of human personality and from that the ultimate equality of all individuals in so far as they are human personalities. We are filled with the utmost repugnance at considering as entirely illusory an idea like that of the rights of man, and to decree the definite impossibility of any universalism in matters of morals and esthetics. On this point, too, there is a very clear divergence between French and Nazi mentality.

On the religious plane in particular the Nazi thesis seems to us to lead to formidable difficulties. Even individuals detached from any positive religion cannot resign themselves to a denial of the possibility of a "religion of humanity" after the manner of Herder and the eighteenth century and of the "primordial religious phenomenon," to use the phraseology of Goethe. As for positive Christianity it seems hardly possible to me that it can renounce its faith in an ecumenical value of Christianity and its belief that Christ died for *all* men. The racialist maintains, however, that each race has its particular soul and its specific religion, in which is expressed its innermost being and in which are manifest the characteristic virtues which it derives from its very blood. If this thesis is pushed to its logical consequences it means that the true religion of the German is the heroic ideal of the ancient Teutons, as expressed in the Nordic myths and the national legends and which is personified in such types as Wotan and Siegfried. If the racialist does not reject Christianity entirely as a religion of an oriental race, and as emphasizing the values of love and mercy instead of honor and heroism, he feels constrained at least to endeavour to "purify" Christianity of its oriental elements in such a way as to render it acceptable to Germans. This is the standpoint which Hitlerism officially supports. I have already indicated the endless controversies which have been occasioned by this attempt. National Socialism finds itself today in open conflict with the confessional churches, Catholic as well as Protestant. These churches accuse the Nazis of desiring to install a new paganism and they maintain that the Nazis have thereby excluded themselves from the Christian community. Will this conflict be pushed to the end or will it result in a compromise? Any prediction is impossible at the moment but the reality of the conflict is patent.

In this conflict I do not believe that the sympathies of very many Frenchmen are with the Nazis. We feel little affinity with either Wotanism or Wotanized Christianity. We have scarcely any desire to change our traditional religion of love for that of a religion of heroism. Finally, the very notion of specifically racial and above all national religions is not sympathetic to us. We refuse to subscribe to the notion that there is a German God and a French God who differ essentially from each other and who might even eventually be at war with each other as was the case during the World War. This concept appears almost sacrilegious to us, in any case irreligious to the highest degree. We instinctively shrink from the racial theory, which in destroying the very idea of a "catholicism" and of "an original religious phenomenon," aims to extend to the domain of religion all the discords of race and nationalism from which the world suffers so cruelly today.

The French reaction toward that other aspect of National Socialism which I have designated as Spartanism, is a bit more hesitant. We are very far from replying with a decided "no" to the German attitude on this question. We too are conscious of the defects of modern civilization and for a long time we too devoted ourselves to pitiless criticism of our typical insufficiencies. We know very well that our hyper-individualism constitutes a grave danger for us, that our sense of discipline and national solidarity often leaves much to be desired, that our civic practices are not to be trusted too much, that often we are wanting in a sense of organization, that we have a sad propensity towards intellectual and esthetic dilettantism, that our system of education is in many respects obsolete and that we do not pay sufficient attention to physical training—to steeling the body—and to the civic education of the French youth. We, therefore, follow the German experiment with a great deal of interest although this does not preclude criticism

286

nor deny that our interest is blended with a great deal of reserve.

First of all there are, for example, the labor camps. Our approval of this organization is unqualified. The excellent appearance of these camps, the incontestable utility of the work they are doing, the goodwill of the participants, the camaraderie which reigns between the workers and their leaders, the strict discipline obtained by persuasion and without punishment, all these merit nothing but praise. We have the impression, however, that a movement like this is possible only in a country where the instinct of social discipline has been developed to the degree found in Germany. We can scarcely believe that an experiment of this kind would have such satisfying results among us. We cannot envisage the French youth voluntarily submitting to the hard and austere existence of these camps, consenting to make manual labor with shovels a mark of honor, acquitting themselves of their work and practicing sport exercises, and maintaining their dormitories and rooms with the perfect neatness which is found in the German camps. It is no credit to us and we need not be proud of an incapacity which has nothing of the glorious about it. But it is, I believe, a fact which must be stated, no matter how regrettable it may be. Even when we take a general view of the measures which the Nazis have undertaken to further marriages and increase births, the more or less witty pleasantries which have been made concerning the "directed marriage" do not do away with the fact that the Germans have obtained results in this domain which we might well envy.

Our reservations are greater with regard to the continuous regimentation of the Nazi, from youth up to middle age or even old age, into a series of associations where he is systematically trained in solidarity with his comrades and in national solidarity. Whereas the German accepts this collective and gregarious existence without difficulty, the Frenchman betrays an instinctive repugnance for the "barracks," from the material and even more so from the spiritual point of view. We are ready to concede that we perhaps have too much individualism and impatience with social and moral constraints. But we are not sure but that there is conversely an excess of "conformism" among the Germans and a too docile submission to the life of the herd.

Our skepticism is even more accentuated when we see artistic life "organized" as they have made it. We do not insist that it is *a priori* impossible to obtain by command a new art which conforms to the Nazi ideals and which the Nazi leaders wish to develop from the German soil. They assure us, for example, that they have obtained very good effects and real artistic value by the use of the *Sprechchöre*. That may be. We shall await the result of the evolution under way. We even admit that the Nazis have obtained certain remarkable results in the organization of grand national festivals and also perhaps in the style of the new public buildings in which the *Führer* is personally interested. In general, however, we retain our doubts on the virtues of a "directed" art and we incline to the belief that in the esthetic domain, at least, it is dangerous to do away with individual liberty.

Our doubts turn into decided opposition when we see National Socialism resolutely subordinating the spirit to politics and proclaiming that all manifestations of thought must be inspired by the national will and that they must aim to exalt "Germanism"; that the entire life of the spirit—including education, the theater, the cinema, literature, the press and the radio—all ought to be "politicized" and considered as within the province of that vast enterprise of national propaganda which aims to spread the National Socialist ideal within and without Germany. Professor Krieck wishes to replace the old humanistic university by a politico-racialist university in which there should be developed a science of the soldier-like and militant type whose ideal mission shall be to work for the integral expansion of the German people. In the same way one of the most eminent philosophers of contemporary Germany, Martin Heidegger, declared in substance at a recent speech: We want ourselves. Science means to know what our people is and in what direction it is tending. The duty of students as well as professors is *to serve the people under the triple form of labor service, military service, and scientific service.*

These theses have been applied in a large measure in the Germany of the Third Reich. We have the feeling that the very aim of culture in Nazi Germany is envisaged from a new angle. It is no longer a matter of freeing the spirit from traditional constraints, of teaching the students to think for themselves, of training them in the free search for truth or of initiating them into free artistic creation. For the Nazi, "truth" is entirely encompassed within the National Socialist conception of the world and of life. The task of the educator is not to discuss it but simply to develop it in all its aspects, diffuse it, fashion the individuals according to the prescribed model, and strengthen in them those principles which will make out of them perfect National Socialists. Under such conditions the true and the beautiful cease to be disinterested ends in themselves, freely pursued. They are nothing more than themes for propaganda which are developed in such a way as to create in the national community as perfect a spiritual conformism as possible.

On this point we are unable to follow National Socialism. Spartanism applied to matters of the spirit, and the subordination of the spiritual to politics appears to us neither desirable nor salutary. We refuse to believe that the function of the spirit is essentially "activist" and that its first duty is to fight for the triumph of race or fatherland—whether it be "Germanism" or "Latinism" matters little.

We can understand how such a notion held sway during the war. It was mobilized at that time in the same way in which armies were mobilized. It engulfed each nation as with a network of barbed wire and with a protective tissue of useful national "legends." But we refuse to believe that it should be retained in this state in times of peace. Of what good is it to aggravate our sorry national conflicts and extend them to the realm of the spirit? Of what good is it to further the development in the souls of individuals of a militant exclusivism which leads them to believe that the various civilizations are fundamentally different from each other and cannot be posed except by fanatically *opposing* each other?

French opinion tends also to maintain an attitude of reserve towards the Nazi regime with respect to another set of facts. This is due to doubts as to the duration and stability of the regime. National Socialism as well as Italian fascism rest essentially on the prestige of *one* leading personality. If this personality disappears for one reason or another no one is able to say what will happen to the regime. This is the common difficulty of all dictatorial regimes. Who will succeed the *Führer* on the day he no longer holds the reins of power in his hands? No prediction is possible. Even if Hitler expressly designates his successor there is no proof that this designation will be accepted without resistance by the other lieutenants of the dictator who at present have submitted without murmur to the leadership of the *Führer*. There is no certainty that it will be supported by the old parties which mysteriously disappeared soon after the advent of the Nazis but which evidently continue in the dark and are only waiting for a favorable moment to return to the scene. Many people are convinced that Hitlerism is not the *true* countenance of Germany and that it might disappear one fine day as suddenly as it came upon the scene.

Even if we admit, however, as most observers do, that in case of a change of regime, sixty to eighty percent of the country will still remain Nazi, there is the question as to how this transformation will take place. On this point agree-

ment is far from being a fact. There is in National Socialism
a revolutionary element by means of which it gives satisfaction to the aspirations of the masses and allies itself to communism or to socialism. But there is also a tendency towards
social conservatism which comes nearer to the old conservatives and the German Nationalists. Hitler's art has been to
harmonize these two tendencies in such a way as to be able
to rally behind him almost the entire German nation. At bottom, however, they remain none the less divergent. By a
skillful game of see-sawing Hitler has been able, up to the
present, to maintain a balance. But the question may always
be raised whether he will not end by veering either to the
right or to the left.

Some people believe that Germany lives today under a
directed economy which approaches socialism in many ways
and that the representatives of big industry who financed this
movement were duped into favoring the advent of a regime
which has greatly reduced all initiative on the part of the
leaders of industry. Others, more numerous, think that Hitler
is really a prisoner of his allies of the right if not a direct
agent of the General Staff, and that he delivered himself up
to them on June 30, 1934, the day when he decimated the
revolutionary wing of his party and struck down with his
own hands his former comrades. Germany, to believe these
people, is more than ever placed under the rule of its old
masters, the Junkers, the army, big industry and the administrative bureaucracy. Hitler is a sort of mascot which these
old privileged classes use to make the secret domination which
they exercise acceptable to the masses. On the day of Hitler's
disappearance the army will naturally take power and, without striking a blow, will re-establish the authoritarian regime
to which the country has in reality been subject all the time.

I admit my own skepticism with regard to all these construc-
tions. I do not believe that Hitler is the "prisoner" of anyone
today. He is invested with *personal* power which he uses ac-

cording to his own inspiration. It does not seem to me that this power need *necessarily* come to an end in the near future nor even that its prestige is already on the decline. The day when for one reason or another he shall cease to exercise power is unpredictable. That day will come sooner or later since I do not believe, as Hitler asserts, that National Socialism will be established in Germany for millenia. But it seems rash to predict the time when the new order will come and unwise to count on a "collapse" which has already been announced so many times. It seems impossible either to fix the time or to foresee the manner in which this will come about. The only reasonable attitude in the face of the Nazi developments is to practice the English precept of "wait and see."

We come, finally, to the important question which dominates the whole record of Franco-German relations. Can we have any confidence in Hitler? What does he wish of us? Is it peace or war which he carries under the folds of his brown shirt? Where do we find his true thoughts with regard to us? In the bellicose pages of *Mein Kampf* which he has never expressly retracted or disavowed, or in the pacific declarations of his recent speeches and in the offers of reconciliation with which he has been so lavish? Is he seeking to allay our mistrust and gain time until his military preparations are complete so that he will then be able to throw off his mask and definitely take his vengeance upon us, or does he really desire amicable relations with us, and even perhaps effective co-operation? Is it necessary to believe that he is resolved to go his way, if possible *with* France, if need be *without* France and if necessary *against* France? French opinion hesitates between these various views. Let us try to discern as sincerely as possible how the question of confidence in Germany poses itself for us.

Let us first of all call attention to an important fact which is made clear today by irreducible evidence. German power is surpassing French power every day. Germany numbers 67 million inhabitants, France, 40. Germany has the advantage over us not only in numbers but also in many other respects such as the energy of the tempo of life, the birth rate, the dynamism, the discipline and aptitude for organization, the power of economic organization, the fanaticism of the racialist ideology which it exalts, the Spartanism which glorifies propaganda and the fact that all power of decision is concentrated in the hands of one leader who can will and act. The superiority of armaments which the Versailles Treaty assured us compensated for these disadvantages for some time. German rearmament has already destroyed that artificial and precarious guarantee. The balance of power was definitely broken to our disadvantage. This too in the face of a nation which always had worshipped the cult of might and which had nothing but scorn for the weak. All that we know. We have always known it even the day following our victory. We know it even too well and we allow it to become too evident. Our incessant preoccupation with security has often appeared ridiculous and ill-suited for a people conscious of its worth. It is a fact nevertheless that dynamically speaking there is no more security for France against Germany. And it is important that no illusions be entertained in this respect either in France or abroad. For us this means a need for incessant vigilance in order to avoid the dangers which our dynamic inferiority inevitably implies.

We have attempted to meet this danger on the one hand by endeavoring to install in place of the reign of might and the struggle of each against all, a regime of international justice and collective guarantee of peace; and on the other hand by attempting to compensate by alliances for our numerical inferiority. Have we succeeded in this? It is very doubtful.

It always seemed rather difficult to believe that the League of Nations and the power of arbitration which it exercises would be sufficient, in the present state of European mentality, to insure a peace of justice. The whole world is rearming today, even Great Britain who had provided striking testimony to her faith in the efficacy of the Covenant by spontaneously carrying out unilateral disarmament. Britain has understood that in the world as it is today, it is not enough to speak of justice. There must also be a force capable of guaranteeing the execution of the orders pronounced by the supreme authority. And while we dare not trust any longer to the League of Nations alone to guarantee the security of all, it does not seem that we have been able to constitute a system of alliances which definitely assures our security and that of the continent. Of what value exactly is the pact with Russia? What remains of the Stresa Front? Who is able to boast today that general peace is effectively guaranteed by a group of powers whose dynamic superiority is shown in undisputable fashion?

It is Hitler's well known thesis that this security which we cannot attain either in the League of Nations or in a system of pacts can immediately be obtained through direct accord with him. By a series of difficult steps Germany has reconquered her liberty, her full sovereignty and the free disposition of her own territory. She has broken the chains of the Versailles Treaty and repudiated the Locarno agreement. There is no litigation between Germany and France any more, says Hitler. He asks only one thing; definitely to bury the hatchet of war with the French nation and conclude a pact with us which would guarantee peace for twenty-five years. He extends his hand to us today in all sincerity. And the German people approved at Stuttgart his initiative by unanimous and enthusiastic acclamation. The time has come, he says, for us to pass the sponge over the past and accept frankly the hand which is offered to us. We must finally free ourselves, he says, from that psychosis of mistrust which paralyses us and we must admit the good faith of Germany. If we dare to take this step it will open up a new era for us and for Europe. If we persist in our pessimistic skepticism we allow to pass once more an occasion which may never be repeated. What should one think of this thesis which Hitler presented with persuasive eloquence and with dramatic show in several speeches to the German people?

I have indicated above (p. 122) the reasons why I think neither Hitler nor the army nor above all the German people want or desire war with France. The *Führer* is, therefore, sincere when he affirms his will for peace and this sincerity gives his declarations an accent which has gained many adherents for him. It would be an error on our part, I believe, if we continue to look upon this as nothing but a snare and dissimulation. But it would also be an error to see in it assurance for definite security. Hitler does not wish to declare war against us. Well and good. But war can come between Germany and France if a well carried out propaganda and the pleading of an eloquent tribune were to convince the Germans that they were not the aggressors but the victims, in the same way in which they have recently demonstrated that it was not *they* but *we* who violated the Locarno agreement. This is the real danger which threatens us and threatens Europe. This danger too is not imaginary. Whatever can be surmised from German designs discloses the fact that there are many motives for conflict which might arise in the near or distant future.

Germany has reconquered its place among the great free European powers. But is she "sated"? In no way. She has not ceased proclaiming that she is the "*Volk ohne Raum,*" that she is stifled within the limits which have been assigned to her and that she is not in any position to insure the subsistence of her population through her own resources. She claims her "place in the sun." Who can tell how far this vital, animating impulse will lead her? Will she demand from England and France her lost colonies? Will she cling to the will which Hitler has loudly proclaimed of uniting all the Germans into a "greater Germany"? Such a prospect has nothing reassuring for us. The realization of the Great Germany of a hundred million inhabitants encompassing all the countries in which reside peoples of German language and culture, cannot be carried out without provoking new wars.

Is Hitler, perhaps, still orienting his ambitions towards the east, as he said in his *Mein Kampf*, and is he aiming, with the co-operation of Poland, to extend his influence over Russia, where he could find immense resources of raw materials and important outlets for his export industries? Might not Germany pursue the design of establishing its hegemony over the Danubian region by relying on Hungary whose present government seems won over to it; over Austria where National Socialism will triumph without difficulty on the day when Italy ceases to guard the Brenner Pass, over the Germans of Czechoslovakia, who recently gained significant electoral victories, and over Jugoslavia where the Germans are carrying on considerable propaganda and are engaged in important commercial relations? These are hardly agreeable prospects for France, who is bound by treaties with Russia and with Czechoslovakia and who would view with concern the resumption by Germany of her projects of expansion towards the east or of hegemony in Central Europe. These policies raised alarm in European diplomacy before the World War. How far then will German ambitions go? In what degree are they compatible with French security? In what way does she intend to realize these ambitions? For all these questions there is no response. In a world ever more chaotic, where more than ever the law of the jungle reigns, where "scraps of paper" have only a problematic value,—who can be astonished that France maintains her reserve and is on guard against a neighbor whose attitude toward us began by being openly menacing, whose behavior during the last years toward us has been frankly unkind and whose views of the future remain veiled in mystery and may eventually involve grave risks for the general peace?

This does not mean that I hold any kind of Franco-German *rapprochement* to be an illusion and a deception. Geographic fate has made the Germans our immediate neighbors. It is impossible to ignore this. We have the choice either of continuing to battle each other or else of attempting to reach an agreement or at least of giving support to each other. I do not belong to those pessimists who, taking the irrevocable hostility of Germany as an accepted fact, consider the first alternative as inevitable, and who think that there is nothing left for us to do but to tighten our reins for the next war. I urge, therefore, that negotiations be carried on with Germany and that no opportunity of an entente with her be neglected. On one condition, however, that we never lose sight of the inequality of forces which exist between us and Germany, and that we never forget the need of incessant vigilance which this fact imposes upon us. Under all circumstances, even that of collaboration, we must be ready for all eventualities. Our independence would be seriously threatened, even in peace, if we would give the impression that we are not ready to defend it with all our energy and all our will.

The future, certainly, is not very reassuring. The hopes of those who, following the war, believed in the advent of a humanity made wise by the great lesson of the world cataclysm, and in which there would be more justice and a better peace, have all gone up in smoke. The world remains a jungle in which peoples, retreating within themselves and armed to the teeth, struggle for their daily bread or for power, and where the triumph of the strongest seems to be the supreme law. The League of Nations, weakened by repeated checks, scarcely seems able to offer the weak any reliable guarantee. There are moments when it seems to be threatened even as to its own existence. We see a new iron age opening up before us. Nazi Germany is engaged in it with sturdy energy, to the acclamations of a people who have faith in their vitality, in their might, in their masses and in their future. She presents herself in our new Europe as a new Sparta, hardened by the experiences of the past, systematically trained for manual labor and works of war, animated by a powerful dynamism, in possession of a military establishment of formidable efficiency, animated by a profound disdain for "bourgeois" civilization and the ideologies of the past, full of scorn for the formalism, the complexities and the delays of the old diplomacy, wearied by the long procrastination and ready for direct action, and gathered with all its strained energies in the hands of one leader who disposes of an immense popularity.

It is idle to recriminate against this fact. It would be dangerous to count on the immediate dissolution of this regime. It is confronted with certain difficulties, no doubt. But it has carried off some astonishing successes and its prestige among the masses seems intact. Nothing remains for us except also to affirm our individuality in the face of the Germanic personality. That does not mean collision. Understanding between French and Germans has always been difficult. The development of Germany towards National Socialism has not facilitated this mutual understanding. It has increased the divergences, which I have indicated in all sincerity. But perhaps it is possible for two peoples very different from each other to understand one another and to esteem each other even in their differences, and, according to the English formula, "agree to disagree." This demands vigor, coolness and moderation. We should like to hope that this is not too much for human powers.

APPENDIX

1. *The Program of the Nationalsozialistische Deutsche Arbeiterpartei*

THE Program of the German Workers' Party is a program for the times. The leaders have no intention, once the aims announced in it have been achieved, of setting up new ones, merely in order to ensure the continued existence of the party through artificially stimulated discontent of the masses.

1. We demand the union of all Germans to form a Great Germany on the basis of the right of self-determination of nations.

2. We demand the equality of Germany with other nations, and the abolition of the Peace Treaties of Versailles and Saint-Germain.

3. We demand land and territory (colonies) for the sustenance of our people and for settling our superfluous population.

4. None but members of the nationality may be citizens of the state. None but those of German blood, irrespective of religion, may be members of the nationality. No Jew, therefore, is a member of the nationality.

5. Anyone who is not a citizen of the state may live in Germany only as a guest and must be subject to the law for aliens.

6. The right to determine the leadership and laws of the state is to be enjoyed only by citizens of the state. We demand, therefore, that all public offices, of whatever kind, whether in the Reich, in the states, or in the municipalities, shall be filled only by citizens of the state. We oppose the corrupt parliamentary system of filling posts merely with a view to party considerations and without reference to character or ability.

7. We demand that the state shall make it its first duty to promote the industry and the livelihood of the citizens of the state. If it is not possible to maintain the entire population of the state then the members of foreign nations (non-citizens) must be expelled from the Reich.

8. All further immigration of non-Germans must be prevented. We demand that all non-Germans who entered Germany subsequent to August 2, 1914, shall be forced to leave the Reich forthwith.

9. All citizens shall enjoy equal rights and duties.

10. The primary duty of every citizen is to work either intellectually or physically. The activities of the individual must not clash with the interests of the community but must be realized within the frame of the whole and to the advantage of all.

The Third Reich

We therefore demand:

11. Abolition of incomes unearned by either work or effort.

Breaking of the Bonds of Interest Slavery

12. In view of the enormous sacrifices of property and life demanded of a people in every war, personal enrichment through war must be regarded as a crime against the nation. We demand, therefore, ruthless confiscation of all war profits.

13. We demand nationalization of all trusts.

14. We demand profit sharing in large concerns.

15. We demand the extensive development of old age pensions.

16. We demand the creation and maintenance of a healthy middle class, immediate communalization of department stores, and their lease at cheap rates to small merchants and extreme consideration for all small merchants in purchases by the federal government, states and municipalities.

17. We demand land reform adapted to our national needs, the enactment of a law for confiscation without compensation of land for public purposes; abolition of land interest and prevention of all speculation in land.*

18. We demand a most ruthless struggle against those whose activities are injurious to the public interest. Base crimes against the nation, usurers, profiteers, etc., irrespective of creed or race, must be punished with death.

19. We demand the substitution of a German common law for the materialistic cosmopolitan Roman law.

20. In order to make it possible for every talented and diligent German to acquire a higher education and thus be able to occupy leading positions, the state must carry out a thorough reconstruction of our entire educational system. The curricula of all educational institutions must be adapted to the needs of practical life. The comprehension of political ideas, from the beginning of a child's understanding, must be the goal of the school (through civic education). We demand the education of intellectually gifted children of poor parents without regard to class or occupation, and at the expense of the state.

21. The state must take care of improvement in public health through protection of mothers and children, through prohibiting child labor, through increasing physical development by obligatory gymnastics and

* The following statement is necessary to clear up the false interpretations given by our opponents to point 17 of the program of the N.S.D.A.P. In view of the fact that the N.S.D.A.P. holds to the view of private property, it is self-evident that the phrase "confiscation without compensation" refers only to the creation of legal means whereby land which was acquired in illegal ways or which is not being administered to the best interests of the nation's welfare might be expropriated if necessary. This is directed primarily against Jewish land-speculation companies.

Munich, April 13, 1928.   Signed: Adolf Hitler.

Appendix I

sports laid down by law, and by the extensive support of all organizations concerned with the physical development of young people.

22. We demand the abolition of mercenary troops and the formation of a national army.

23. We demand a legal battle against deliberate political lies and their dissemination by the press. In order to make possible the creation of a German press we demand:

    (a) All editors and contributors of newspapers appearing in the German language must be members of the German nationality.

    (b) Non-German newspapers must require express permission of the state before they appear. They must not be printed in the German language.

    (c) Non-Germans must be forbidden by law to participate financially in German newspapers or to influence them. As punishment for violation of this law we demand that such a newspaper be immediately suppressed and the non-German participating in it be immediately expelled from the country. Newspapers which give offense to the national welfare must be suppressed. We demand legal battle against any tendency in art and literature which exercises a disintegrating influence on our national life. Institutions which violate the above mentioned demands must be shut down.

24. We demand liberty for all religious confessions in the state, in so far as they do not in any way endanger its existence or do not offend the moral sentiment and the customs of the Germanic race. The party as such represents the standpoint of positive Christianity without binding itself confessionally to a particular faith. It opposes the Jewish materialistic spirit within and without and is convinced that permanent recovery of our people is possible only from within and on the basis of the principle of:

General Welfare Before Individual Welfare

25. In order to carry out all these demands we call for the creation of a strong central authority in the Reich with unconditional authority by the political central parliament over the entire Reich and all its organizations, and the formation of chambers of classes and occupations to carry out the laws promulgated by the Reich in the various individual states of the federation. The leaders of the party promise that they will fight for the realization of the above mentioned points and if necessary even sacrifice their lives.

Munich, February 24, 1920.

After due consideration the general membership of the party decided on May 22, 1926 that "This program is never to be changed."

11. *The Horst Wessel Song*

Die Fahne hoch, die Reihen dicht geschlossen,
S.A. marschiert mit ruhig festem Schritt.
Kam'raden, die Rotfront und Reaktion erschossen,
Marschieren im Geist in unsern Reihen mit.

Die Strasse frei den braunen Bataillonen!
Die Strasse frei dem Sturmabteilungsmann!
Es schaun aufs Hakenkreuz voll Hoffnung schon Millionen,
Der Tag für Freiheit und für Brot bricht an.

Zum letzten Mal wird nun Appel geblasen,
Zum Kampfe stehn wir alle schon bereit.
Bald flattern Hitlerfahnen über allen Strassen,
Die Knechtschaft dauert nur noch kurze Zeit.

Die Fahne hoch, die Reihen dicht geschlossen,
S.A. marschiert mit ruhig festem Schritt.
Kam'raden, die Rotfront und Reaktion erschossen,
Marschieren im Geist in unsern Reihen mit.

English Translation

Raise the flag aloft, keep your ranks closed; S.A. marches on with calm, firm step. Our comrades who were shot by Red Front and reaction; March on in spirit within our ranks.

Clear the streets for the brown battalions; Clear the streets for the S.A. man. Millions now gaze with hope on the swastika; For the dawn of the day of freedom and bread.

For the last time now the alarm is sounded; We all stand prepared for the battle. Soon Hitler flags will flutter over all the streets; Our bondage will last for but another short while.

Raise the flag aloft, keep your ranks closed; S.A. marches on with calm, firm step. Our comrades who were shot by Red Front and reaction; March on in spirit within our ranks.*

* The Horst Wessel song was the fighting song of the Nazi movement before they assumed power. After taking over the government this song was given equal status with *Deutschland über Alles* as the official national anthem of the Third Reich.

III. *Law for the Reorganization of the Reich January 30, 1934*

Article 1

THE popular assemblies of the states are hereby abolished.

Article 2

(1) The sovereign rights of the states are hereby transferred to the Reich.

(2) The governments of the states are subordinate to the Reich government.

Article 3

The *Reichsstatthalter* are subject to the supervision of the Reich Minister of Interior.

Article 4

The Reich government may lay down new constitutional laws.

Article 5

The Reich Minister of Interior is to issue the necessary legal decrees and administrative measures for the carrying out of this law.

Article 6

This law becomes effective on the day it is promulgated.

IV. *The Law Regarding Labor Service*
June 26, 1935

THE Reich government has decided upon the following law which is hereby promulgated:

Article 1

(1) The Reich Labor Service is a service of honor to the German people.

(2) All young Germans of both sexes are obliged to serve their nation in the Reich Labor Service.

(3) The Reich Labor Service is to educate the German youth in the spirit of National Socialism in order that they may acquire a true national community feeling, a true conception of labor and, above all, a proper respect for manual labor.

(4) The Reich Labor Service is organised for the carrying out of public welfare works.

Article 2

(1) The Reich Labor Service is under the jurisdiction of the Reich Minister of Interior. Subordinate to him the Reich Labor Leader exercises supreme authority over the Reich Labor Service.

(2) The Reich Labor Leader is at the head of the Reich administration of the Labor Service; he determines the organisation, supervises the distribution of work and directs training and education.

Article 3

(1) The *Führer* and Chancellor of the Reich determines the number of people to be called annually for service and he determines the length of service.

(2) Obligation for service begins at the earliest with the completion of the eighteenth year and terminates at the latest with the completion of the twenty-fifth year.

(3) Those subject to compulsory service will as a rule be called for Reich Labor Service in the calendar year in which they complete their nineteenth year. Voluntary enrollment in the Reich Labor Service at an earlier age is possible.

Appendix IV

(4) Those subject to compulsory service and those serving voluntarily are subject to more than thirty days imprisonment if they leave the Reich Labor Service in ways other than provided in Article 16.

Article 4

Those subject to compulsory service are drafted by the recruiting offices of the Reich Labor Service.

Article 5

(1) The following are excluded from Labor Service:
   a) Those who were punished with penal servitude.
   b) Those who are not in possession of the rights of citizenship.
   c) Those subject to the measures for protection and improvement of Article 42a of the Criminal Code.
   d) Those expelled from the National Socialist Labor Party because of dishonorable activities.
   e) Those punished by court for treasonable activity.

(2) The Reich Minister of Interior may make exceptions to (c) and (e) of Section 1.

(3) Those subject to compulsory service in the Labor Service who were deprived of eligibility to hold public offices may be called for service only after the expiration of the period of sentence.

Article 6

(1) No persons shall be recruited for the Labor Service who are completely unfitted for the Reich Labor Service.

(2) Those subject to Labor Service who live abroad or who desire to go abroad for a longer period may be relieved of the duty of labor service for up to two years, in exceptional cases permanently, and in any case for the period of the stay abroad.

Article 7

(1) No one shall be allowed to serve in the Reich Labor Service who is of non-Aryan descent or who is married to a person of non-Aryan descent. Non-Aryan descent is determined according to the instructions of the Reich Minister of Interior of August 8, 1933 to Article 1a, Section 3 of the Reich Law Concerning State Officials (*Reichsgesetzblatt* I, p. 575).

(2) Non-Aryans who by Article 15, Section 2 of the Army Law have been declared worthy of military service may also be allowed to serve in the Reich Labor Service. They cannot, however, become superiors in the Reich Labor Service.

Article 8

Upon showing cause for pressing occupational reasons those subject to Labor Service may have their service postponed from the two-year period to a period of five years.

307

The Third Reich

Article 9

The provisions for the Labor Service duties of young women remain subject to special legal regulations.

Article 10

(1) Members of the Reich Labor Service are:
  a) the permanent staff,
  b) those recruited for the Labor Service,
  c) volunteers in the Labor Service.
(2) For performance of definite services in the inside service persons may also be engaged by labor contracts.

Article 11

(1) The permanent staff consists of the regular leaders and officials as well as the candidates for these posts. The regular leaders and officials are active professionally in the Reich Labor Service.
(2) A candidate for leader must, before his elevation to regular troop leader, give written engagement to serve continuously for at least ten years and must supply proof of his Aryan descent; he must furthermore have completed his active service in the army.
(3) Regular leaders and officials are retired upon attainment of definite age limits.
(4) Officials of other departments who are transferred to the Reich Labor Service retain all the salary rights which they had up to then acquired.
(5) The *Führer* and Reich Chancellor appoints and dismisses all members of the Reich Labor Service from the rank of Work Leader upwards. All other members of the permanent staff are appointed and dismissed by the Reich Minister of Interior on the recommendations of the Reich Labor Leader. He may yield these powers to the Reich Labor Leader.

Article 12

(1) A regular leader or official may be dismissed from service at any time
  a) in reasonable cases upon his own request;
  b) if he no longer possesses the physical or intellectual powers necessary for the exercise of his duties and if, according to the statement of the physician of the Labor Service, he cannot expect to regain these necessary powers within the year's term;
  c) if in the judgment of his superior leader he no longer possesses the capabilities for the exercise of his duties.
(2) Dismissal is obligatory if reasons barring membership in the Labor Service as indicated in Articles 5 or 7 are subsequently discovered.
(3) Notice of dismissal and reasons therefore in cases indicated in Sec-

tion 1, letters (b) and (c), are to be given three months in advance for members of the permanent staff who have served more than five years; for other members of the permanent staff one month in advance. In all other cases there is no definite time period for dismissal notice necessary.

Article 13

Membership in the Reich Labor Service lasts from the day of entrance or calling in (day of presentation) up to the expiration of the day of dismissal.

Article 14

Membership in the Reich Labor Service is no ground for any labor or service status in the meaning of the labor law and Article 11 of the decree for welfare administration.

Article 15

Members of the Reich Labor Service are subject to the disciplinary measures of the Reich Labor Service.

Article 16

(1) Those subject to compulsory Labor Service and volunteers may be dismissed from the Reich Labor Service ahead of time
    a) upon application; if after having been called, a reason for post-ponement according to Article 8 is involved,
    b) if the necessary physical and intellectual powers for the exercise of their duties are no longer possessed.
(2) Advance dismissal of compulsory and voluntary members of the Labor Service is obligatory if reasons barring membership in the Reich Labor Service as indicated in Articles 5 and 7 are subsequently established.

Article 17

(1) Members of the Reich Labor Service are not to engage in any active service in the National Socialist Labor Party or in any of its affiliates. This is not to prejudice their membership in the party.
(2) Members of the Reich Labor Service must have permission for soliciting or exercising membership in organizations of any sort as well as for the formation of organizations within or without the Reich Labor Service.

Article 18

Members of the Reich Labor Service must secure permission to marry.

Article 19

Members of the Reich Labor Service must secure permission to take over the direction of a business either for themselves or for the members of their family, as well as for accepting any additional occupation involving remuneration.

Article 20

(1) Members of the Reich Labor Service may refuse positions as guardian, co-guardian, trustee, advisor or any honorary activity in the Reich, state or municipal service or in the party service.

(2) To assume such positions permission must be secured. Such permission may be denied only in exceptional cases.

Article 21

In case of sickness or accident, members of the Reich Labor Service are entitled to free medical attention and nursing according to separate regulations.

Article 22

Salaries of members of the Reich Labor Service are regulated by the salary decree of the Reich Labor Service.

Article 23

(1) Claims pertaining to the rights of property which derive from membership in the Reich Labor Service are regulated by the appropriate ordinances for Reich officials. The supreme agency in the sense of these ordinances is the Reich Labor Leader.

(2) Decisions by the agencies of the Reich Labor Service on matters of enlistment (Articles 5, 6, 7), replacement (Article 8) and dismissal (Articles 12 and 16) are binding for courts-of-law. The same applies to decisions regarding temporary removals.

Article 24

Pensions for persons injured in service and for members of the permanent staff retiring after at least ten years of service and their survivors are regulated by the Law on Pensions for the Reich Labor Service.

Article 25

(1) The *Führer* and Reich Chancellor or any agency empowered by him may permit retiring members of the Reich Labor Service to wear the uniform of the Reich Labor Service, subject to recall.

(2) This right may be granted only after honorable service of at least ten years duration.

Article 26

The Reich Minister of Interior will issue the legal and administrative decrees for the carrying out and amplification of this law.

Appendix IV

Article 27

This law goes into effect on July 1, 1935.

The Reich Minister of Interior is empowered to determine a later date for several provisions of this law to take effect.

Berlin, June 26, 1935.

v. The Nuremberg Laws on Citizenship and Race

I. THE REICH CITIZENSHIP LAW OF SEPTEMBER 15, 1935

THE Reichstag has adopted unanimously the following law which is herewith promulgated.

Article 1

(1) A subject of the state is he who belongs to the protective union of the German Reich and who, therefore, has particular obligations towards the Reich.

(2) The status of subject is acquired in accordance with the provisions of the Reich and State Law of Citizenship.

Article 2

(1) A citizen of the Reich is only that subject who is of German or kindred blood and who, through his conduct, shows that he is both desirous and fit to serve faithfully the German people and the Reich.

(2) The right to citizenship is acquired by the granting of Reich citizenship papers.

(3) Only the citizen of the Reich enjoys full political rights in accordance with the provisions of the laws.

Article 3

The Reich Minister of the Interior in conjunction with the Deputy to the *Führer* will issue the necessary legal and administrative decrees for the carrying out and amplification of this law.

Promulgated: September 16, 1935. In force: September 30, 1935.

I a. FIRST SUPPLEMENTARY DECREE OF NOVEMBER 14, 1935

On the basis of Article 3 of the Reich Law of Citizenship of September 15, 1935, the following is hereby decreed:

Article 1

(1) Until further provisions regarding citizenship papers all subjects of German or kindred blood who possessed the right to vote in the Reich-

312

stag elections at the time the Law of Citizenship came into effect shall for the time being possess the rights of Reich citizens. The same shall be true of those upon whom the Reich Minister of Interior in conjunction with the Deputy to the *Führer* shall bestow citizenship.

(2) The Reich Minister of the Interior, in conjunction with the Deputy to the *Führer* may revoke citizenship.

Article 2

(1) The provisions of Article 1 apply also to subjects who are of mixed Jewish blood.

(2) An individual of mixed Jewish blood is one who is descended from one or two grandparents who were racially full Jews, in so far as he does not count as a Jew according to Section 2 of Article 5. As full-blooded Jewish grandparents shall be considered those who belonged to the Jewish religious community.

Article 3

Only citizens of the Reich, as bearers of full political rights, can exercise the right of voting in political affairs, and can hold public office. The Reich Minister of the Interior or any agency empowered by him can make exceptions during the transition period with regard to occupying public office. These measures do not apply to affairs pertaining to religious organizations.

Article 4

(1) A Jew cannot be a citizen of the Reich. He cannot exercise the right to vote; he cannot occupy public office.

(2) Jewish officials are to be retired as of December 31, 1935. In case these officials served at the front in the World War either for Germany or her allies, they shall receive as pension, until the attainment of the age limit, the full salary last received, on the basis of which their pension would have to be computed; they do not however advance according to seniority grades. After they reach the age limit their pension is to be calculated anew according to the salary last received on the basis of which their pension was to be computed.

(3) Affairs of religious organizations are not concerned therewith.

(4) The conditions of service of teachers in public Jewish schools remain unchanged until the new regulation of the Jewish school system.

Article 5

(1) A Jew is anyone who is descended from at least three grandparents who were racially full Jews. . . .

(2) A Jew is also one who is descended from two full-Jewish grandparents if:

(a) he belonged to the Jewish religious community at the time this law was issued or who joined the community later.

(b) at the time the law was issued he was married to a person who was a Jew or was subsequently married to a Jew.

(c) he is the offspring from a marriage with a Jew, in the sense of Section 1, which was contracted after the coming into effect of the Law for the Protection of German Blood and Honor of September 15, 1935.

(d) he is the offspring of an extra-marital relationship with a Jew, according to Section 1, and will be born out of wedlock after July 31, 1936.

Article 6

(1) In so far as there are, in laws of the Reich or decrees of the National Socialist Labor Party and its affiliates, certain requirements for the purity of the German blood which go beyond Article 5, the same remain untouched.

(2) Other requirements for the purity of the blood that go beyond Article 5 may be submitted only with the consent of the Minister of the Interior and the Deputy to the *Führer*. All such requirements already in existence will be discarded after January 1, 1936 unless they have been allowed by the Minister of the Interior together with the Deputy to the *Führer*. Proposals for admission are to be presented to the Reich Minister of Interior.

Article 7

The *Führer* and Chancellor of the Reich is empowered to release anyone from the provisions of these administrative decrees.

II. THE LAW FOR THE PROTECTION OF GERMAN BLOOD AND HONOR, SEPTEMBER 15, 1935

Imbued with the knowledge that the purity of the German blood is the necessary condition for the continued existence of the German people, and animated by the inflexible will to ensure the existence of the German nation for all future times, the Reichstag has unanimously adopted the following law which is hereby promulgated:

Article 1

(1) Marriages between Jews and subjects of German or kindred blood are forbidden. Marriages concluded despite this law are invalid, even if they are concluded abroad in order to circumvent this law.

(2) Proceedings for annulment may be initiated only by the Public Prosecutor.

Appendix V

Article 2

Extra-marital relations between Jews and subjects of German or kindred blood are forbidden.

Article 3

Jews may not employ in domestic service female subjects of German or kindred blood who are under the age of 45 years.

Article 4

(1) Jews are forbidden to display the Reich and national flag or to show the national colors.

(2) The display of the Jewish colors, however, is permitted for them. The exercise of this right is protected by the state.

Article 5

(1) Whoever acts in violation of the prohibition of Article 1 will be punished with penal servitude.

(2) The man who acts in violation of Article 2 will be punished with either imprisonment or penal servitude.

(3) Whoever acts in violation of Articles 3 or 4 will be punished with imprisonment up to one year and with a fine or with either of these penalties.

Article 6

The Reich Minister of Interior in conjunction with the Deputy to the *Führer* and the Reich Minister of Justice, will issue the necessary legal and administrative decrees for the carrying out and amplification of this law.

Article 7

This law goes into effect on the day following promulgation except for Article 3 which shall go into force on January 1, 1936.

VI. *Law Making the Hitler Youth a State Agency, December 1, 1936*

THE future of the German people depends upon its youth. The entire German youth must, therefore, be prepared for its future duties. The Reich government, therefore, has decided upon the following law which is hereby decreed:

Article 1

The entire German youth within the territory of the Reich is brought together within the Hitler Youth.

Article 2

The entire German youth, outside of their homes and school, is to be educated in the Hitler Youth physically, spiritually and morally in the spirit of National Socialism and for service to nation and national community.

Article 3

The task of educating the entire German youth within the Hitler Youth is entrusted to the Reich Youth Leader of the National Socialist Labor Party. He thereby becomes "Youth Leader of the German Reich." He has the status of a chief Reich office with its seat in Berlin and he is immediately responsible to the *Führer* and Reich Chancellor.

Article 4

The legal decrees and general administrative measures necessary for carrying out and amplifying this law will be issued by the *Führer* and Reich Chancellor.

Berlin, December 1, 1936.

VII. The German-Japanese Agreement on Communism Signed at Berlin November 25, 1936 *

THE German Government and the Japanese Government, recognizing that the aim of the Communist Internationale known as the Comintern is directed at disrupting and violating existing States with all means at its command and convinced that to tolerate the Communist Internationale's interference with the internal affairs of nations not only endangers their internal peace and social well-being but threatens world peace at large, animated by a desire to work in common against Communist disruptive influences, have arrived at the following agreement:

1. The high contracting parties agree to mutually inform each other concerning the activities of the Communist Internationale, to consult with each other concerning measures to combat this activity, and to execute these measures in close cooperation with each other.

2. The two high contracting States will jointly invite third parties whose domestic peace is endangered by the disruptive activities of the Communist Internationale to embark upon measures for warding these off in accordance with the spirit of this agreement or to join in it.

3. For this agreement, both the German and Japanese texts are regarded as original versions. It becomes effective the day of signing and is in force for a period of five years.

The high contracting State will, at the proper time before expiration of this period, arrive at an understanding with each other concerning the form this cooperation is to take.

Supplementary Protocol

A. The competent authorities of both high contracting parties will cooperate most clearly in connection with the exchange of information concerning the activities of the Communist Internationale, as well as in connection with publicity and defense measures against the Communist Internationale.

* Reprinted by permission of The Associated Press, from *The New York Times*, November 26, 1936.

B. The competent authorities of both high contracting parties will, within the framework of existing laws, take strict measures against those who, at home or abroad, directly or indirectly, are active in the service of the Communist Internationale or lend a helping hand to its disruptive work.

With a view to facilitating the cooperation of the competent authorities of both high contracting parties, specified in (A), a permanent commission will be created. In this commission the further defensive measures necessary for combating the disruptive work of the Communist Internationale will be considered and deliberated upon.

Berlin, November 25, 1936; that is, the November 25 of the eleventh year of the Showa Period.

RIBBENTROP,
MUSHAKOJI.

VIII. *Letter of Resignation as High Commissioner for Refugees Coming from Germany*

By James G. McDonald

London, December 27, 1935.
The Secretary General of the League of Nations, Geneva, Switzerland,

Sir:

On October 26, 1933, the President of the Council of the League of Nations did me the honor to appoint me High Commissioner for Refugees (Jewish and Other) Coming from Germany, to "negotiate and direct" the "international collaboration" necessary to solve the "economic, financial and social problem" of the refugees. I hereby beg to submit through you to the Council of the League my resignation from this office, to become effective as from December 31, 1935.

2. In the period of over two years since the establishment of the office, conditions in Germany which create refugees have developed so catastrophically that a reconsideration by the League of Nations of the entire situation is essential. The legislation and administrative and party action against "non-Aryans" were steadily intensified, and culminated in the autumn of 1935 when a series of new laws and decrees initiated a fresh wave of repression and persecution of a character which was not envisaged in 1933.

The intensified persecution in Germany threatens the pauperization or exile of hundred of thousands of Germans—men, women, and children—not only Jews but also the "non-Aryan" Christians treated as Jews, and Protestants and Catholics who in obedience to their faith and conscience dare to resist the absolute will of the National Socialist State.

3. Apart from all questions of principle and of religious persecution, one portentous fact confronts the community of States. More than half a million persons, against whom no charge can be made except that they are not what the National Socialists choose to regard as "Nordic," are being crushed. They cannot escape oppression by any act of their own free-will, for what has been called "the membership of non-Aryan race" cannot be changed or kept in abeyance.

Tens of thousands are today anxiously seeking ways to flee abroad;

but except for those prepared to sacrifice the whole or greater part of their savings, the official restrictions on export of capital effectively bar the road to escape, and the doors of most countries are closed against impoverished fugitives. Nevertheless, if the present pressure is not relieved, it is inconceivable that those who can flee will remain within Germany.

The task of saving these victims calls for renewed efforts of the philanthropic bodies. The private organizations, Jewish and Christian, may be expected to do their part if the governments, acting through the League, make possible a solution. But in the new circumstances it will not be enough to continue the activities on behalf of those who flee from the Reich. Efforts must be made to remove or mitigate the causes which create German refugees. This could not have been any part of the work of the High Commissioner's office; nor, presumably, can it be a function of the body to which the League may decide to entrust future administrative activities on behalf of the refugees. It is a political function, which properly belongs to the League itself.

4. At the last meeting, on October 16, 1935, of the permanent committee of the governing body of the High Commission, at which my intention to resign was fully discussed, action was taken to liquidate the office of the High Commissioner at the end of January, 1936, or sooner if before that date the council of the League had made other provision for the coordination of the activities on behalf of the refugees coming from Germany. It was the expectation of the permanent committee that the committee of experts provided for by the assembly of 1935 to study the reorganization of the activities on behalf of the "German" and of the "Nansen" refugees would complete its investigations in time to present a plan for consideration, and, it was hoped, for action, by the Council at its meeting in January, 1936.

It has been the sense of the governing body that the work of assistance in the countries of refuge could be better carried forward by an organization directly under the authority of the League. It is now clear that the effectiveness of the High Commissioner's efforts was weakened from the beginning by the compromise which was agreed upon at the time his office was set up—that is, the decision to separate it definitely from the League. This compromise was accepted in order to avoid the veto of Germany, which was then an active member of the League.

5. Progress has been made during the last three years in settling the refugees from Germany. Of the more than 80,000 who have already left the Reich, approximately three-fourths have now found new homes —more than half of these in Palestine—or have been repatriated to their countries of origin. This accomplishment has been primarily the work of refugees themselves and of the philanthropic organizations—Jewish and Christian—whose devoted labors have been ceaselessly carried on in many parts of the world. Probably not more than 15,000 refugees now re-

main unplaced. (An account of the work done for the refugees since April, 1933, is being published.)

6. The care and the settlement of these remaining thousands of refugees could and would be borne by the already heavily burdened private organizations were they not fearful that the number of refugees may be increased many times by new flights from Germany.

The facts which arouse these apprehensions are indisputable. They are evidenced clearly in the German laws, decrees, judicial decisions and party pronouncements and practices during the last two years. The culmination of these attacks on the Jews, the Christian "non-Aryans," and the political and religious dissenters was the new legislation announced at the Party Congress at Nuremberg last September. The core of that enactment was the law limiting citizenship to those who are "of German or cognate blood," and who also conform to the National Socialist conception of loyalty to the State. As the direct result in Germany not only the Jews, who now number about 435,000, but also tens of thousands of Christian "non-Aryans" who are classified as Jews, lost their citizenship, were disfranchised, and made ineligible to hold public office. Indirectly, through this new law, a constitutional basis was laid for unrestricted discriminations against all those whom the party may wish to penalize.

The denationalization by the German Government of thousands of German citizens has added to the hardships both of those remaining in Germany and of the refugees, and is an increasing burden on States which have admitted the refugees while in possession of German nationality.

7. Relentlessly the Jews and "non-Aryans" are excluded from all public offices, from the exercise of the liberal professions, and from any part in the cultural and intellectual life of Germany. Ostracized from social relations with "Aryans," they are subjected to every kind of humiliation. Neither sex nor age exempts them from discrimination. Even the Jewish and "non-Aryan" children do not escape cruel forms of segregation and persecution. In party publications, directly sponsored by the government, "Aryan" children are stirred to hate the Jews and the Christian "non-Aryans," to spy upon them and to attack them, and to incite their own parents to extirpate the Jews altogether.

8. It is being made increasingly difficult for Jews and "non-Aryans" in Germany to sustain life. Condemned to segregation within the four corners of the legal and social Ghetto, which has now closed upon them, they are increasingly prevented from earning their living. Indeed, more than half of the Jews remaining in Germany have already been deprived of their livelihood. In many parts of the country there is a systematic attempt at starvation of the Jewish population. In no field of economic activity is there any security whatsoever. For some time it has been impossible for Jewish business men and shopkeepers

321

to carry on their trades in small towns. The campaign against any dealings with Jews is now systematically prosecuted in the larger towns. Despite the restrictions upon migration from the provinces into the few largest cities where Jewish economic activity is not yet completely excluded, the Jews are fleeing to those cities because there only can they hope to escape, at least for a time, from the more brutal forms of persecution.

This influx has exhausted already the resources of the Jewish philanthropic and educational institutions in Germany. The victims of the terrorism are being driven to the point where, in utter anguish and despair, they may burst the frontiers in fresh waves of refugees.

9. Again, as so often during their long heroic and tragic history, the Jewish people are used as the scapegoat for political and partisan purposes. The National Socialists level against them charges of the most outrageous and untenable kind. They ignore all of the facts of the continuous loyalty of the Jews in Germany: for example, during the empire when Jews helped to unify Germany and to make it strong; during the war, when a percentage of Jewish youth as high as that of any other religious community in the Reich gave their lives for the Fatherland, and Jewish scientists and men of affairs helped so notably to enable Germany to prolong the struggle; and under the republic, when Jewish leaders aided in saving Germany from some of the worst effects of defeat.

Instead, it has been found useful to attribute to the Jews the responsibility for the misery and dejection which the German people suffered during the last years of the war and the decade that followed. Though less than a one-hundredth part of the total population, the Jews are held responsible for all the adversity which the German people had to undergo. As in the Middle Ages, when they were massacred and expelled from German States as the cause of the Black Death, so today they are eliminated from the economic and cultural life of Germany and degraded on the ground that they were the cause of the German humiliation. So far does this hatred extend that even the Jewish war veterans, who fought and were wounded in the front-line trenches, have been forced from their positions in the public services, and the names of the Jewish war dead may no longer be engraved on war memorials.

10. The attitude of the German Government is based not only on the theory of "Nordic race" supremacy and the desire to eliminate "foreign racial" elements from the life of the country; it rests also on the conception of the absolute subordination of the individual to the State. An influential section of the party is actively promoting a revival of neo-Paganism which sets itself against both the Old Testament and parts of the New Testament. The conceptions of "blood, race, and soil," propagated with fanatical enthusiasm, menace not alone

322

the Jews, but all those who remain defiantly loyal to the old ideals of religious and individual freedom.

Party leaders violently attack religious freedom in the State and threaten the church with political domination. Outstanding thinkers of the two great Christian communities in Germany and abroad raise their voices in protest against this attack which threatens to increase the number of refugees.

11. The developments since 1933, and in particular those following the Nuremberg legislation, call for fresh collective action in regard to the problem created by persecution in Germany. The moral authority of the League of Nations and of States members of the League must be directed toward a determined appeal to the German Government in the name of humanity and of the principles of the public law of Europe. They must ask for a modification of policies which constitute a source of unrest and perplexity in the world, a challenge to the conscience of mankind, and a menace to the legitimate interests of the States affected by the immigration of German refugees.

12. Apart from the Upper Silesia convention of May, 1922, Germany does not appear to be expressly bound by a treaty obligation providing for equal citizenship of racial, religious, or linguistic minorities. But the principle of respect for the rights of minorities has been during the last three centuries hardening into an obligation of the public law of Europe. That principle was recognized in some of the most important international instruments of the nineteenth century. I may refer to the provisions of the Congress of Vienna, the treaty of guarantee following upon the union of Belgium and Holland, the collective recognition of the independence of Greece, the creation of the autonomous principalities of Moldavia and Wallachia. It was affirmed at the Congress of Berlin in 1878 in relation to newly recognized States. It was deliberately reaffirmed in the Peace Settlement of 1919 and in a series of special minorities treaties as a vital condition both of international justice and of the preservation of the peace of the world. In the case of newly created States its express recognition constituted a condition of admission to the League of Nations.

Neither was the attitude of Germany in this matter open to any doubt. During the peace conference, the German delegation, in urging the adoption of the principle of protection of minorities for the German population in the territories detached from Germany, declared spontaneously that "Germany on her part is resolved to treat minorities of alien origin in her territories according to the same principles." The Allied and Associated Powers expressly took note of that declaration. From the moment of her admission to the League Germany took the lead in securing the effectiveness of the principles of international protection of minorities.

13. The Assembly of the League in 1922 adopted a resolution which

expressed the hope that "States not bound by specific legal obligations in the matter of minorities will nevertheless observe in the treatment of their own minorities at least as high a standard of justice and toleration as is required by the treaties in question." The Assembly in 1933, when considering the question of the persecution of Jews in Germany in connection with the discussion on minorities, reaffirmed that resolution; and in order to dispel doubts whether it applied to the Jews in Germany, voted, with the single dissent of Germany, in favor of a further resolution that the principle "must be applied without exception to all classes of nationals of a State which differ from the majority of the population in race, language, or religion."

The German Jews, although not claiming or desiring to be a minority, are within the scope of this principle because, as was stated at the Assembly, as soon as there is legal discrimination, a minority exists within the meaning of modern law.

14. It is not within my province to state to what extent the practice in this matter of the community of nations in the last hundred years and of the League of Nations has become a rule of customary international law; neither am I called upon to judge how far the declarations and the conduct of Germany prior to 1933 are in themselves sufficient to establish legal presumptions. But both, I believe, are sufficient to establish an appeal to those broad considerations of humanity and of international peace which are the basis of the public law of Europe in the matter of racial and religious minorities.

The growing sufferings of the persecuted minority in Germany and the menace of the growing exodus call for friendly but firm intercession with the German Government, by all pacific means, on the part of the League of Nations, of its member States, and other members of the community of nations.

Pity and reason alike must inspire the hope that intercession will meet with response. Without such response, the problems caused by the persecution of the Jews and the "non-Aryans" will not be solved by philanthropic action, but will continue to constitute a danger to international peace and a source of injury to the legitimate interests of other States.

15. The efforts of the private organizations and of any League organization for refugees can only mitigate a problem of growing gravity and complexity. In the present economic conditions of the world, the European States, and even those overseas, have only a limited power of absorption of refugees. The problem must be tackled at its source if disaster is to be avoided.

This is the function of the League, which is essentially an association of States for the consideration of matters of common concern. The Covenant empowers the Council and the Assembly to deal with any matter within the sphere of activity of the League or affecting the peace of the world. The effort of the League to insure respect for human personality, when not grounded on express provisions of the Covenant or international treaties, has a sure foundation in the fact that the protection of the individual from racial and religious intolerance is a vital condition of international peace and security.

16. I am appending to this letter a comprehensive analysis of the German legislation, administrative decrees and jurisprudence, as well as of their effects on the problems of refugees.

17. I feel bound to conclude this letter on a personal note. Prior to my appointment as High Commissioner for Refugees Coming from Germany, and in particular during the fourteen years following the war, I gave in my former office frequent and tangible proof of my concern that justice be done to the German people. But convinced as I am that desperate suffering in the countries adjacent to Germany, and an even more terrible human calamity within the German frontiers are inevitable unless present tendencies in the Reich are checked or reversed, I cannot remain silent. I am convinced that it is the duty of the High Commissioner for German Refugees, in tendering his resignation, to express an opinion on the essential elements of the task with which the Council of the League entrusted him. When domestic policies threaten the demoralization and exile of hundreds of thousands of human beings, considerations of diplomatic correctness must yield to those of common humanity. I should be recreant if I did not call attention to the actual situation and plead that world opinion, acting through the League and its member States and other countries, move to avert the existing and impending tragedies.

I have the honor to be, Sir,

Your obedient servant,

JAMES G. McDONALD,

High Commissioner for Refugees (Jewish and Other) Coming from Germany.

IX. The Twenty-five Theses of the German Religion

A CATECHISM

By Professor Ernst Bergmann*

1. The German has his own religion, which flows like the living water of his own perception, feeling and thought, and is rooted in his species. We call it the German religion, or the religion of the German people and understand thereby a German faith expressing the peculiarity and integrity of our race.

2. The German religion is the form of faith appropriate to our age, which we Germans would have today if it had been granted to us to have our native German religion developed undisturbed to the present time.

3. The German of today requires a healthy and natural religion which makes him brave, pious and strong in the struggle for people and fatherland. Such a religion is the German religion.

4. The German religion recognizes no dogmas, for it is a religion.

5. The German religion is not a religion of revelation in the Christian sense. It rests rather upon a natural "revelation" of the divine forces in the world and in the human mind.

6. The German religion is a religion of the people. It has nothing to do with free thought, atheist propaganda and the disintegration of religion. We who are genuine followers of the German religion take our stand on the basis of a positive religion.

7. The German religion is not hostile to a Church. It seeks a German Church on the basis of a religious people.

8. God is a moral idea to which we are bound by the eternal creative force of Nature, which works in the world and man. Belief in an other-worldly God is not of Indo-Germanic but of Semitic origin. This kind of God-belief is not a condition of true religion and piety.

* Professor Bergmann is one of the leading figures in the German neo-pagan movement. This catechism is taken from his *Die 25 Thesen der Deutschreligion* (Breslau 1934). The English version of this document is reprinted from number 39 of the Friends of Europe, *Publications* (London, 1936).

Appendix IX

9. In the lap of the divine, living world the knowing Being or Mind grows. Mind is a natural growth of the world of reality. It is not a finished thing at the beginning, but at the end at the height of world development.

10. To God's Being belong will, understanding and personality. These are, however, unique in man. Hence man is the place of God in the world.

11. Man is not God. But he is God's birthplace. God exists and grows in man. If God does not come in man, He never comes. Hence the German religion is the religion of high faith in man.

12. The German religion recognizes no dualism or conflict between body and soul, any more than duality and conflict between God and the world and God and man. We think of the being, body-soul, as a natural unity and entity.

13. The living world is the womb-mother of the high human mind. Knowing, Being and Mind is a birth of the All-Mother. The mother-child thought is hence the right indication of the God-world secret. We speak in a modern nature religion of the Mind-child God, who rests in the womb of the All-Mother.

14. The feelings of union, holiness and blessedness are the basic religious feelings. The Christian feelings of sin, guilt and repentance are not religious feelings at all. They are artificially engendered complexes in man.

15. The ethics of the German religion condemn all belief in inherited sin, as well as the Jewish-Christian teaching of a fallen world and man. Such a teaching is not only non-Germanic and non-German, it is immoral and non-religious. Whoever preaches this, menaces the morality of the people.

16. Whoever forgives sin, sanctions sin. The forgiving of sin undermines religious ethics and destroys the morale of the people.

17. At the heart of the German religious ethics stands concern for the welfare of people and fatherland, not for the blessedness of the individual. The German ethic is not one for the salvation of the individual like the Christian ethic, but one for the welfare of the people as a whole.

18. He who belongs to the German religion is not a slave of God, but lord of the divine within him. German ethics, therefore, reject making man passive for receiving grace, as non-German.

19. In the German religion there is no escape from life, but only release into life. For it, the statement is valid: Whoever loves man heals him before he is born, not before he dies. The genuine Saviour turns his care towards pre-natal man.

20. The ethics of the German religion is an heroic ethics. It rests on three ancient German virtues: bravery, chivalry and fidelity, all of which spring from honor.

21. We of the German religion demand the introduction of religious

327

instruction in the schools. Christian instruction can no longer be regarded as adequate or valid, since Christianity is in our sense no longer a religion.

22. We of the German religion construe the Divine in images true to life—a manly-heroic and a woman-motherly.

23. One of the two religious forms of the German religion is the Nordic Light-Hero as the embodiment of heroic manliness. This Nordic Light-Hero is the image of the high human Mind and of the heroic and helping leader, which goes struggling and triumphant ahead as the Moral Ideal of his people.

24. The Mother with the Child is the truest, most loving, sacred and happiness-bringing of all the symbols of world and life. The Mother figure is the original religious figure from which indeed the God-Father figure derives its splendor. In the German church there must be alongside the manly-heroic figure the dear and faithful picture of the most blessed Mother, if the church is to rest on the laws of life of a people's church.

25. The cult forms of the German religion and of the German People's Church must adapt themselves to the living laws of thought which underlie them. The life of the family, of the state and of the whole nation must be reflected in a natural way in these cult forms of the church, if the church is to be a modern people's church with life flowing through it.

x. Evangelical Church Letter Submitted to Chancellor Hitler in June, 1936*

THE German Evangelical Church, represented by the spiritual members of its provisional administration and by the council supporting it, offers to the Fuehrer and Chancellor respectful greeting.

The German Evangelical Church is closely associated with the Fuehrer and his advisers through the intercession that it makes publicly and in private for the people, the State, and the government. The provisional administration and the council of the German Evangelical Church consider, therefore, that they may undertake to give expression in the present document to the anxieties and fears cherished by many Christians in the communities, by the Councils of Brethren, and by the church leaders in regard to the future of the Evangelical faith and of the Evangelical Church in Germany, and on which they have meditated long and earnestly.

The provisional administration of the German Evangelical Church publishes this document in obedience to the divine charge laid on it to hold forth His word and to bear witness to His commands fearlessly before all the world—even before the sovereigns and rulers of the peoples. It is confident that God accords it the wisdom to fulfil its task so clearly and so unequivocally that its solicitude concerning the Christian conscience and its love for the German people will be both unmistakably discerned.

In presenting these expositions, however, we know that we are impelled only by the one duty, as were our predecessors in office with their declaration of April 11, 1935, that unfortunately had no traceable effect, to help the suffering, confused, and imperiled members of the Evangelical Church by mediating for them. It imports us all that the government of the Reich shall hear clearly and distinctly the voice speaking out of anxiety for the souls intrusted to the church.

The Lord of the church says: For what is a man profited, if he shall gain the whole world and lose his own soul? or what shall a man give in exchange for his soul? These words show how great and serious is the service required by God of the church, and they remind us at the same time of the limits set to all earthly powers and their strivings. They point

* Reprinted by permission from *International Conciliation*, No. 324 (November, 1936).

out finally the danger constantly menacing unnumbered people, including members of the church.

1. Danger of De-Christianization

The provisional administration appreciates what it signified in the year 1933 and in later years that those responsible for the National Socialist revolution could declare emphatically that "In gaining our victory over Bolshevism we overcame at the same time the enemy that combated Christianity and the Christian churches and threatened to destroy them." What we now see, however, is that the Christian church is being combated actively and keenly by a section of the German people as it never was since 1918.

No power in the world, by whatever name it may be called, is able to destroy or to protect the church of God against His will; this is God's concern. It is the part of the church, however, to take up the cause of the consciences of its members that are attacked.

Many baptized Christians are menaced by the distress and confusion produced by the religious combats of the present day with temporal and eternal adversity. When even high authorities in the State and in the party publicly assail the Christian faith (see, among others, speech by Dr. Ley), church members who are already estranged from the church and its message are more and more enmeshed in their unbelief, the waverers and the doubters are made completely uncertain and are driven to defection. Grave danger, as a matter of fact, exists that the Evangelical youth will be prevented from coming to Him who is the only Saviour of German as well as of other boys and girls.

Against such an imperilment of members of the churches all church leaders conscious of their responsibility must offer strenuous resistance, and to this opposition belongs the clear question to the Fuehrer and Chancellor whether the attempt to de-Christianize the German people is to become the official policy of the government through the further cooperation of responsible statesmen or perhaps by simply looking on, letting things take their course.

2. "Positive Christianity"

We sincerely hope that in order to prevent the aggravation of the religious combats in Germany the government of the Reich will listen to what the Evangelical Church has to say. When the National Socialist party declared in its program that it stood on the basis of a "positive Christianity" the whole church population could not but understand and was intended to understand that the Christian faith, in conformity with the confessions and the preaching of the church, should be accorded freedom and protection in the Third Reich, and even help and encouragement.

Later on, however, authoritative persons in the State and in the party have given quite an arbitrary interpretation to the words, "positive Christianity." The Reich Minister for Propaganda and National Enlightenment, for example, declared positive Christianity to be merely humanitarian service, and joined to this interpretation occasionally an attack on the Christian churches and their allegedly inadequate achievements in the domain of Christian charity, although the State itself had considerably restricted them by its prohibitions since the year 1933.

(N. B.: Speeches by Dr. Goebbels in connection with the winter relief work, and on other occasions: "If the churches were animated by a real Christian spirit they would never have left it to the State to assist the poor in this winter against hunger and cold. . . . I believe that Christ Himself would discover more of His teaching in what we are doing than in this theological hair-splitting. . . . The people would perhaps better understand if the church concerned itself with true Christianity.")

Then Herr Rosenberg, Reich organization leader, proclaimed his mystic doctrine of the blood to be positive Christianity, and, following his example, other notable party leaders defamed as being negative the Christianity as confessed by believers.

(N. B.: Rosenberg: "We recognize today that the general ideas of the Roman and of the Protestant Churches are negative Christianity, and do not, therefore, accord with our soul, and we see that they stand in the way of the organized forces of the nations following nordic-racial principles, that they have to make room for these forces, and that they must allow themselves to be transformed within the meaning of Germanic Christianity.")

(Letter from the 11th Brigade of the S.A. to the administration: "No positive Christian is to be dismissed from the S.A., but the negative Christians who, being bound up with medieval dogmas, are in discord with National Socialism, may be removed. . . . The negative Christian fights for the church, to the detriment of the people, he fights for the church's dogmas, and in support of the lies of the priests, and thus for the devil. . . . To be an S.A. man and to belong to the confessional front of those who confess such a faith is absolute contradiction. . . . If we as positive Christians do not think so badly of our fellow men, we, nevertheless, secure ourselves against the intrusion of spies and of the elements of disintegration.")

Other members of the Reich Government have, under the cloak of positive Christianity, divested of their confessional character categorical conceptions of the Christian faith, such as belief, love, eternity, prayer, resurrection, and have given them a new, purely worldly, psychological interpretation. This has been done even by Herr Kerrl, Reich Minister for the Churches.

(N. B.: General Goering: "We have informed the church that we stand on the basis of positive Christianity. We have shown the church by our religious zeal, by the firmness of our belief, what faith really is." Reich Minister Kerrl: "That (the profession to positive Christianity) has nothing to do with dogmas, it is an independent faith, and is the love that is practical deeds, which enjoins on us to say: 'Lord, forgive them, for they do not know what they do.' The essence of National Socialism is faith, its deeds are love, and National Socialist positive Christianity is love for the neighbor.")

The harm done by such statements is all the greater as the church is never permitted the possibility to refute with similar publicity the misrepresentations of the Christian faith proclaimed from high quarters.

3. Destruction of the Ecclesiastical System

The methods by means of which the German people are to be de-Christianized will be understood in their full association when the statement by Herr Rosenberg, the Reich Organization Leader, is recalled, namely, that in the striving for a German faith "the opposing party must not be spared, it must be overcome intellectually, from the organization standpoint it must perish, and politically it must be kept impotent." (Mythus, page 636.) It is on this standpoint that action has been taken.

Officially, it is true, intervention in any form in the internal structure and in the religious life of the Evangelical Church is disclaimed.

(N. B.: Speeches by Reich Ministers Goering and Kerrl: "If in the course of the past two years there have been disturbances within the Evangelical Church these can have been caused only by individuals, and never by the party as such and never by the State as such." Dr. Goebbels, Reich Minister for Propaganda: "When we preach the unity of the Protestant Church we do so because we consider it to be impossible that in a time when the whole Reich is united twenty-eight national churches can continue to exist. In this we are bringing no dogmas to bear, and we do not meddle with the interpretation of the Gospel. God's command in regard to the exposition of the Gospel should be placed higher than the command of human intermediaries. In the interpretation of political expediency we hold ourselves to be the instrument of God." Herr Hitler: "The party never intended and does not intend today to combat Christianity in Germany in any way whatever. On the contrary, it has endeavored to create a great Evangelical Reich Church by uniting impossible Protestant national churches, and without meddling in the slightest degree in confessional questions." [At the party rally on September 11, 1935.])

As a matter of fact, one interference has followed the other until today since the elections forced on the church in July, 1933.

(N. B.: The most important of these interferences are: 1. The installation of the State Commissar in Prussia on June 24, 1933, and of State Commissars in Bremen, Hesse, Lippe, Mecklenburg, and Saxony. 2. Ordainment of universal church elections by the law of the Reich, promulgated on July 15, 1933. 3. Speech by the Fuehrer in favor of German Christians, broadcast on July 22, 1933. 4. Prohibition to publish anything concerning church affairs by decree (unpublished) of the Reich Minister of the Interior on November 6 and 7, 1934. 5. Establishment of the State Finance Department by the Prussian law of March, 1935. 6. Establishment of an authority over resolutions by Reich law, in June, 1935. 7. The law of September 24, 1935, to secure the German Evangelical Church, and the church committees set up thereupon by the State.

Against individual clergy: 1. Arrest of the Bishop of Wurttemberg and Bavaria in 1934. 2. Conveyance of clergy into concentration camps, especially in Saxony and in Nassau-Hessen. 3. Expulsion of clergy from their parishes, at times from their home province, especially in Prussia. 4. Arrest of 700 pastors (Pfarrer) in Prussia, in connection with the reading from the pulpits, ordered by the Old Prussian Synod in March, 1935, of the proclamation against modern paganism. 5. Permanent prohibition to hold confessional church services, clergymen and laymen forbidden to speak in public, in some cases over the whole of Germany. And others.)

The Evangelical public, who had been guaranteed freedom for the church by the Fuehrer just before the compulsory elections (N. B.: Telegram to the Reich President on July 12, 1933), could be informed only very inadequately concerning the progress of the church strife.

The so-called "Work of Reconciliation," that had started with the creation of the Reich Church Ministry and the setting up of the church committees, remedied, it is true, some abuses occasioned by state officials and members of the party and tolerated by the State.

The Evangelical Christian who looks more closely into the matter sees, however, that by means of this conciliatory work the church is kept in dependence on the State in regard to administration and finances, it is deprived of freedom of speech and of organization, and it is forced to tolerate the teaching of forced doctrine. For him it must be a severe shock to read in the preamble to the "Reconciliation" law of September 24, 1935, that there is no truth in the statement that disquietude prevails in the German Evangelical Church, and that interferences in church matters by the State are not really interferences, but services rendered by the State to the church.

This course of procedure by the State lays a burden that they can hardly bear on the shoulders of the Evangelical Church members who stand by the revealed word of God, who hold to their fathers' profession of faith, and who, because they do this, know what they, as Christians, owe to their people and its government.

4. De-confessionalizing

A movement has been started with the watchword "De-confessionalizing" or "to overcome the confessional disunion," which is intended to render impossible the public work of the church.

The Evangelical Church's own youth organization was long since taken away from it by an agreement between the Reich Youth Leader and the Reich Bishop, who was in no sense entitled to enter into such an agreement. Even the full rights accorded by that arrangement are frequently not permitted to the Evangelical members of the National Socialist Youth Organization.

The chief leaders of the organized youth and, following this example, all persons holding any post of authority in the organization continually hold up their church to the Evangelical youth as being contemptuous and suspicious, and endeavor to undermine the youths' faith in their religion. (N. B., among others: Chief district order 8-35 of the chief district of the girls' organization, dated December 5, 1935: "From this present date I forbid not only the girl and women leaders but also all girls to help in any form of confessional work" [helpers at children's services, etc.]. On the signboard of the Hitler Youth at Halle on the Saale: "Where are the enemies of our Hitler Youth? They are the religious fanatics, who still today fall on their knees with wistful looks directed upward, who spend their time attending churches and praying. We, as Hitler boys, can regard only with contempt or derision young people who still today run to their ridiculous Evangelical or Catholic clubs to give themselves up to eminently superfluous religious reveries." Baldur von Schirach, the Reich Youth Leader, on November 5, 1935: "Rosenberg's way is also the way of the German youth.")

While the State holds today officially to positive Christianity, its new organizations, such as the year on the land or the labor service, not only themselves provide no opportunity for pastoral work among the persons engaged in fulfilling that service, but they deliberately prevent any communication between the pastors of the parishes to which the young people belong. The pastors are refused permission to visit the members of their congregation, and are also forbidden to send them any Evangelical literature. (N. B. among others: Letter from the representative of the government [Regierungs-Praesident] in Breslau, dated October 22, 1935: "In reply to your letter of October 15, to camp-leaderess Schädel concerning the sending of religious literature, I inform you that the Reich and Prussian Minister for Science, for Training, and for the Education of the People emphasized in his decree that the sending of religious publications to persons who are serving their year on the land is forbidden.")

The circumstance that, for example, the Evangelical persons in a Labor Service camp were refused permission to attend a church service on Good Friday shows how far in some cases the de-Christianization has advanced. The regulations concerning the religious care of children in the year on the land speak a very clear language. The de-confessionalization of the schools is deliberately furthered by the State.

In violation of the rights of the church the confessional schools are being abolished, and in this respect the strongest pressure is brought to bear on the conscience of the parents. The course of lessons for religious instruction that has been approved by the authorities is frequently ignored, and in many places today essential portions of Biblical instruction are simply expunged from the religious course (Old Testament), or un-Christian material is put in its place (Old-German Paganism). (N. B. among others: Citation of a decree of the Ministry of State for Anhalt, against which the women of the German Evangelical Church have protested in vain.) Religious services in the schools, and school prayers are neglected ever more frequently, or they are transformed to mark the de-Christianization even of the outer forms of scholastic life.

The education of the coming race of theologians in the universities is intrusted more and more to professors and lecturers who have proved themselves to be teachers of false doctrine; the destruction of the theological faculties in Prussia throws a strong light on this picture. The Ministry for Science and for the Education of the People has demanded the reinstatement of teachers of false doctrine as members of the examining boards of the universities. De-Christianization is in reality the deconfessionalization of public life, which suppresses ever more and more Christian influence and Christian cooperation by means of the radio, the daily newspapers, and of public lectures.

5. National Socialist View of Life

The National Socialist organizations require of their evangelical members that these shall pledge themselves without any qualification or restriction to the National Socialist view of life. (N. B.: Ley, Labor Front leader: "The party claims the totality of the soul of the German people. It can and will not suffer that another party or point of view dominates in Germany. We believe that the German people can become eternal only through National Socialism, and therefore we require the last German, whether Protestant or Catholic.") This view of life is frequently presented and described as a positive substitute for Christianity that has to be vanquished.

When blood, race, nationality, and honor are thus raised to the rank of qualities that guarantee eternity the Evangelical Christian is bound, by the first commandment, to reject the assumption. When the "Aryan" human being is glorified, God's Word bears witness to the sinfulness of all men. When, within the compass of the National Socialist view of life, an anti-Semitism is forced on the Christian that binds him to hatred of the Jew, the Christian injunction to love one's neighbor still stands for him opposed to it.

The members of our Evangelical community have to submit to an especially severe conflict in their conscience when, in compliance with their duty as parents, they have to combat the penetration of these anti-Christian ideals in their children's minds.

6. Morality and Justice

We see with profound anxiety that a system of morality essentially foreign to Christianity is circulating among our people, and threatens to disintegrate it. We know perfectly well that in his speech on March 23,

335

The Third Reich

1933, the Fuehrer acknowledged the moral importance of the Christian confessions for the life of the people, but the power of the new morality has up to the present been greater than that declaration.

On all sides what is of advantage to the people is regarded as being good. (N. B.: From the paper read before the Juridical Congress at Leipzig, 1936, by Dr. Barth, leader of the department for legal policy in the National Socialist party: "Reich Minister Dr. Frank established the legal-political principle that 'Right is what serves the people; wrong what is detrimental to them,' and in this principle are points of discernment of the innermost connection between the vital necessities of the nation and its consciousness of justice.")

With the knowledge of Herr Derichsweiler, leader of the Reich Department, it could be declared that the expression "positive Christianity" in Article 24 of the party program was used only in the manner in which the full truth is withheld from a person who is ill. Such an attitude places considerations of expediency above the truthfulness required in God's commandment.

This contempt of the command to be sincere and truthful, emanating from the spirit of morality based on what is advantageous to the people, will be especially evident to the Evangelical Christian from the manner in which the church strife is officially represented (see above), from the treatment accorded to the Evangelical press and to the question of Evangelical assemblies, from the perversion of the idea of voluntariness to its opposite in connection with assemblies and with canvassing for entrance into organizations, etc.

The Evangelical Church welcomes with gratitude, in view of Christ's commands, in the Sermon on the Mount, the fact that the number of oaths in the law courts has dwindled under the dominion of the present State to a fragment. It must, however, deplore, as a fresh victory for the anti-Christian spirit, the fact that the oath is being applied to an alarming extent in swearing allegiance and as a pledge, and has thus depreciated in value to an alarming extent. Seeing that every oath in God's eyes is a declaration or assurance given under the eyes of God, even when God's name is not expressly used, the circumstance that many persons are made to swear one after the other at very short intervals must rob the oath of its dignity, and lead to the profanation and abuse of the name of God.

Evangelical parents consider it to be absolutely intolerable that pledges of the nature of an oath are taken from their children at a very early age. (N. B.: The wording of the pledge given by the Hitler Youth: "I promise solemnly to be loyal to the Fuehrer Adolf Hitler and to serve unselfishly in the Hitler Youth. I promise solemnly to stand up at all times for the unity and comradeship of the German youth. I promise solemnly obedience to the Reich youth leader and to all leaders of the Hitler Youth. I promise solemnly by our sacred flag that I will always endeavor to be worthy of it. So help me, God.")

Appendix X

In the discharge of our Christian duties we hear ever more frequently of persons declaring that they did not feel bound by an oath which it would have threatened their very existence to refuse. The Evangelical Church would be able to combat more easily such a manner of thinking among its members that runs counter to the Christian requirement, if it were permitted to the Christian to give the natural explanation that no oath can cover proceedings that are contrary to God's commandments.

It has actually happened that earnest Christians, who, under God's will, were fully ready to work in obedience to their superiors, have been dismissed from their posts because they claimed the right to that explanation. It is thus very difficult for many officials to maintain an absolutely sincere attitude.

The value attached to the voting paper in the last Reichstag elections caused many Evangelical Christians pangs of conscience. That value is founded on the fact that the advantage of the people is placed above veracity. Evangelical Christians, who acknowledge sincerity in their decisions were ridiculed, or even maltreated.

Evangelical Christians are convinced, on the foundation of the Holy Scriptures, that God is the protector of the right and of those without rights, and so we regard it as turning away from Him when arbitrary dealing creeps into affairs of law, and things occur that "are not right before the Lord." To these things belong not only the many circumstances in the Church combat, but also what is ultimately denial of justice by the institution and the demeanor of the Ecclesiastical Decree center. (The law of the Reich, dated June 24, 1935, concerning the procedure of the center in German Evangelical Church matters deprives church disputes of the right to judicial decision, and substitutes for this the decision of a political functionary, who, according to an authoritative member of the decree center, sets himself the task to promote political construction. This decree center has been in existence for a year and has not yet decided one of the seventy cases that have been laid before it. The persons concerned in these cases are thus practically deprived of legal rights.)

The Evangelical conscience, that shares the responsibility for the people and the government, is most heavily burdened by the fact that there are still concentration camps in Germany, that describes itself as a country in which justice is administered, and that the measures and actions of the secret State police are exempt from any judicial control. Evangelical Christians faithful to their confession whose honor may be assailed are often not accorded the protection of their honor that is afforded to the other citizens.

Evangelical Christianity sees in these matters also the danger of an anti-Christian spirit gaining the ascendancy over our moral and juridical reasoning.

We have endeavored to justify publicly the great anxiety felt in widespread Evangelical circles over the circumstances that authoritative forces in this country are prosecuting the suppression of the Evangelical Church, the disintegration of its faith, and the setting aside of the Evangelical morality, in short, de-Christianization on the widest scale. We cannot permit ourselves to be reassured in regard to this view of the state of affairs that we have arrived at on the basis of careful observations by the presentation of opposing statements and facts.

We beg the government of the Reich to consider whether it can be permanently beneficial to our people that the path hitherto taken shall be followed farther. The coercion of the consciences, the persecution of Evangelical conviction, the mutual spying and eavesdropping already exert a baleful influence.

Even a great cause, if it places itself in opposition to the revealed will of God, must finally bring the people to ruin. God's church will continue to exist, even if millions of Evangelical Christians sink under the endeavor to de-Christianize the German people. The German people have, however, not been given the promise that the poison of an anti-Christian spirit shall not harm them, even if they realize only perhaps after a long time that they have been defrauded of their best inheritance by those who took Christ from them.

Our people threaten to break down the barriers set up by God; they wish to make of themselves the measure of all things. That is human arrogance, that rises up against God.

In this connection we must make known to the Fuehrer and Chancellor our uneasiness over the fact that he is often revered in form that is due to God alone. It is only a few years ago that the Fuehrer himself disapproved of his picture being placed on Evangelical altars. His judgment is taken to be the standard unrestrainedly today not only in political decisions, but also in regard to morality and justice in our people, and he himself is vested with the dignity of the national priest, and even of the mediator between God and the people.

(N. B.: Dr. Goebbels on April 19, 1936: "When the Fuehrer addressed his last appeal to the people on March 28, it was as if a profound agitation went through the whole nation; one felt that Germany was transformed into one single House of God, in which its intercessor stood before the throne of the Almighty to bear witness. . . . It seemed to us that this cry to heaven of a people for freedom and peace could not die away unheard. That was religion in its profoundest and most mystical sense. A nation then acknowledged God through its spokesman, and laid its destiny and its life with full confidence in His hand." See also Goering's speeches.)

We beg, however, that our people may be free to pursue their way in future under the sign of the cross of Christ, that our grandchildren may not one day curse the fathers for having built up a state on the earth for them and left it behind, but shut them out of the kingdom of God.

What we have said to the Fuehrer in this memorandum we had to say under the responsibility of our office. The church is in the hands of the Lord.

338

Appendix X

The ecclesiastical members of the provisional administration of the German Evangelical Church. (Signed) Mueller, Albertz, Bohm, Forck, Fricke.

The Council of the German Evangelical Church. (Signed) Asmussen, Lucking, Middendorff, Niemoller, Von Thadden.

XI. *German Evangelical Church Manifesto of August 23, 1936*[*]

To Evangelical Christians and the Authorities in Germany.

Brethren and Sisters:

The German people is facing a decision of the greatest historical importance.

The question is whether the Christian faith is to retain its right to exist in Germany or not. Today the gospel of Jesus Christ is being attacked here systematically with unequaled violence. This is being done not only by those who reject any belief in God, but also by those who do not wish to deny God, but think they can reject the revelations of Jesus Christ. Powers of the State and of the party are being used against the gospel of Jesus Christ and against those who profess it.

It is hard for us to say this.

The Evangelical Church knows that it is bound to our people and its authorities by the word of God and has its duties toward them. On every Sunday divine aid is asked for the Fuehrer and the Fatherland in the Evangelical Church services. Three years ago millions of Evangelical Germans welcomed the new beginning in the life of our people with warm hearts. They did so with all the more joy because the government of the nation had said in its first proclamation of February 1, 1933, that it would "firmly protect Christianity as the basis of our whole moral system."

It is absolutely fantastic for Evangelical Christians to think that official organs in the German Fatherland turn against the gospel of Jesus Christ. But it is happening, nevertheless.

We have kept silence about this for a long time. We have allowed ourselves to be told that it was only the action of a few individuals who would be called to order. We have waited; we have made representations. And the Fuehrer has been told what was weighing down the hearts and consciences of Evangelical Christians.

Already on October 4, 1935, the then acting management of the German Evangelical Church, the National Council of Brothers, and the church governing bodies and councils of brothers affiliated with the acting manage-

[*] Reprinted by permission from *International Conciliation*, No. 324 (November, 1936).

ment directed a communication to him in the name of the whole Confessional Church of Germany. It sounds like a cry of the deepest distress when this communication begins as follows:

> It has gone so far among the German people that the honor of German citizens is being trampled in the dust because they are Christians. The Christian population of Germany notes with great perturbation that it is being ridiculed and scorned in every way (in the press, theatres, lectures, and mass meetings) for its faith in the will of Jesus Christ, and its German sentiments and trustworthiness are being doubted.
>
> Especial objects of such suspicions are those who are determined to cling loyally to the gospel. All attempts to improve this situation have remained vain, while at the same time we are being deprived in an ever-increasing degree of practically all possibility of public defense.

During this year the present acting management and the Council of the German Evangelical Church have sent to the Fuehrer a memorandum making apparent the whole misery and trouble of the Evangelical population. This memorandum is backed up point for point with detailed evidence. With the greatest conscientiousness, this memorandum and its contents were kept secret from the public, indeed even from the members of the Confessional Church, in order to give an opportunity to the Fuehrer of the Reich to give it a thorough examination and at the same time to avoid public misuse of this memorandum. Against our will and without the responsibility of the Confessional Church, this memorandum was published in the foreign press and thus became known also in Germany.

Now we are forced publicly to stand by our word. Now we must prove to the church what motivates us in connection with our people and our church. It is the duty of the Christian Church freely and publicly to oppose attacks upon the gospel, without fear of man. It is its duty especially to open the eyes of the rising generation to the danger menacing us all. It is in this sense of duty that we speak. What the result will be we leave in the hands of Him who has called us to His service. He has commanded it; He will take care of it.

The truth of the gospel is being attacked most openly, even by leading men of the State. We draw attention to the speech of National Director Dr. Ley [Dr. Robert Ley, head of the German Labor Front] on May 1, 1936, which was broadcast over the air and published in the whole German press.

The Evangelical Church is not permitted to repel such attacks before the general public. In the training camps the conception of the world contained in the Rosenberg Mythus, which exalts man and demeans God, frequently is taught.

With complete candor it already is being announced on occasion that this point of view is irreconcilable with the Christian faith and that it is destined to replace that faith. Even those Christians who have the honest desire to serve their people must be fought. Thus it was said in a students' training camp: When the party program mentions "positive Christianity" it really does not mean Christianity, but just a positive religious feeling in general. It was not wished to say this openly right at once, because the doctor cannot tell the whole truth to a sick man.

These expressions have been expressly verified by National Office Director Albrecht Derichsweiler. They have become known to hundreds of thousands. Never have they been officially denied. The totalitarian pretension of this point of view places innumerable Evangelical believers in a difficult position with their conscience and in constant temptation to be hypocrites and liars.

Under the slogan "De-confessionalization of public life," the church is being forced more and more to limit all its activities to within the church walls. In the country of Martin Luther the Evangelical Christians are being prevented from bearing witness to the gospel in public gatherings.

Preaching and spiritual consolation, as they exist in the Regular Army, are not permitted in the camps of the Labor Service. The Evangelical school is being opposed. Ministration to the souls of the rising generation is being made almost impossible. At the same time, however, the young people are being accustomed to the disparagement and even the mockery of the Christian faith.

In the writings of the Hitler Youth, in newspapers and magazines, like the "Schwarze Korps," etc., there are repeatedly found fresh insults to the Christian faith which are not fit to be reproduced. He who rebels against this war upon the Christian faith must expect to be branded as an enemy of the State. The Evangelical Christian frequently finds no ear among the State officials when his conscience forces him to oppose things contrary to God's plain commandment, as, for example, the mass swearing in of children on April 20, 1936.

Such oppression of conscience, made worse by constant espionage, produces hypocrisy and a slavish spirit and, finally, the genuine moral ties are dissolved.

We say all this in deep sorrow. We are ready to sacrifice our property and our lifeblood in the interest of the State and of our German people, but we do not want to be told before the throne of God's judgment: "When the gospel of Jesus was being attacked in the German lands, you remained silent and turned your children over to a strange spirit without resistance." In the face of what is happening today in our midst, we bear witness to the eternal truths of God before the German people.

The Lord our God is a holy God and does not allow himself to be mocked. He has revealed Himself in His Son Jesus Christ, who was crucified and arose from the dead. There is no God other than this one, who is the father of Jesus Christ. His Word contains eternal verities and saving

342

grace for all. It demands and creates faith and therewith an obedience that entrusts one's entire life to the mercy of God.

God's salvation, also for the German people, is found in this Christ and in no other than him. He says: "For what shall it profit a man if he shall gain the whole world and lose his own soul?" No exterior advance, no economic, political, and social improvement, can compensate for failure to care for the soul of a people. Righteousness exalts a people, but sin is the people's ruination. This is the eternal truth of God.

Christians are in duty bound to obey the authorities in so far as they do not demand anything against the commands of God. It is the mission of the church of Jesus Christ to proclaim the word of the living God to all the people, not merely to those who attend the divine services of the congregations. Christ says: "That which ye have spoken in the ear in closets, proclaim from the housetops. Go forth and preach the gospel to all creatures." The church is bound by these words.

We appeal to all the authorities over the German people. The National Government unequivocally promised to give firm protection to Christianity as the basis of our entire moral system. And just as definite were the words pronounced in the German Reichstag on March 21, 1933: "The right of the church continues to exist; nothing will be changed in its relation to the State."

Protection for Christianity cannot mean that the gospel must be protected by human power. The gospel enjoys a higher protection! But it must mean that disparagements of the gospel be kept aloof from the public life of the German people and that the faith to which the church bears witness be not systematically destroyed in our young folk. This we demand, in the name of the living God, from all those holding office in Germany.

We must have the right publicly and freely to bear witness before the German people of the faith of its fathers. The continual spying upon the work of the church must cease. The ban upon church meetings in public rooms must be lifted; the fetters placed upon the church press and the works of Christian charity must be removed. Above all must a halt be called upon State officials continually interfering in our internal affairs in the interest of those who, by their life and acts, are bringing about the destruction of the Evangelical Church.

A stop must be put to making it impossible for many evangelical Christians to attend divine service through parades, triumphal processions, demonstrations, and other affairs just on Sunday forenoon. It must be demanded that the German youth be not so in demand for political and sport service as to prejudice Christian family life and to leave no time for showing loyalty to the church.

This whole matter involves the right of the church of Jesus Christ to exist in this world. We ask all the authorities over the German people to bear in mind that they must give an accounting to the living God for all that they are doing. We entreat them to do nothing and to leave nothing undone that is against the will of God and against the freedom of conscience contained in the word of God.

We appeal to the entire Evangelical Christianity in Germany. We urge its members, true to the exhortations of the gospel: Do not allow yourselves to become embittered against the State and the people if you have to suffer for conscience's sake! Always and under all circumstances the Evangelical Christian owes loyalty to his State and to his people. And it also is loyalty when the Christian resists an order that conflicts with the word of God and thus recalls his authorities to obedience to God.

We entreat all evangelical Christians to pay attention to the rising generation and to maintain in it reverence for the gospel that gave strength and support to the German people through a thousand years of history. We call upon all evangelical Christians to confess firmly and openly their faith in the gospel of Jesus Christ. In this decisive hour Jesus Christ wants upright believers and resolute disciples. Now the following words hold good: "He who acknowledges me before men, him will I also acknowledge before my Heavenly Father."

We appeal to the servants of the church to bear witness to the gospel of Jesus Christ firmly and openly, without compromise and without fear of men. Many, for example, have lain in jail and in concentration camps and have had to endure banishment and other things. We do not know what still lies before us. But, come what may, we are bound to obey our Heavenly Father!

Let us do what we must and let us live in the joyous faith that men who fear only God and nothing else in the world are the best servants of their people.

We raise our hands to God the Father, the Son and the Holy Ghost! Be merciful to our people! Let Thy truth remain with us! Help it to victory! Amen.

The Council of Brothers of the Denominational Synod of the German Evangelical Church.

(Signed) D. KOCH

The Acting Management of the German Evangelical Church.

(Signed) MUELLER-DAHLEM

XII. *Encyclical of Pope Pius XI*

TO THE VENERABLE
ARCHBISHOPS AND BISHOPS OF GERMANY
AND OTHER ORDINARIES IN PEACE
AND COMMUNION WITH THE APOSTOLIC SEE

ON THE CONDITION OF THE CHURCH IN GERMANY*

POPE PIUS XI

VENERABLE BRETHREN

GREETING AND APOSTOLIC BENEDICTION

1. With deep anxiety and increasing dismay, We have for some time past beheld the sufferings of the Church, and the steadily growing oppression of those men and women who, loyally professing their faith in thought and deed, have remained true to her amidst the people of that land to which St. Boniface once brought the light and glad tidings of Christ and the Kingdom of God.

2. This anxiety of Ours has not been lessened by the accurate reports dutifully brought to Us by the representatives of the most reverend episcopate, who came to visit at Our sick-bed. They related much that is consoling and edifying about the struggle for religion that is being waged by the faithful, and yet, despite their love for their people and their fatherland, with every possible attempt to reach a dispassionate judgment, they could not pass over much that is bitter and sad. After receiving their accounts, We could say in great thankfulness to God: "I have no greater grace than this, to hear that my children walk in truth."[1] But the frankness befitting Our responsible apostolic office, and the desire to place before your eyes and those of the entire Christian world the actual facts in all their gravity, require Us to add: A greater anxiety, a more bitter suffering

---

* Reprinted by permission from the text published by the National Catholic Welfare Conference.

[1] III John, 1, 4.

345

in Our pastoral care, We have not, than to hear "many leave the way of truth."[2]

3. In the summer of 1933, Venerable Brethren, We accepted the offer made by the Government of the Reich to institute negotiations for a Concordat in connection with a proposal of the previous year, and to the satisfaction of you all brought them to a conclusion with a solemn agreement. In this We were guided by the solicitude incumbent on Us to safeguard the freedom of the Church in the exercise of her apostolic ministry in Germany and the salvation of the souls entrusted to her, and at the same time by the sincere wish of rendering an essential service to the progress and prosperity of the German people.

4. In spite of many serious misgivings at the time, We forced Ourselves to decide that We should not withhold Our consent. We wished to spare Our faithful sons and daughters in Germany, so far as was humanly possible, the anxiety and suffering which, in the given circumstances, We would certainly have otherwise had to expect. Through Our act We wished to prove to all, that seeking only Christ and the things of Christ, We do not refuse the hand of peace of Mother Church to anyone who does not himself reject it.

5. If the tree of peace which We planted with pure intention in German soil has not borne the fruit We desired in the interests of your people, no one in the wide world who has eyes to see and ears to hear can say today that the fault lies with the Church and her Head. The lessons of the past years make it clear where the responsibility lies. They disclose machinations that from the beginning had no other aim than a war of extermination. In the furrows where We labored to plant the seeds of sincere peace, others were sowing—like the enemy in Holy Scripture[3]—the tares of distrust, of discord, hatred, calumny, of secret and open enmity against Christ and His Church, an enmity in principle, fed from a thousand springs and working with every means at its disposal. With them and only with them, as well as with their open and silent supporters, lies the responsibility that now, instead of the rainbow of peace, the storm-clouds of destructive religious conflicts are visible on the German horizon.

6. We have not tired, Venerable Brethren, of portraying to the responsible guides of the destinies of your country the consequences that necessarily follow if such trends are left unhindered and much more if they are viewed with favor. We have done everything to defend the sanctity of a word solemnly pledged, to protect the inviolability of obligations, freely undertaken, against theories and practices which, if officially approved, must destroy all confidence and render valueless any word that might also be pledged in the future. When once the time shall have come to place before the eyes of the world these Our endeavors, all right minded persons will know where they have to look for those who kept the peace, and

[2] II Peter, 2, 3.
[3] Matthew, 13, 25.

where for those who broke it. Everyone in whose mind there is left the least perception of the truth, in whose heart there is a trace of feeling for justice, will then have to admit that in these grievous and eventful years after the signing of the Concordat, in every word and in every action of Ours, We have stood faithful to the terms of the agreement. But with amazement and deep aversion he will be obliged to admit that to change the meaning of the agreement, to evade the agreement, to empty the agreement of all its significance, and finally more or less openly to violate the agreement, has been made the unwritten law of conduct by the other party.

7. The moderation We have shown in spite of everything was neither dictated by considerations of human expediency nor motivated by unseemly weakness, but simply by the desire that We might not perchance tear up valuable wheat with the tares; by the intention not to pronounce judgment openly until minds were made ready for the inevitability of this judgment; by the determination not to deny definitively the good faith of others before the hard language of facts had torn away the coverings under which a systematic camouflage has been able and is able to disguise the attack on the Church. Even today, when the open campaign waged against the denominational school guaranteed by the Concordat, when the nullification of the freedom of the vote for Catholics who should have the right to decide in the matter of education, shows the dreadful seriousness of the situation in a most important field of the Church's life and the unparalleled torment of conscience of believing Christians, Our pastoral care for the salvation of souls counsels Us not to leave unheeded even the slight prospects of return to a loyal adherence to a responsible agreement. In compliance with the prayers of the Most Reverend Episcopate, We shall not weary in the future also of pleading the cause of outraged right with the rulers of your people. Unconcerned with the success or failure of the day and obeying only Our conscience and in accordance with Our pastoral mission, We shall oppose an attitude of mind that seeks to stifle chartered right with open or covered violence.

8. The purpose of the present letter, however, Venerable Brethren, is a different one. As you kindly visited Us as We lay on Our bed of sickness, so today We turn to you and through you to the Catholic faithful of Germany, who, like all suffering and oppressed children, are particularly close to the heart of the Common Father. In this hour, when their faith is being tried like pure gold in the fire of tribulation and concealed and open persecution, when they are surrounded by a thousand forms of organized bondage in matters of religion, when the lack of true information and absence of the customary means of defense weigh heavy on them, they have a double right to words of truth and spiritual comfort from him, to whose first predecessor the significant words of the Saviour were spoken: "But I have prayed for thee, that thy faith fail not; and thou being once converted, confirm thy brethren."[4]

[4] Luke, 22, 32.

True Belief in God

9. Take care, Venerable Brethren, that first of all belief in God, the primary and irreplaceable foundation of all religion, be preserved true and unadulterated in German lands. He is not a believer in God who uses the word of God rhetorically but he who associates with the sacred word the true and worthy idea of God.

10. He who, in pantheistic vagueness, equates God with the universe, and identifies God with the world and the world with God does not belong to believers in God.

11. He who replaces a personal God with a weird impersonal Fate supposedly according to ancient pre-Christian German concepts denies the wisdom and providence of God, that "reacheth from end to end mightily and ordereth all things sweetly"[5] and directs everything for the best. Such a one cannot claim to be numbered among those who believe in God.

12. He who takes the race, or the people, or the State, or the form of Government, the bearers of the power of the State or other fundamental elements of human society—which in the temporal order of things have an essential and honorable place—out of the system of their earthly valuation, and makes them the ultimate norm of all, even of religious, values, and deifies them with an idolatrous worship, perverts and falsifies the order of things created and commanded by God. Such a one is far from true belief in God and a conception of life corresponding to true belief.

13. Beware, Venerable Brethren, of the growing abuse in speech and writing, of using the thrice holy name of God as a meaningless label for a more or less capricious form of human search and longing. Work among your faithful that they may be vigilant to reject this aberration as it deserves. Our God is the personal, superhuman, almighty, infinitely perfect God, one in the Trinity of persons, threefold in the unity of the Divine essence, the Creator of the universe, the Lord and King in whom the history of the world finds fulfillment, Who suffers and can suffer no other god beside Him.

14. This God has given His commandments in His capacity as Sovereign. They apply regardless of time and space, country or race. As God's sun shines on all that bear human countenance, so does His law know no privileges or exceptions. The rulers and the ruled, crowned and uncrowned, high and low, rich and poor, all alike are subject to His law. From the sum total of His rights as Creator flows connaturally the sum total of His claims to obedience on the part of the individual and every kind of society. This claim to obedience comprehends every walk of life, in which moral questions demand a settlement in harmony with God's law and consequently the adjustment of transitory human legislation to the structure of the immutable law of God. Only superficial minds can lapse into the heresy of speaking of a national God, of a national religion; only

[5] Wisdom, 8, 1.

such can make the mad attempt of trying to confine within the boundaries of a single people, within the narrow blood stream of a single race, God the Creator of the world, the King and Lawgiver of all peoples before whose greatness all peoples are small as a drop of a bucket.[6]

15. The Bishops of the Church of Christ set up "for the things that appertain to God"[7] must be watchful that such pernicious errors, which are usually followed by more pernicious practices, find no foothold among the faithful. It is the holy duty of your office, as far as in you lies, to do everything to bring it about that the commandments of God shall be regarded and obeyed as the obligatory basis of morally ordered private and public life, that the sovereign rights of God, the name and the word of God, be not blasphemed;[8] that the blasphemies—in word, writing and picture, at times countless as the sands by the sea—be made to cease; that over against the defying Promethean spirit of deniers, scorners and haters of God the propitiatory prayer of the faithful never falters but that, like incense, it may rise hour after hour to the Most High and stay His hand raised to punish.

16. We thank you, Venerable Brethren, your priests and all the faithful, who have done and continue to do their duty in defending the sovereign rights of God against the aggressive neo-paganism—that unfortunately in many instances is favored in influential quarters. Our thanks are doubly sincere and coupled with admiration and approval of those who in the exercise of their duty were found worthy of making earthly sacrifices for God's sake and of enduring earthly suffering.

True Belief in Christ

17. No belief in God will in the long run be preserved pure and genuine, if it is not supported by belief in Christ: "No one knoweth the Son, but the Father; neither does any one know the Father, but the Son and he to whom it shall please the Son to reveal him."[9] "This is eternal life: that they may know Thee, the only true God and Jesus Christ, whom Thou hast sent."[10] Hence no one may say: I am a believer in God; that is religion enough for me. The words of the Saviour allow no room for this kind of evasion. "Whosoever denieth the Son, the same hath not the Father. He that confesseth the Son hath also the Father."[11]

18. The fulness of divine revelation has appeared in Jesus Christ, the incarnate Son of God. "God, Who at sundry times and divers manners spoke in times past to the fathers through the prophets, in the fulness of time hath spoken to us by his Son."[12] The sacred books of the Old Testament are all God's Word, an organic part of His revelation. Correspond-

[6] Is., 40, 15.
[7] Heb., 5. 1.
[8] Tit., 2, 5.
[9] Matthew, 11, 27.
[10] John, 17, 3.
[11] John, 2, 23.
[12] Hebrews, 1, 1.

ing to the gradual unfolding of the revelation, the dimness of the time preceding the full noon day of the redemption hovers over them. As is inevitable in the case of books of history and law, they are the reflections in many particulars of human imperfection, weakness and sin. Side by side with infinitely much that is high and noble, they relate the dissipation and worldliness that occurred time and again among the covenanted people who bore the revelation and promise of God.

19. Yet for every eye not blinded by prejudice and passion out of the human failings, of which the Bible history speaks, shines forth all the more clearly the divine light of the work of salvation finally triumphant over all defects and sin. God's pedagogy of salvation develops on such a background oftentimes dark into perspectives that point the way, warn, fill with dread, elevate and make happy at the same time. Only blindness and pride can close their eyes to the treasures of instruction for salvation, that are in the Old Testament. He who wants to see the Biblical history and the wisdom of the Old Testament banished from the Church and school, blasphemes the Word of God, blasphemes the Almighty's plan of salvation, makes the narrow and limited mind of man judge over the divine plan of history. He denies belief in the real Christ, Who appeared in the flesh, Who took His human nature from that people which was to nail Him to the cross. He stands uncomprehendingly before the world-drama of the Son of God Who opposed to the felony of His crucifiers the Divine high-priestly action of the Redeemer's death and thus brought the Old Testament to its fulfilment and completion in the New, by which it is superseded.

20. The climax of revelation reached in the Gospel of Jesus Christ is definite, is obligatory for ever. This revelation knows no addition from the hand of man, above all, knows no substitution and no replacement by arbitrary "revelations" that certain speakers of the present day wish to derive from the myth of blood and race. Since Christ, the Anointed, accomplished the work of redemption, broke the dominion of sin, and merited for us the grace of becoming children of God—since then no other name has been given under heaven to men, through which they can be saved, but the name of Jesus.[13] No man, though all knowledge, all power, all outward might on earth should be embodied in him, can lay any other foundation than that which is already laid in Christ.[14] He who sacrilegiously disregarding the yawning abyss of essential distinction between God and creature, between the God-Man and the children of men, dares to place any mortal, were he the greatest of all times, beside Christ, or worse, above Him and against Him, must be told that he is a false prophet, in whom the words of Scripture find terrible application: "He that dwelleth in heaven, shall laugh at them."[15]

[13] Acts, 4, 12.
[14] I Cor., 3, 11.
[15] Ps., 2, 4.

350

Appendix XII

True Belief in the Church

21. Belief in Christ will not be preserved true and genuine, if not supported and protected by belief in the Church, "the pillar and ground of the truth."[16] Christ Himself, Godpraised forever in the ages, has erected this pillar of faith. His command, to hear the Church,[17] to hear His own words and commandments[18] in the words and commandments of the Church, is meant for the men of all times and places. The Church founded by the Redeemer is one—for all peoples and nations. Beneath her vault, that like God's firmament arches over the whole earth, there is a place and home for all peoples and tongues; there is room for the development of all the particular qualities, points of excellence, missions and callings, that God has assigned to individuals and peoples. The heart of Mother Church is wide and big enough to see in the development, according to God's purpose, of such special qualities and gifts rather the richness of variety than the danger of separation. She rejoices in the intellectual advancement of individuals and peoples. With the joy and pride of a mother she sees in their genuine achievements the fruits of education and progress, that she blesses and furthers whenever she can in conscience do so. But she knows, too, that limits are set to this freedom by the majesty of God's law that has willed and founded this Church one and indivisible in all essentials. He who touches this unity and indivisibility, takes from the Bride of Christ one of the diadems with which God Himself has crowned her. He subjects her divine structure that rests on eternal foundations to the re-examination and remodeling of architects, to whom the Heavenly Father has granted no plenipotentiary powers to build.

22. The divine mission of the Church that works among men and must work through men may be lamentably obscured by human failings that again and again sprout up as tares amid the wheat of God's kingdom. He who has heard the Saviour's word about scandals and those who give scandal, knows how the Church and each individual has to judge on what was sin and is sin. But because of these deplorable discrepancies between believing and living, between word and deed, between the outward conduct and the interior disposition of individuals—even though there might be many such—to forget the immense sum of sincere pursuit of virtue, of the spirit of sacrifice, of brotherly love, of heroic striving after holiness; or worse, to conceal all this knowingly, is to display regrettable blindness and injustice. When it becomes perfectly clear that the hard standard applied to the hated Church is forgotten the very moment there is question of societies of a different nature, felt to be akin in sentiment or interest, then the one who so acts and pretends that he has been offended in his sense of cleanliness, shows that he is related to those who in the cutting words of the

[16] I Timothy, 3, 15.
[17] Matthew, 18, 17.
[18] Luke, 10, 16.

351

The Third Reich

Saviour see the mote in their brother's eye, but do not see the beam in their own. Questionable as is the intention of those who make a career, and in many instances a low profession, of busying themselves with human failings in the Church, and though it be true that the authority of him who holds ecclesiastical office is founded on God and is independent of his human or moral standing; nevertheless, no period of time, no individual, no community is free from the duty of sincere examination of conscience, of unrelenting, of thorough renewal in mind and deed. In Our encyclical on the priesthood, in Our letters on Catholic Action, We pointed out with adjuring insistence the sacred duty of all members of the Church, and particularly members of the priesthood and religious state, that they should bring their belief and conduct into the agreement required by the law of God and demanded by the Church with emphasis. And today We earnestly repeat: It is not enough to be counted a member of the Church of Christ. One must be also a living member of this Church—in spirit and in truth. And only they are such, who are in the grace of the Lord and ever walk in His presence—in innocence or in sincere and efficacious penance. If the Apostle of the Gentiles, the "Vessel of Election," kept his body under the rod of chastisement and mortification in order that he might not, after preaching to others, become himself a castaway,[19] can there be any other way but that of the closest union of apostolate and personal sanctification for the others to whose hands is committed the keeping and increase of the kingdom of God? Only in this way can it be proved to the present generation, and especially to the adversaries of the Church, that the salt of the earth has not lost its savor, that the leaven of Christendom has not become stale, but is capable and ready to bring to the people of today who are caught in doubt and error, in indifference and perplexity, in weariness in believing and in separation from God, the spiritual renewal and rejuvenation of which they stand, whether they admit it or not, in greater need than ever before. A Christianity that enters into itself in all its members, that strips off all mere outward show and worldliness, that takes the commandments of God seriously, and proves itself in love of God and active love of one's neighbor, can and must be the pattern and leader to a world sick to its very heart and seeking for support and guidance if unspeakable misfortune and a cataclysm far beyond all imagination is not to burst over it.

23. In the final analysis every true and lasting reform has proceeded from the sanctuary; from men who were inflamed and driven by love of God and their neighbor. From their magnanimity and readiness to hearken to every call of God and to realize that call first of all in themselves, they grew in humility and in the conviction of their calling to be luminaries and renewers of their times. When zeal for reform did not spring from the pure source of personal singleness of heart, but was the expression and outbreak of passionate frenzy, it caused confusion instead of bringing light,

[19] I Cor., 9, 27.

352

tore down instead of building up; and not seldom was the point of departure for errors more disastrous than were the evils that it was the intention or the pretended intention to correct. True, the spirit of God breatheth where He will.[20] He can raise up stones to prepare the way for His design.[21] He chooses the instruments of His will according to His Own plans, and not according to those of men. But He Who founded His Church and called it into being in the storm of Pentecost, does not blast the foundation of the establishment He Himself intended for salvation. Those who are moved by the spirit of God have of themselves the proper inward and outward attitude towards the Church, which is the precious fruit on the tree of the Cross, the Pentecostal gift of God's spirit to a world in need of guidance.

24. In your districts, Venerable Brethren, voices are raised in ever louder chorus urging men on to leave the Church. Among the spokesmen there are many who, by reason of their official position, seek to create the impression that leaving the Church, and the disloyalty to Christ the King which it entails, is a particularly convincing and meritorious form of profession of loyalty to the present State. With cloaked and with manifest methods of coercion, by intimidation, by holding out the prospect of economic, professional, civic and other advantages, the loyalty of Catholics and especially of certain classes of Catholic officials to their faith is put under a pressure that is as unlawful as it is unworthy of human beings. All Our fatherly sympathy and deepest condolence We offer to those who pay so high a price for their fidelity to Christ and the Church. But here We reach the point of supreme importance, where it is a question of safety or destruction, and where, consequently, for the believer the way of heroic fortitude is the only way of salvation. When the tempter or oppressor comes to him with the Judas-like suggestion to leave the Church, then, even at the cost of heavy, earthly sacrifices he can only reply in the words of the Saviour: "Begone, Satan: for it is written: The Lord thy God thou shalt adore and Him only shalt thou serve."[22] But to the Church he will say: Thou my Mother from the days of my childhood, my comfort in life, my intercessor in death, may my tongue cleave to my palate, if I, yielding to earthly enticements or threats, should turn traitor to the promises of my baptism. But to those who think that they can continue outward leaving of the Church with inward loyalty to the Church, let the Saviour's words be earnest warning: "He that shall deny Me before men, I will also deny him before My Father Who is in heaven."[23]

The Belief in the Primacy

25. Belief in the Church will not be kept pure and genuine if it is not supported by belief in the primacy of the Bishop of Rome. At the very

[20] John, 3, 8.
[21] Matthew, 3, 9; Luke, 3, 8.
[22] Matthew, 4, 10; Luke, 4, 8.
[23] Matthew, 10, 33.

moment when Peter, foremost of all the Apostles and disciples, confessed faith in Christ, the Son of the living God, the answer of Christ rewarding his faith and his confession was the word that speaks of the building of His Church, the one Church, and on Peter the Rock.[24] Belief in Christ, in the Church, in the Primacy are thus connected in the holiest way. Real and lawful authority is everywhere the bond of unity, a source of strength, a security against disruption and dissolution, a pledge for the future; it is so in the highest and holiest sense in the case for the Church where alone to such authority the guidance of grace by the Holy Ghost and His assistance against which nothing can prevail have been promised. When people who do not even agree on their faith in Christ hold before you as a thing to be desired or allure you with the picture of a German national church, know this: it is nothing but the denial of the Church of Christ, a manifest apostasy from the command to evangelize the whole world, to whose fulfilment only a universal church can be commensurate. The history of other national churches, their spiritual torpor, their attachment to or enslavement by earthly powers, shows the hopeless sterility that comes over every branch that separates itself from the living vine of the Church. To be on the alert right from the very start and to oppose an unflinching "No" to such sophistries, is to serve not only the purity of one's faith in Christ, but also the well-being and vital forces of one's people.

No Changing the Sense of Holy Words and Ideas

26. You must be especially alert, Venerable Brethren, when fundamental religious conceptions are robbed of their intrinsic content and made to mean something else in a profane sense.

27. Revelation, in the Christian sense, is the word of God to man. To use the same word for the "whispered inspirations" of blood and race, for the manifestations of the history of a people, is confusing in any case. Such false coinage does not deserve to be received into the vocabulary of a believing Christian.

28. Faith is the certain holding as true what God has revealed and through His Church proposes for belief, "the evidence of things that appear not."[25] The joyous and proud confidence in the future of one's people, dear to everyone, means something quite different from faith in the religious sense. To play one off against the other, to try to replace one by the other, and thereupon demand to be recognized as a "believer" by the convinced Christian, is an empty play on words or a wilful effacing of distinctions, or worse.

29. Immortality in the Christian sense is the continuance of the life of a man after temporal death, as a personal individual, to be rewarded or punished eternally. To designate with the word immortality the collective continued enjoyment of life in association with the continued existence of

[24] Matthew, 16, 18.
[25] Hebrews, 11, 1.

354

one's people on earth for an undetermined length of time in the future, is to pervert and falsify one of the principal truths of the Christian faith and strike at the foundations of every religious philosophy that demands a moral ordering of the world. If they do not want to be Christians, at least they should forego enriching the vocabulary of their unbelief from the Christian treasure of ideas.

30. Original sin is the inherited, though not personal, fault of the descendants of Adam, who sinned in him;[26] loss of grace, and therewith loss of eternal life, with the propensity to evil that each one must combat and overcome by grace, penance, struggle and moral endeavor. The passion and death of the Son of God redeemed the world from the inherited curse of sin and death. Faith in these truths that today are clearly scorned in your country by the enemies of Christ belongs to the inalienable substance of the Christian religion.

31. The Cross of Christ, though the mere name may have become to many a folly and a scandal,[27] is still for the Christian the hallowed sign of redemption, the standard of moral greatness and strength. In its shadow we live. In its kiss we die. On our graves it shall stand to proclaim our faith, to witness our hope turned towards the eternal light.

32. Humility in the spirit of the Gospel and prayer for the help of God's grace are compatible with self-respect, self-confidence and heroic purpose. The Church of Christ, that in all ages up to the present time counts more confessors and voluntary martyrs than any other body, does not need to receive instruction from such quarters about heroic purposefulness and heroic achievement. In its shallow twaddle about Christian humility being self-abasement and unheroic conduct, the disgusting pride of these reformers mocks itself.

33. Grace, in the loose sense of the term, can be said to be everything that the creature receives from the Creator. Grace in the proper and Christian sense of the word embraces, however, the supernatural manifestations of divine love, the loving kindness and working of God, whereby He raises men to that inward participation of life with Himself, that is called in the New Testament sonship of God. "Behold what manner of charity the Father hath bestowed upon us, that we should be called and should be the sons of God."[28] The repudiation of this supernatural elevation of grace on account of the supposedly peculiar German type of being, is an error and an open challenge to a fundamental truth of Christianity. To put supernatural grace on the same level with the gifts of nature robs the vocabulary fashioned and sanctified by the Church. The pastors and guardians of God's people will do well to act with vigilance against this looting of the sanctuary and this work of confusing minds.

[26] Romans, 5, 12.
[27] I Cor., 1, 23.
[28] I John, 3, 1.

The Third Reich

Moral Doctrine and Moral Order

34. The moral conduct of mankind is grounded on faith in God kept true and pure. Every attempt to dislodge moral teaching and moral conduct from the rock of faith, and to build them on the unstable sands of human norms, sooner or later leads the individual and the community to moral destruction. The fool who hath said in his heart there is no God, will walk the ways of corruption.[29] The number of such fools, who today attempt to separate morality and religion, has become legion. They do not or will not see that by expelling confessional, i.e. clear and definite, Christianity from instruction and education, from the formation of social and public life, they are treading the ways of spiritual impoverishment and decline. No coercive power of the State, no mere earthly ideals, though they be high and noble in themselves, will be able in the long run to replace the final and decisive motives that come from belief in God and Christ. Take the moral support of the eternal and divine, of comforting and consoling belief in the Rewarder of all good and the Punisher of all evil, from those who are called on to make the greatest sacrifices, to surrender their petty self to the common weal, the result will be in countless instances not the acceptance, but the shirking, of duty. The conscientious observance of the ten commandments of God and the commandments of the Church—the latter are only the practical applications of the principles of the Gospel—is for every individual an incomparable schooling of systematic self-discipline, moral training and character formation—a schooling that demands much, but not too much. The God of kindness, Who as lawgiver says: "Thou shalt," gives in His grace also the power to do. To disregard such profound and efficacious factors in moral training, or knowingly to bar their way to the field of popular education, is inexcusable cooperation in the religious undernourishment of the community. To hand over moral teaching to subjective human opinions that change with the trend of the time, instead of anchoring it to the holy will of the Eternal God and to His commandments, is to open wide the door to the forces of destruction. Thus to have ushered in the betrayal of the eternal principles of an objective morality for the schooling of conscience, for the ennoblement of every sphere and branch of life, is a sin against the future of the people, whose bitter fruits the coming generations will taste.

Recognition of the Natural Law

35. It is part of the trend of the day to sever more and more not only morality but also the foundation of law and jurisprudence, from true belief in God and from His revealed commandments. Here We have in mind particularly the so-called natural law that is written by the finger of the Creator Himself in the tables of the hearts of men[30] and which can be read

[29] Ps., 13, 1.
[30] Cf. Rom., 2, 15.

356

on these tables by sound reason not darkened by sin and passion. Every positive law, from whatever lawgiver it may come, can be examined as to its moral implications, and consequently as to its moral authority to bind in conscience, in the light of the commandments of the natural law. The laws of man that are in direct contradiction with the natural law bear an initial defect that no violent means, no outward display of power can remedy. By this standard must we judge the principle: "What helps the people is right." A right meaning may be given to this sentence if understood as expressing that what is morally illicit can never serve the true interests of the people. But even ancient paganism recognized that the sentence, to be perfectly accurate, should be inverted and read: "Never is anything useful, if it is not at the same time morally good. And not because it is useful, is it morally good, but because it is morally good, it is also useful."[31] Cut loose from this rule of morality, that principle would mean, in international life, a perpetual state of war between the different nations. In political life within the State, since it confuses considerations of utility with those of right, it mistakes the basic fact that man as a person possesses God-given rights, which must be preserved from all attacks aimed at denying, suppressing or disregarding them. To pay no heed to this truth is to overlook the fact that the true public good is finally determined and recognized by the nature of man, with his harmonious coordination of personal rights and social obligations, as well as by the purpose of the community which in turn is conditioned by the same human nature. The community is willed by the Creator as the means to the full development of the individual and social attainments, which the individual in give and take has to employ to his own good and that of others. Also those higher and more comprehensive values, that cannot be realized by the individual but only by the community, in the final analysis are intended by the Creator for the sake of the individual, for his natural and supernatural development and perfection. A deviation from this order loosens the supports on which the community is placed, and thereby imperils the tranquillity, security and even the existence of the community itself.

36. The believer has an inalienable right to profess his faith and put it into practice in the manner suited to him. Laws that suppress or make this profession and practice difficult contradict the natural law.

37. Conscientious parents, aware of their duty in the matter of education, have a primary and original right to determine the education of the children given to them by God in the spirit of the true faith and in agreement with its principles and ordinances. Laws or other regulations concerning schools that disregard the rights of parents guaranteed to them by the natural law, or by threat and violence nullify those rights, contradict the natural law and are utterly and essentially immoral.

38. The Church, the guardian and exponent of the divine natural law, cannot do otherwise than declare that the registrations which have just

[31] Cicero, De officiis, 3, 30.

taken place in circumstances of notorious coercion are the result of violence and void of all legality.

To Youth

39. As the vice regent of Him who said to the young man of the gospel: "If thou wilt enter into life, keep the commandments,"[32] do We especially address fatherly words to youth. By a thousand tongues today a gospel is preached in your ears that is not revealed by your Heavenly Father. A thousand pens write in the service of a sham Christianity that is not the Christianity of Christ. Day by day the press and the radio overwhelm you with productions hostile to your faith and Church and, with no consideration or reverence, attack what must be to you sacred and holy.

40. We know that many, very many, of you for the sake of loyalty to your religion and Church, for the sake of belonging to Church associations guaranteed by the Concordat, have borne and still endure bitter days of misunderstanding, of suspicion, of contempt, of denial of your patriotism, of manifold injury in your professional and social life. We are aware that many an unknown soldier of Christ stands in your ranks, who with heavy heart but head erect bears his lot and finds comfort solely in the thought of suffering reproach for the Name of Jesus.[33]

41. Today, when new perils and conflicts threaten, We say to this youth: "If anyone preach to you a gospel, besides that which you have received" at the knees of a pious mother, from the lips of a Catholic father, from the education of a teacher true to his God and his church, "let him be anathema."[34] If the State founds a State-Youth to which all are obliged to belong, then it is—without prejudice to the rights of Church associations—an obvious, an inalienable right of the young men themselves, and of their parents responsible for them before God, to demand that this obligatory organization should be cleansed of all manifestations of a spirit hostile to Christianity and the Church, which, up to the recent past and even at the present moment, place Catholic parents in hopeless conflicts of conscience, since they cannot give to the State what is demanded in the name of the State without robbing God of what belongs to God.

42. No one has any intention of obstructing the youth of Germany on the road that is meant to bring them to the realization of true popular union, to the fostering of the love of freedom, to steadfast loyalty to the fatherland. What We object to, and what We must object to, is the intentional and systematically fomented opposition which is set up between these educational purposes and those of religion. Therefore we call out to youth: Sing your songs of freedom, but do not forget the freedom of the sons of God while singing them. Do not allow this noble freedom, for which there is no substitute, to pine away in the slave chains of sin and

[32] Matthew, 19, 17.
[33] Acts, 5, 41.
[34] Gal., 1, 9.

sensuality. He who sings the song of loyalty to his earthly country must not, in disloyalty to God, to his church, to his eternal country, become a deserter and a traitor. You are told a great deal about heroic greatness, in designed and false contrast to the humility and patience of the Gospel. Why is silence kept about the heroism of moral struggle? Why is it not told you that the preservation of baptismal innocence represents an heroic action which should be assured of the appreciation it deserves in the religious and moral sphere? A great deal is told you of human weaknesses in the history of the Church. Why is nothing said of the great deeds that accompany her on her way through the centuries, of the Saints she has produced, of the blessings which came from the living union between this Church and your people and enriched the culture of the west? You are told a great deal of the exercises of sport. Undertaken with discretion, the cult of physical fitness is a benefit for youth. But now so much time is devoted to it, in many cases, that no account is taken of the harmonious development of mind and body, of what is due to family life, of the commandment to keep holy the Lord's day. With a disregard bordering on indifference, the sacredness and peace that are in the best tradition of the German Sunday are taken from it. With confidence We expect from practicing Catholic youth that, in the difficult circumstances of obligatory State organization, they will insist unflinchingly on their right to keep Sunday in a Christian manner, that in the cult of physical fitness they will not forget the interests of their immortal souls; that they will not allow themselves to be overcome by evil, but will strive to overcome evil by good;[35] that their highest and holiest ambition will be so to run the race towards immortal life as to achieve the crown of victory.[36]

To Priests and Religious

43. We address a special word of recognition, encouragement and exhortation to the priests of Germany, on whom, in subordination to their Bishops, there rests the task of showing the flock of Christ in a trying time and under difficult circumstances, the right paths, by precept and example, by daily sacrifice and apostolic patience. Be not weary, beloved sons and sharers in the holy mysteries, in following the eternal High Priest, Jesus Christ, Who bestows love and care like the good Samaritan. Keep yourselves day by day in conduct undefiled before God, in unremitting discipline and perfection, in merciful care for all entrusted to you, especially for those endangered, the weak and the wavering. Be the leaders of the faithful, the support of the stumbling, the teachers of the doubtful, the consolers of those who mourn, the unselfish helpers and counsellors of all. The trials and sorrows through which your people have passed since the war have left their mark on its soul. They have left behind conflicts and bitterness that can be healed only slowly, that can be overcome only

[35] Rom., 12, 21.
[36] Cf. I Cor., 9, 24.

in the spirit of unselfish and active charity. This charity, which is the indispensable armor of the apostle, especially in the world of the present day stirred up and distorted with hate, We pray and beg the Lord to bestow on you in superabundant measure. This apostolic love will make you, if not forget, at least forgive the many undeserved offenses that more plentifully than ever before are strewn in the path of your priestly ministration. This comprehending and merciful charity towards the erring, and even towards the contemptuous, does not mean and cannot mean, that you renounce in any way the proclaiming of, the insisting on, and the courageous defense of the truth and its free and unhindered application to the realities about you. The first and obvious duty the priest owes to the world about him is service to the truth, the whole truth, the unmasking and refutation of error in whatever form or disguise it conceals itself.

44. To Catholic religious of both sexes We likewise express Our fatherly thanks, together with our utmost sympathy in the fate that, in consequence of regulations against the religious Orders, has taken them out of the work of their chosen career, which they had loved and made rich in blessing. If individuals have fallen short and proved themselves unworthy, their misdeeds, punished by the Church herself, do not lessen the merits of the overwhelming majority, who, in unselfishness and voluntary poverty, were striving to serve their God and people in the spirit of sacrifice. The zeal, fidelity, striving after virtue, active charity and readiness to help on the part of the Orders engaged in the ministry, hospitals and schools are, and remain, a praiseworthy contribution to private and public prosperity, to which undoubtedly a later and quieter time will accord more justice than the troubled present. We feel confident that Superiors of religious communities will take occasion from their trials and difficulties to call down from the Almighty fresh blessing and fruitfulness on their heavy work through redoubled zeal, deepened life of prayer, holy earnestness in their vocation and religious discipline.

To the Faithful of the Laity

45. Before our eyes stands the countless throng of faithful sons and daughters, for whom the suffering of the Church in Germany and their own suffering has in no way diminished their devotion to the cause of God, their tender love for the Father of Christendom, their obedience to their Bishops and priests, their cheerful readiness, come what may, to remain true in the future to what they have believed and have received from their forefathers as a sacred inheritance. From a heart that is deeply moved We send them all our paternal greeting.

46. And this, first and foremost, to the members of the Church associations, who courageously and oftentimes at the cost of painful sacrifice have kept true to Christ and did not give up the rights which a formal agreement, made in good faith and trust, had guaranteed to the Church and themselves.

360

47. We address a particularly heartfelt greeting to Catholic parents. Their God-given rights and duties in education are this present moment at the very center of a struggle which could not conceivably be fraught with graver consequences for the future. The Church of Christ cannot wait until her altars have been overthrown, until sacrilegious hands have set the houses of God on fire, before she begins to mourn and lament. When the attempt is made to desecrate the tabernacle of a child's soul sanctified in baptism by an education that is hostile to Christ; when from this living temple of God the eternal lamp of belief in Christ is cast out and in its place is brought the false light of a substitute faith that has nothing in common with the faith of the Cross, then the time of spiritual profanation of the temple is at hand, then it is the duty of every professing Christian to separate clearly his responsibility from that of the other side, to keep his conscience clear of any culpable cooperation in such dreadful work and corruption. The more the opponents are at pains to deny and gloss over their dark intentions, all the more is vigilant distrust called for, and distrustful vigilance that has been aroused by bitter experience. The formal maintaining of religious instruction, especially when controlled and shackled by those who are not competent, in the framework of a school that in other departments systematically and invidiously works against the same religion, can never be a justification for a believing Christian to give his free approval to such a school that aims at destroying religion. We know, beloved Catholic parents, that there can be no question of such willingness on your part. We know that a free and secret ballot would in your case be equivalent to an overwhelming vote for the religious school. And therefore We shall not weary in the future of representing to responsible parties the injustice of the coercive measures so far adopted, and the obligation of allowing free expression of a free will. Meanwhile do not forget this: from the bond of responsibility established by God that binds you to your children, no earthly power can loose you. No one of those who today are oppressing you in the exercise of your rights in education and pretend to free you from your duty in this matter, will be able to answer for you to the Eternal Judge when He asks you the question: "Where are those I have given you?" May everyone of you be able to answer: "Of them thou hast given me, I have not lost anyone."[37]

48. Venerable Brethren, We are certain that the words which We address to you, and through you to the Catholics of the German Reich, in this decisive hour, will awaken in the hearts and actions of Our loyal children the echo that answers to the loving solicitude of the Common Father. If there is anything that We beseech of the Lord with particular fervor, it is this, that Our words may also reach the ears and hearts of those who have already begun to allow themselves to be inveigled by the enticements and threats of those who take their stand against Christ and His holy Gospel and cause them to reflect.

[37] John, 18, 9.

49. Every word of this letter has been weighed in the scales of truth and of charity. We did not desire to share any accountability, by reason of untimely silence, for a want of enlightenment, nor, by needless severity, for the hardening of heart of any one of those who are placed under Our pastoral responsibility and are no less included in Our pastoral charity because at the moment they are walking estranged in the ways of error. Though many of those who adapt themselves to the ways of their new environment, who have for their deserted Father's house and for the Father Himself only words of disloyalty, ingratitude or even insult; though they forget what they have cast behind them, the day will dawn when the horror of being in spiritual dereliction far from God will strike the hearts of these prodigal sons, when homesickness will drive them back to the "God who rejoiced their youth" and to the Church whose maternal hand pointed out for them the way to the Heavenly Father. To hasten this hour is the object of Our unceasing prayers.

50. Just as other times of the Church, so will this be the harbinger of new advance and inward purification, if the readiness to suffer and confess the faith on the part of Christ's faithful is great enough to oppose to the physical violence of the persecutors of the Church the intransigeance of inward faith, the inexhaustibleness of hope that rests on eternity, the commanding power of active charity. The holy seasons of Lent and Easter, that preach recollection and penance and direct more often than at other times the eyes of the Christian to the Cross, but at the same time to the glory of the Risen Christ, may they be for all and every one of you a joyfully welcomed and eagerly used occasion to fill heart and mind with the spirit of heroism, patience and victory that shines forth from the Cross of Christ.

Then—of this We are certain—will the enemies of the Church, who fancy that her hour has come, soon recognize that they rejoiced too soon and were too quick to dig her grave. Then will the day come when, instead of the too hasty songs of victory raised by the enemies of Christ, the *Te Deum* of liberation can rise to heaven from the hearts and lips of Christ's faithful; a *Te Deum* of thanks to the Highest; a *Te Deum* of joy, that the German people, even in its erring sons of today, has trodden the way of religious home-coming, that they once more bend the knee in faith purified by suffering before the King of time and eternity, Jesus Christ, and that they prepare to fulfill that calling which the designs of the Eternal God point out to them, in the struggle against the deniers and destroyers of the Christian west, in harmony with all right-minded people of other nations.

51. He Who searches the heart and reins[88] is Our witness, that We have no more heartfelt wish than the restoration of a true peace between Church and State in Germany. But if, through no fault of Ours, there shall not be peace, the Church of God will defend her rights and liberties in the Name of the Almighty, Whose arm even today is not shortened. Trusting in Him

[88] Ps., 7, 10.

Appendix XII

"We cease not to pray and beg[39] for you, the children of the Church, that the days of anguish may be shortened and that you may be found true in the day of searching; and We pray also for the persecutors and oppressors; may the Father of all light and all mercy grant them an hour of enlightenment, such as was vouchsafed to Paul on the road to Damascus, for themselves and all those who with them have erred and err.

52. With this prayer of supplication in Our heart and on Our lips, We impart as a pledge of divine assistance, as a help in your difficult and weighty decisions, as strength in the struggle, as consolation in suffering, to you, the episcopal Pastors of your loyal flock, to the priests and religious, to the lay apostles of Catholic Action, to all your diocesans, finally to the sick and imprisoned, in fatherly love, the Apostolic blessing.

Given at the Vatican, on Passion Sunday, March 14th, 1937.

PIUS PP. XI.

[39] Coloss., 1, 9.

XIII. Exchange of Letters Between Romain Rolland and the Editors of the Kölnische Zeitung*

May 14, 1933.

Dear Editor:

The lines which the *Kölnische Zeitung* devoted to me in its issue of May 9 (no. 251) have been brought to my attention.

It is true that I love Germany and that I have always defended her against the injustice and lack of understanding on the part of other nations. But the Germany which I love and which had fructified my spirit is the Germany of the great citizens of the world—of those "who experienced the fortunes and misfortunes of other nations as their own"—of those who worked for the union of nations and spirits.

This Germany is being trampled under foot, is being stained with blood and is being derided by her "national" ruling powers of today, by the Germany of the swastika which is rejecting the free spirits, the Europeans, the pacifists, the Jews, the socialists, and the communists who wish to establish the international of labor. Do you not see that national-fascist Germany is the worst enemy of the true Germany and that it is denying this Germany? Such a policy is a crime not only against the human spirit but also against your own nation. You withdraw from her a large portion of her energies and you remove from her the great respect of her best friends in the world. Your leaders have succeeded in bringing about the artful creation of a union of nationalists and internationalists of all lands against you. You do not care to see that. You prefer to speak of a conspiracy against Germany. But you, you yourselves, have conspired against yourselves.

I have proclaimed the injustice of which Germany became the victim after the victory of 1918. I demanded the revision of the Treaty of Versailles which was imposed upon you by force. I called for the equality of

* The letter by Romain Rolland and the reply by the editors was published in the *Kölnische Zeitung* on May 21, 1933. The paper then invited Rudolf Binding, Baron Robert Fabre-Luce, Otto Wirz, Wilhem von Scholz and Erwin Kolbenheyer to supply statements on the letter of Rolland. All these letters were then brought together in the pamphlet, *Sechs Bekenntnisse zum neuen Deutschland* (Hamburg, 1933).

Germany with all other nations. But do you believe that I demanded all this for the sake of a still greater injustice, of a Germany which herself violates the equality of human races and all human rights which are sacred to us? The stubborn opponents of treaty revision could not exert a more powerful influence against Germany than you, you yourselves, have done. The future will enlighten you—too late—regarding your murderous mistake, for which there is only one excuse, the fever of despair into which the blindness and severity of the victors of Versailles dragged your people.

Despite you and against you I will retain my sympathy for Germany, for the true Germany which is dishonored by the terrorism and the aberrations of Hitlerite fascism. And I shall continue to carry on my work, as I have done all my life, not for the egotism of one single nation but for all nations together, for the international of spirits and peoples.

ROMAIN ROLLAND

P.S. You treat the accusations of the foreign press against Hitlerite fascism as calumnies. We have a whole bundle of proofs concerning proscribed individuals and the most atrocious horrors by brown shirts which were never punished or denounced by any official statement. But let us not talk of that here! The official texts are enough for us. Can you deny the very pronouncements of your leaders, Hitler, Göring, Goebbels, which have been published in the press and disseminated by the radio; their incitement to violence, their proclamations of racialism which denounce other races like the Jews—this decaying smell which belonged to a middle age long passed in the West? Do you deny the vulgar intrusion of politics into the universities and academies? Do you not believe that the great anathema of science and art outbalances on the scales of world opinion the ridiculous excommunications of your inquisitors?

R. R.

II. THE REPLY OF THE KÖLNISCHE ZEITUNG

May 20, 1933.

DEAR HERR ROLLAND,

We were not particularly surprised on this occasion to have received from you such a blunt reply to the lines regarding you which appeared in the *Kölnische Zeitung*. We know that present-day Germany enjoys very little sympathy in the world, even among her former friends, and that serious attempts at understanding have become extremely rare. This does not dishearten us, however, and for you in particular, we shall repeat gladly the attempt to meet the serious charges which you raise against Germany and her leaders. We still remember with gratitude the many works, both of a literary character and of immediate practical concern, which you have dedicated to the German cause. We still know your novel, *Jean Christoph*, in which your love for things German found such beautiful expression; we still know your profound writings on Goethe and Beethoven, your ready aid during the war and in the difficult years immediately following the war, your attacks upon the immoderate brutality of the victors and your courageous stand for a just peace. All that we shall not forget and it is the memory of that which now inspires our writing.

Germany has experienced a revolution; a revolution which is inspired not only by the fulfillment of an age-old German dream—the creation of a strong unified state—but which goes beyond administrative innovations and reveals deep spiritual transformations. The significance of such an elemental occurrence is well known to you from history. You yourself attempted to portray it in your drama, *Danton*. When this play was performed some years ago in Berlin the scene which made the deepest impression on the spectators was that before the Revolutionary Tribunal in which Danton is forced to retire and the people become the hero. Stamping, shouting and waving flags it makes its entrance and fills the scene with its wave of enthusiasm.

From this historic event in the history of your fatherland the German revolution differs in that very thing which you so erroneously misunderstand: in its disciplined and bloodless course. Certainly there were some excesses; these are to be deplored and they were branded as such by the official authorities; excesses of individual hot-spurs and acts of violence which are to be explained by the long persecution of their perpetrators. Many rash words, too, were uttered at the beginning of the revolution. Viewed as a whole, however, the leaders held the course of political events firmly in their hands. The well-being of a single individual in the storm of a revolution can hardly be taken as the measure of events—you have portrayed this dramatically in your *Danton*—yet we were spared that cruel fate which befell large sections of the French people in 1789 and which now in Russia still drives thousands into the arms of a meaningless death. Compared with the French past and with the conditions in Russia, Germany stands without shame before the bar of history, for the German revolution took place with less bloodshed than any other previous revolution.

In a world which is filled with the lies of atrocity propaganda even the most unprejudiced will not believe this and nothing will convince them except their personal observations. We invite you heartily, Herr Rolland, to come here and we believe that we can assure you that you will not suffer any embarrassment because of your attitude towards our government. We know the sources of these lies too well and we know how to distinguish between willful slanderers and those who are merely led astray.

Supposing then that we succeeded somehow in convincing you that Germany is "not stained with blood," there still remains the charge that she has violated the "sacred human rights" of liberty and equality. Our reply to that is that schematic adherence to these rights was precisely what brought Germany as well as all Europe to the brink of ruin. For under the cover of legally sanctioned liberty and equality the communists in Germany were able to undermine the bourgeois order and, as has been

366

proved, prepared to convert it into bloody chaos. Had this plan succeeded it would undoubtedly also have spread to other countries and who knows if your peaceful abode on Lake Geneva, which during the war was called "the sole refuge of reason," would have continued to remain such. To have averted the danger of new woes for Europe is the great service of Hitler and his ministers, and if the world is not yet ready to recognize this now, then history will some day render a more just verdict.

Liberty and equality, you say further, are not accorded the Jews by the present-day Germany. You fail to recognize that our situation is quite different from that existing in other countries of Europe. Many of the key positions in science, art and economic life were occupied in Germany by Jews and the latter exploited this fact in a way in which they on their side did not recognize the equality of races but rather furthered the interests of their racial brethren. Added to these there came the elements from Eastern Europe, which streamed across the German border after the war and which took advantage of our weakness and poverty. They intensified the opposition which was then released in the national revolution and which received new sustenance when Jewish writers abroad initiated a veritable witches' Sabbath against Germany. Of course here too the excitement in Germany caused unjust hardships and many a tragic fate. But if you examine the German laws your desire for objective justice cannot remain in doubt.

You speak, Herr Rolland, of the "Germany of the great world-citizens," which alone commands your love and which today has been dishonored by "racialism" and other "crimes." It is just we, the intellectuals of Germany, who must reject this charge. We wish to retain with true vitality a rightly-understood cosmopolitanism. We do not conceive of it so abstractly that it seems either possible or desirable to eradicate one's own nationality; we know that it is only the firm attachment to homeland and fatherland which makes people capable of contributing something valuable to the intellectual co-operation of nations. This we are taught by those German poets and thinkers whom you honor and who were not only universal but who educated the people also in patriotic feeling. Your countrymen, Herr Rolland, have willfully denied this. To cite but one example, they preferred to see in Goethe the world-citizen and not also the man whose most powerful talents grew out of the German cultural soil. They thus believed that they could have less respect for the people and homeland of Goethe and they thus gave fuel to that unholy chauvinism which is completely un-German in concept and in word and which is aroused among us only under unbearable pressure from without. Such chauvinism in itself is far removed from the German and that there will be no change in the future along these lines is clearly revealed in the speech which Hitler addressed to the world on Wednesday, March 17, 1933. Germany places the peaceful co-operation of nations above all aspirations which spring only from the blind hunger of a nation for power. The German government has given yet another indication of its cosmopolitan attitude; think of the invitations recently sent out to all nations for participation in the Olympic games, All of this clearly indicates that Germany has never rejected pacifism as such. She merely refuses to give heed to that rootless and aimless intellectualism which makes more difficult Germany's struggle for her most essential rights to life.

Foreign nations will indeed have to become accustomed to this fact, that German cosmopolitanism rooted in the national idea has its limits when the question is that of the internal character of the German state. There can be no intervention in this sphere, and it ill-befits the representatives of democracy abroad to concern themselves with how Germany arranges her own house and to make this purely German matter a pretext for extreme vilification. You too, Herr Rolland, cling to democracy and you believe that you must rage against the new order in Germany. This order is being created by leaders who more than ever before have won the confidence of the people. It is, therefore, thoroughly democratic, even though not in the sense of a parliamentary regime. The latter, moreover, is revealing certain manifestations of a crisis in your own country and in other European states which still cling to such a system. But you must not overlook the democratic basis of the German revolution. You must no longer declare that "Germany provides us with a terrible example of oppression," as you did in that anti-fascist declaration which called forth our original comment. If you were right there would no longer be any independent *Kölnische Zeitung*, then we could not dare to publish your violent attacks upon the German government, then we could not carry on this free and candid conversation with you across the border. But we do possess this possibility and we shall utilise it further in order thereby to exhaust those sorry and secret sources which disseminate hatred and calumny in Europe today. In these critical times such efforts are doubly necessary. Such a discussion can be fruitful and stimulating for both parties only if certain preliminary questions are clarified. Above all this false talk of "German barbarism" and "fascist terror" must be quieted. That you too fell victim to this talk, despite your usual incorruptible judgment, we regret very much, but it only spurs us on all the more to earn understanding on your part and to continue the battle for truth.

Editors of the Kölnische Zeitung.

xiv. *The Poet and His Times*

By Ernst Wiechert*

It is almost two years now since I here gave an account to the young people and to myself of my position with regard to one of the most important relationships between people: the relation of poet to youth. I confess gladly that the echo which I found in your hearts gave me the deepest consolation in my many hours of care. Only he who is entirely alone is without consolation.

Time has elapsed in the meantime. Not all Heavens have been stormed by the youth and not all the old people have descended to Hell as many might have desired. Many books have been written, many speeches delivered, many bonfires kindled, many tears wept in secret. . . .

Less than ever does it seem right to me to-day for the poet, who is called before a gathering of inquiring individuals, to be satisfied merely with opening his works and bringing up before them images to provide animation and violent commotion for the hearts of men. It befits us no longer to emerge from our solitude and, like enchanters who are beyond all time, merely throw our images on a white curtain as if we were still living in happy childhood days. It befits us no longer because there are too many among us who receive no reply to their many questions. These people may feel that although the poets in the main are good-natured fools, nevertheless because they look at the world in a different way they might perhaps have an answer to much that brings unrest to their hearts.

And so it seemed to me that of the relationships concerning which I might have something to say, the one closest to me was that between the two worlds in which I too am living—that between poetry and the times. You know as well as I do that this is a dangerous subject, because there is always danger where human self-conceit and sensitiveness are touched. You know too that this is a subject which concerns us all. In the tension between the two, you—the young people among you—have a share which is not to be overlooked. Not only because, I am convinced, at some time—and perhaps soon—there will be placed in your hands the decision as to

* This address was delivered to students of the University of Munich on April 16, 1936. Its publication was forbidden by the authorities and it was disseminated in typewritten form.

what is temporary and what is eternal in poetry (a decision which will benefit neither you nor poetry), but also because from youth has come the most passionate attack upon the poetry which does not in every verse reflect the times and the immediate present.

Far be it from me to maintain that right rests only with one side. Right on this imperfect earth almost never rests with one side alone. We ought to advance gradually to wiser judgments than the childish formula of "I am right."

Let me tell you something out of my childhood, something which I wrote on another occasion and which no doubt is known to some of you.

It happened forty years ago when I was a child and perhaps it was only a trifle. We were celebrating a summer holiday in our woods—relatives and friends. In the evening we went out in many boats on a dark lake. The boats carried paper lanterns, the girls sang duets and my uncle, whom they called the count because of his frivolity, shot one sky-rocket after another towards the stars above. The boats glided by one behind another and we thus came upon a fisherman who had cast his nets upon the dark waters. His hand held the long net and let it slide slowly over the edge of the boat. His hair was white, his shoulders drooped and he appeared altogether as a stranger amidst our riotous merriment. When our boat came near to his he lifted his eyes once and looked at us with cool, distant and quite serene gaze. "Mother," I asked, "what is that man doing?" "He is catching fish to feed the five thousand," answered my mother.

I have never forgotten that; neither the slight sense of shame which came over me, nor the almost sacred reverence for this strange man at whom I looked back for a long while. To-day as I search for an image of what I might say this comes to my mind again. "He is catching fish to feed the five thousand"—is it not a beautiful image for the poet among the peoples? In the same fashion everything rushes by him: the celebrations of men and their defeats, their humiliations and their revolutions. Occasionally he raises his gaze and looks at it all with a distant and quite serene contemplation. Is he not concerned with it all? Is he a stranger to his times? Ah, no, it is not that. But already he has borne all this within him before it actually happened: the lanterns and the songs, the celebrations and the defeats, the humiliations and revolutions. In the fate of his characters all that already happened, all was fought out and battled over, cleansed and transfigured. He has dimmed the light like the sadness and beneath all the loud words and songs of the day he searches for the quiet and the imperishable, for the food for the starving, whom he wants to give their fill, when all words and song have died away.

And the poet in the midst of his times? He is like one who ties his boat to a shrieking tug and forgets all about the nets with which he was to catch the food. But the poet beyond his times, he is the one for whom the starving are waiting. For there are many hungry ones in our day who would not like to stand aloof because their nation's fate is, in burning fashion, their own fate, and yet who must stand aloof because they were so reared that weddings and burials are for them hushed occasions, and of all, the most hushed occasion is a resurrection. When the stone is rolled off from a grave, then children and birds may scream; the poet, however, raises his hands before his eyes—what appears is bound in rags, the Lazarus of nations. And while the others lift the resurrected one on their shoulders and carry him about in triumph, the poet moves softly aside, back to the quiet field where man's bread grows, and there he sits down, head in hand, reflecting how to transform the mad rush of time into one small word of eternity.

This, my friends, seems to me to be the calling of the poet. There never was any other calling. It is not as many might believe that the meaning of revolutions consists in beginning anew with the first day of creation. Down deep below the foundations of all human convulsions and high above their stars the imperturbable and eternal elements of all nations calmly pursue their course—nature, for example, or God, or the love of a mother for her children. . . .

I know—and the post-man in Ambach knows it too—that Germany is bubbling over with poets to-day. When I was young, our bards were old like Jordan or Felix Dahn, and the wicked generation of Arno Holz did what the young generation of to-day does or would like to do: it arranged a grand funeral for them while they were still alive, because they held that the throne of poetry belongs only to youth and the times. To-day our bards are young—between twenty and twenty-five. They also would like to count us among the "justly dead," because in our scanty works we deal only with such defunct matters as God, or justice, or love, or even the Great War. And there are some among these who with all their twenty-five years traverse the German land and sing not only their songs of blood but also tell the story of their lives. And there are many, yes thousands, who listen reverently to these songs and to these lives; for we are, as is well known, a courageous people who have learned to assert our manly pride even before royal thrones.

No, dear friends, this is good neither for us nor for our times. . . . Our time, threatened by the hate, envy and lies of an entire world, should at least be freed from menace by its poets. At certain times one can say to every young person: win or die; but one cannot say to every young person: sing or die. In most cases it would be better that he die than sing. Dying may always be beautiful if accompanied by dignity and decorum, but singing needs a few more things besides dignity and decorum.

This is also not altered by the fact that we have in Germany already, a camp for the training of poets in which Herr Roman Hoppenheit—and none less than he—educates the future bards to give up the "individualistic art of a remnant of supposedly prominent figures in art" (*individualistischen Kunstgetriebe einer restbeständigen Kunstprominenz*) in favor of an "anonymous community art" in order . . . "to preserve the national treasures

which are found in the talents and use them for the welfare of the whole."
Any of you who know something of the poetry and culture of Soviet
Russia will also know that Herr Roman Hoppenheit is on the same road
which they successfully adopted in Russia and which we, antiquated individuals, call the assassination of the soul. . . .

. . .

Do not think, my friends, that here stands one who raises his voice only
for his own domain. There are many other fields in which the same thing
is happening. In the field of criticism, for example, the question is not
asked if a poem, a novel or a drama can hold its own in the forum of art
but rather if it can stand the test of the forum of political opinion. And
the justice which I meted out to Fallada in my strong criticism of his
book, *Im inneren Reich*, brought me a letter in which the writer told me
that for cultural-political reasons I would have done better had I emphasized the few good things which I found in Fallada.

There is the field of education in which the same things occur. Here
too they turn to the youth because they know that only with the aid of
the youth can the world, which they wish to change, be changed. Some
time ago in a book issued by the association of philologists there appeared
an essay by a superintendent of schools concerning future instruction in
German. In this essay the goal of transforming the world was expressed in
unconcealed fashion. This reckless world-reformer demanded in his essay
that the youth be educated from now on in a new heroism. It is quite immaterial if the hero of a poem or of a group be noble or ignoble, if his
action be good or bad; the only thing that counts is that he act. That the
youth be guided by reverence for moral greatness is but a demand which
belongs to times which have since been transcended. The youth of to-day
. . . is to be educated "to affirm with cold contemplation the anarchy of
the moral world."

. . .

Poets, as I conceive them to be, are even more wonderful people than
philologists. They may not always be right but they desire that right reign
upon the earth. They do not want all people to read their books but they
want whoever reads them to believe them. They want the blurred and
opaque world to appear simple and clear in the reflected image which they
set up. They want before the eyes of man those things in the world which
are beclouded and too often prostituted to be exalted: truth, justice, liberty, goodness, love and above all the meaning and law of a great world
order. They want to make men better, more confident, braver and
purer. . . . If a part of the conscience of our nation still lives within me—
and I feel painfully enough how much it does—then it cannot be immaterial to me whether the youth is reared in Goethean reverence or that it
"affirms with cold contemplation the anarchy of the moral world." All
poetry speaks of heroism, but let Fallada and his Johannes Gaentschow—

let alone other examples—assert that it is immaterial whether the heroes act nobly or ignobly. This has never been asserted by any of those from whom, for thousands of years, the German soul has drawn its nourishment. . . .

It is indeed the fate of all revolutions that those who run along with and after the revolution falsify the meaning of the revolution. They not only do away with the monarchy, they also want the head of the monarch; they not only depose the priests, they also depose God; and they believe that every sixth-class boy must be given a German oak in his hand in order to "act." They do not know that the history of a people already bears eternal characteristics which the hands of no subaltern can change. They do not know that the stream of centuries-old blood cannot be deflected by phrases into another channel. They do not know how the genuinely heroic walks the earth—although they would only have to look into the faces of the people who silently carried out and endured their heroism for twenty years. They have long forgotten with what reverence and quiet and humility Pestalozzi taught his children.

Yet it may well be that a nation ceases to distinguish between right and wrong and that it considers every battle to be right. Such a people, however, stands already on the level of heavy decline and its doom is already sealed. It may still win gladiatorial renown and set up in fits a sort of ethics which we may call "boxer's ethics," but for such a people the scales are already weighted and on every wall appears the hand which writes with letters of fire. . . .

BIBLIOGRAPHY

Bibliography

FOR A GENERAL BACKGROUND OF GERMAN PROBLEMS

Lichtenberger, Henri, *Germany and Its Evolution in Modern Times* (New York 1913).

Meinecke, Friedrich, *Weltbürgertum und Nationalstaat*, 7th ed. (Munich 1928).

Pinson, Koppel S., *Pietism and the Rise of German Nationalism* (New York 1934).

Reynaud, Louis, *L'Ame allemande* (Paris 1933).

Rosenberg, Arthur, *The Birth of the German Republic* (New York 1931).

Schnabel, Franz, *Deutsche Geschichte im neunzehnten Jahrhundert*, vols. i-iv (Freiburg 1929-36).

For further references for the problems of German nationalism see:

Pinson, Koppel S., *A Bibliographical Introduction to Nationalism* (New York 1935).

THE REVOLUTION OF 1918 AND THE WEIMAR REPUBLIC

Bernstein, Eduard, *Die deutsche Revolution* (Berlin 1921). An uncompleted work by one of the leaders of the Independent Socialist Party.

Bernhard, Georg, *Die deutsche Tragödie* (Prague 1933). A history of the Weimar republic by the former editor of the liberal *Vossische Zeitung*.

Clark, R. T., *The Fall of the German Republic* (London 1935).

Daniels, H. G., *The Rise of the German Republic* (London 1927).

Kosok, Paul, *Modern Germany* (Chicago 1933).

Price, M. P., *Germany in Transition* (London 1923).

Quigley, H., and Clark, R. T., *Republican Germany* (New York 1928).

Rosenberg, Arthur, *A History of the German Republic* (London 1936).

Stampfer, Friedrich, *Die 14 Jahre* (Carlsbad 1936). By the former editor of the Berlin Socialist daily, *Vorwärts*.

Stroebel, Heinrich, *The German Revolution and After* (New York 1923).

Toller, Ernst, *I Was a German* (New York 1935). Particularly interesting for the description of the suppression of the Bavarian Soviet Republic.

THE NATIONAL SOCIALIST MOVEMENT BEFORE 1933

Goebbels, Joseph, *Der Angriff, Aufsätze aus der Kampfzeit* (Munich 1935).

———, *Das erwachende Berlin* (Munich 1933).

———, *Kampf um Berlin* (Munich 1932).

The Third Reich

Goebbels, Joseph, *My Part in Germany's Fight* (London 1935). A translation of his diary.

The above works of the present Minister of Propaganda are concerned primarily with his part in the Nazi movement in Berlin, where he was editor of the *Angriff*, Berlin district leader and Reich propaganda leader.

Heiden, Konrad, *Geschichte des Nationalsozialismus* (Berlin 1932).

———, *Geburt des dritten Reiches* (Zurich 1934).

———, *A History of National Socialism* (New York 1934). This is a condensed version of the two preceding German books. It is not as good as the first German work.

———, *Adolf Hitler* (New York 1936).

Heuss, Theodor, *Hitler's Weg* (Stuttgart 1932). A critical analysis by a Christian Democrat.

Hitler, Adolf, *Reden* (Munich 1933). A collection of Hitler's speeches delivered before 1933.

Miltenberg, Weigand von (Herbert Blank), *Adolf Hitler, Wilhelm III* (Berlin 1932). A most valuable character study by a former follower who later joined the Strasser *Schwarze Front*.

Naziführer sehen dich an (Paris 1934). Thirty-three biographies of Nazi leaders by emigré authors.

Olberg, Oda, *Nationalsozialismus* (Vienna 1932). A socialist appraisal.

Olden, Rudolf, *Hitler* (New York 1936). A critical biography by a former editor of the *Berliner Tageblatt*.

Ottwalt, Ernst, *Deutschland Erwache. Geschichte des Nationalsozialismus* (Vienna 1932). A very hostile work.

Röhm, Ernst, *Die Geschichte eines Hochverräters* (Munich 1928). The autobiography of the former chief-of-staff of the S.A.

Schmidt-Pauli, Edgar von, *Die Männer um Hitler* (Berlin 1932). A pro-Nazi account of the leading figures in the movement.

Strasser, Otto, *Ministersessel oder Revolution?* (Berlin 1930). An account by the leader of the *Schwarze Front* of his break with Hitler.

NAZI IDEOLOGY AND GENERAL PRINCIPLES

Amtsblatt des Bischöflichen Ordinariats Berlin, *Studien zum Mythus des XX. Jahrhunderts* (Cologne 1935). An official Catholic analysis of Alfred Rosenberg's *Mythus*.

Dietrich, Otto, *Die philosophischen Grundlagen des Nationalsozialismus* (Breslau 1935).

Feder, Gottfried, *Der deutsche Staat auf nationaler und sozialer Grundlage*, 3d ed. (Munich 1932).

———, *Hitler's Official Program* (London 1934).

Historicus, *Der Fascismus als Massenbewegung* (Carlsbad 1934).

Hitler, Adolf, *Mein Kampf*, vol. i (Munich 1925); vol. ii (Munich 1926); first complete ed. (Munich 1930). This work is the Bible of National Socialism. Complete translation of this work into other languages has

378

never been permitted. The English version (Boston 1933) is a mutilated version. A complete translation into French was published by the Nouvelles Editions Latines (Paris 1934) but the publishers were sued in court and forbidden to distribute the book.

Jung, Rudolf, *Der nationale Sozialismus* (Troppau 1919). One of the most important early expositions of National Socialist principles.

Jünger, Ernst, *Der Arbeiter, Herrschaft und Gestalt* (Hamburg 1932). While not officially a Nazi, Jünger stands close to the movement and is one of the most brilliant of the nationalist writers.

Künneth, Walter, *Antwort auf den Mythus* (Berlin 1935). A Protestant reply to Rosenberg's *Mythus*.

Leers, Johann von, *Spenglers weltpolitisches System und der National-sozialismus* (Berlin 1934).

Moeller van der Bruck, Arthur, *Das dritte Reich* (Berlin 1923). This work was one of the most important influences in paving the way for the diffusion of Nazi ideology, particularly among certain groups of intellectuals. Moeller van der Bruck was a "conservative revolutionary."

Reventlow, Graf E., *Deutscher Sozialismus,* new ed. (Weimar 1933). Count Reventlow belongs to the left wing of the Nazi movement and is one of the most serious and sincere intellectuals in the party.

——, *Nationaler Sozialismus im neuen Deutschland* (Berlin 1932).

Rosenberg, Alfred, *Der Mythus des XX. Jahrhunderts,* 4th ed. (Munich 1932). This is the most elaborate attempt to build a system of Nazi ideology.

——, *An die Dunkelmänner unserer Zeit* (Munich 1935). A reply to his critics.

——, *Das Wesengefüge des Nationalsozialismus* (Munich 1932).

——, *Blut und Ehre; Reden und Aufsätze 1919-1933* (Munich 1936).

Scheunemann, W., *Der Nationalsozialismus* (Berlin 1931).

Strasser, Gregor, *Kampf um Deutschland* (Munich 1932). Important addresses by the former Reich Party Leader and leader of the socializing wing of the party.

Unger, Erich, *Das Schrifttum des Nationalsozialismus 1919-1934* (Berlin 1934). An official bibliography of Nazi literature.

NAZI RULE

American Jewish Congress, *The Case of Civilization Against Hitlerism* (New York 1934).

Armstrong, Hamilton Fish, *Hitler's Reich. The First Phase* (New York 1933).

Beer, M., *Die auswärtige Politik des dritten Reiches* (Zurich 1935).

Brown Network (London 1935). An account of Nazi activities outside of Germany.

Dietrich, Otto, *Mit Hitler in die Macht* (Munich 1933).

Ermarth, Fritz, *The New Germany* (Washington 1936).

The Third Reich

Förtsch, H., *Die Wehrmacht im nationalsozialistischen Staat* (Hamburg 1935).
Frei, Lothar, *Deutschland Wohin?* (Zurich 1934).
Friedrichs, Axel, ed., *Dokumente der deutschen Politik*, vols. i-iii (Berlin 1935-36).
Henri, Ernst, *Hitler over Europe* (New York 1934).
Holt, John G., *Under the Swastika* (Chapel Hill 1936).
Hoover, Calvin B., *Germany Enters the Third Reich* (New York 1933).
Lévy, Paul, *La Germanisme a l'étranger* (Paris 1933).
Lowenstein, Prince Hubertus, *The Tragedy of a Nation, Germany 1918-1934* (New York 1934).
Pascal, Roy, *The Nazi Dictatorship* (London 1934).
Pollock, J. K. and Henemann, J. H., *The Hitler Decrees* (Ann Arbor 1934).
Reed, Douglas, *The Burning of the Reichstag* (New York 1934).
Schuman, Frederick L., *The Nazi Dictatorship*, 2d ed. (New York 1936).
Shuster, George N., *Strong Man Rules* (New York 1934).
Strasser, Otto, *Die deutsche Bartholomäusnacht* (Zurich 1935). An account of the purge of June 30, 1934, not altogether reliable but full of a great deal of interesting material.
Wheeler-Bennett, John Wheeler, *Wooden Titan; Hindenburg in Twenty Years of German History, 1914-1934* (New York 1936).

TERROR UNDER NAZI RULE

Billinger, Karl, *Fatherland* (New York 1935).
———, *All Quiet in Germany* (London 1935).
Liepmann, Heinz, *Murder Made in Germany* (New York 1934).
Lorant, Stefan, *I Was Hitler's Prisoner* (London 1935).
Seger, Gerhart, *A Nation Terrorized* (Chicago 1935).
World Committee for the Victims of German Fascism, *The Brown Book of the Hitler Terror and the Burning of the Reichstag* (New York 1933).
———, *The Burning of the Reichstag; The Second Brown Book* (New York 1934).

THE PROBLEM OF RACE

Burgdörfer, Friedrich, *Volk ohne Jugend* (Berlin 1934).
Fischer, Eugen, *Der völkische Staat biologisch gesehen* (Berlin 1934).
Glass, D. V., *The Struggle for Population* (London 1937).
Günther, H. K. F., *Rassenkunde des jüdischen Volkes* (Munich 1930).
———, *Rassenkunde des deutschen Volkes* (Munich 1930).
———, *Rassenkunde Europas* (Munich 1933).
Haddon, A. C. and Huxley, Julian, *We Europeans: A Survey of Racial Problems* (New York 1936).
Hertz, Friedrich, *Hans Günther als Rassenforscher*, 2d ed. (Berlin 1930).
———, *Race and Culture* (New York 1928).

Bibliography

THE JEWISH PROBLEM

American Jewish Committee, *The Jews in Nazi Germany* (New York 1935).

Cahiers Juifs, *L'Apporte des Juifs d'Allemagne à la civilisation allemande* (Paris 1933).

Lowenthal, Marvin, *The Jews in Germany* (New York 1936).

Miller, Anton van, *Deutsche und Juden* (Vienna 1936).

Pinson, Koppel S., "The Jewish Spirit in Nazi Germany," in the *Menorah Journal*, vol. xxiv (1936) pp. 228-54. An account of the internal reactions to Nazi rule within the Jewish community.

World Jewish Congress, *Der wirtschaftliche Vernichtungskampf gegen die Juden im dritten Reich* (Paris 1937).

Yellow Spot (London 1936). A collection of facts and documents relating to three years' persecution of German Jews, derived chiefly from National Socialist sources, with an introduction by the Bishop of Durham.

The following are some of the more important pro-Nazi treatments of this problem:

Bartels, Adolf, *Literaturwissenschaft und jüdische Herkunft* (Leipzig 1925). By the leading Nazi literary historian.

Blüher, Hans, *Die Erhebung Israels gegen die christlichen Güter* (Hamburg 1931).

Fritsch, Theodor, *Handbuch der Judenfrage* (Leipzig 1934).

Institut zum Studium der Judenfrage, *Die Juden in Deutschland*, 4th ed. (Munich 1936).

Kittel, Gerhard, *Die Judenfrage* (Stuttgart 1933).

CULTURE AND EDUCATION

Adler, Max, "Crime and Culture in Germany," in the *Socialist Review*, vol. v (1933) pp. 379-84.

Beard, Charles, "Education under the Nazis," in *Foreign Affairs*, vol. xiv (1936) pp. 437-52.

d'Harcourt, Robert, *Evangile de la Force* (Paris 1937).

Kandel, I. L., *The Making of Nazis* (New York 1935).

Kohn, Hans, *Force or Reason* (Cambridge, Massachusetts 1937).

Krieck, Ernst, *Nationalpolitische Erziehung* (Leipzig 1932). Krieck is the leading Nazi educator.

——, *Völkischer Gesamtstaat und nationale Erziehung* (Heidelberg 1933).

Langenbucher, Hellmuth, *Volkhafte Dichtung der Zeit*, 2d ed. (Berlin 1935). A Nazi analysis of contemporary German literature.

Mann, Thomas, *Exchange of Letters* (New York 1937). A letter to the rector of the University of Bonn on the revocation of Mann's honorary degree.

Michaelis, C., Michaelis, H. and Sonin, O. W., *Die braune Kultur* (Zurich 1934). A collection of documents to illustrate Nazi policy with respect to religion, justice, education, culture and science. It is an emigré publication.

Schirach, Baldur von, *Die Hitler-Jugend, Idee und Gestalt* (Berlin 1934). By the Reich Leader of the Hitler Youth.

Sechs Bekenntnisse zum neuen Deutschland (Hamburg 1933). Rudolf G. Binding, E. G. Kolbenheyer, Die Kölnische Zeitung, Wilhelm von Scholz, Otto Winz and Robert Fabre-Luce reply to the attack upon Nazi Germany by Romain Rolland.

Thompson, Dorothy, "Culture under the Nazis," in *Foreign Affairs*, vol. xiv (1936) pp. 407-23.

THE RELIGIOUS PROBLEM

Bergmann, Ernst, *Die deutsche Nationalkirche* (Breslau 1933). By one of the leaders of the neo-Pagan movement.

———, *Die 25 Thesen der Deutschreligion* (Breslau 1934).

Faulhaber, Michael von, Cardinal, *Judaism, Christianity and Germany* (New York 1934). The sermons of the Cardinal in Munich in 1933.

Gurian, Waldemar, *Hitler and the Christians* (London 1936).

Hauer, Wilhelm, *Deutsche Gottschau* (Stuttgart 1934). The most important work by the leading figure in the German Faith movement.

Macfarland, Charles S., *The New Church and the New Germany* (New York 1934).

Reventlow, Graf E., *Wo ist Gott?* (Berlin 1935). A philosophical analysis by a leader of the German Faith Movement.

Shuster, George N., *Like a Mighty Army. Hitler versus Established Religion* (New York 1935).

Tillich, Paul, "*The Totalitarian State and the Claims of the Church*," in *Social Research*, vol. i (1934) pp. 405-33.

AGRARIAN AND ECONOMIC AFFAIRS

Banker, The (London). The issue of February 1937 is devoted to a review of four years of Nazi economic policy.

Darré, Walther R., *Neuadel aus Blut und Boden*, new ed. (Munich 1933). The author is the leading Nazi authority on agrarian problems.

———, *Das Bauerntum als Lebensquell der nordischen Rasse*, 2d ed. (Munich 1933).

David, F., *Ist die NSDAP eine sozialistische Partei?* (Berlin 1933). A communist analysis of Nazi economic theories.

Einzig, Paul, *Germany's Default. The Economics of Hitlerism* (London 1934).

Endemic, Horace, in *The Annalist* (August 7 and 21, 1936) pp. 180-81 and 284-85, 310.

Bibliography

Florinsky, M., *Fascism and National Socialism. A Study of the Economic and Social Policies of the Totalitarian State* (New York 1936).

Franz, Leopold, *Die Gewerkschaften in der Demokratie und in der Diktatur* (Carlsbad 1935).

Holt, John B., *German Agricultural Policy 1918-1934* (Chapel Hill 1936).

Huber, Ernst, *Die Gestalt des deutschen Sozialismus* (Hamburg 1934).

Laum, Bernhard, *Die geschlossene Wirtschaft* (Tübingen 1933).

Reinhardt, Fritz, *Die Arbeitsschlacht der Reichsregierung* (Berlin 1933).

———, *Finanz—und Steuer Politik im nationalsozialistischen Statt* (Berlin 1934).

Reuter, Franz, *Schacht*, 2d ed. (Stuttgart 1937).

Sombart, Werner, *Deutscher Sozialismus* (Berlin 1934).

Starcke, Gerhard, *NSBO und Deutsche Arbeitsfront* (Berlin 1934).

Thomas, Norman, "Labor under the Nazis," in *Foreign Affairs*, vol. xiv (1936) pp. 424-36.

de Wilde, John C., *The German Economic Dilemma* (New York 1937), Foreign Policy Reports, vol. xiii, no. i.

INDEX

Index

Index

Index

Index

Index

391

Index

A NOTE ON THE TYPE
IN WHICH THIS BOOK IS SET

*This book is composed on the lino-
type in Janson. In recutting the
original type issued by Anton
Janson in 1660, its sparkle and
beautiful clarity was retained. The
recutting of Janson was made direct from type cast from the original matrices now in possession of
the Stempel foundry in Frankfort,
A. M.*

THIS BOOK WAS DESIGNED, COM-
POSED, PRINTED, AND BOUND BY
THE HADDON CRAFTSMEN, CAM-
DEN, N. J. THE PAPER WAS MADE
BY THE TILESTON AND HOLLINGS-
WORTH COMPANY, BOSTON, MASS.